WALKING

Shakespeare's
LONDON

20 ORIGINAL WALKS
IN AND AROUND LONDON

NICHOLAS ROBINS

Interlink Books

An imprint of Interlink Publishing Group, Inc.
Northampton, Massachusetts

First American edition published in 2005 by

INTERLINK BOOKS
An imprint of Interlink Publishing Group, Ltd.
46 Crosby Street, Northampton, Massachusetts 01060
www.interlinkbooks.com

Text copyright © Nicholas Robins 2005
Photographs copyright © Eric Nathan 2005
Maps copyright © Globetrotter™ Travel Map London (New Holland Publishers) 2005

ISBN 1-56656-588-X

Reproduction by Pica Digital (Pte) Ltd, Singapore
Printed and bound by Kyodo Printing Co (Singapore) Ltd

Photograph Acknowledgements
All photographs by Eric Nathan
Front cover: The Globe Theatre
Back cover: The Old Vic Theatre
Spine: Detail from the groundling gates of the Globe Theatre
p2: Shakespeare's Memorial in Leicester Square

2 4 6 8 10 9 7 5 3 1

To request our complete 40-page full-color catalog,
please call us toll-free at **1-800-238-LINK**, visit our website
at **www.interlinkbooks.com**, or write to
Interlink Publishing
46 Crosby Street, Northampton, MA 01060
e-mail: info@interlinkbooks.com

CONTENTS

KEY TO MAPS

Each of the walks in the book is accompanied by a map on which the route is shown in blue. Places of interest along the walk, such as historic buildings, churches and pubs, are clearly identified. Where necessary specific route directions have also been included on the maps. In both the text and the maps, certain features have been abbreviated as follows:

	Route		Underground station
CHADWELL ST	Minor road		Toilet
			Church
ST JOHN'S ST	Main road		Park and garden
	Railway line		Building

INTRODUCTION

Everyone knows about Shakespeare's birthplace. Here is the house in which he was born, there is his schoolroom, here the house of his mother. Stratford-upon-Avon rewards the Shakespearean pilgrim with a considerable material legacy. Even the site of vanished New Place, the family house Shakespeare bought in 1597 and lived and died in, and which was pulled down in 1759, is teasingly evocative. In the town of his birth the very stones prate of his whereabouts.

But what of his workplace, the city in which he spent the greatest part of his life? Shakespeare's London: the squalid, recently brutalized, beautiful, theatrical City so painstakingly inventoried by John Stow, has left hardly a trace. Burned by the Great Fire, bombed in the Second World War and the subject of more calculated depredations by property developers over the last four centuries, London has wiped out half of its history, 'like', as V. S. Pritchett said, 'some promiscuous jade, some bedraggled old Madame wiping the gin off her lips.' The contrast with its great Italian contemporaries – 16th-century Venice, say, or Verona, so indifferently evoked by Shakespeare but still so materially present – is stark. The most evocative 'Shakespearean' building in London is also one of its most recent – the new Globe Theatre, opened in 1997.

This makes looking for Elizabethan London in the modern City a bit like trying to recover the words of a song whose tune you can just remember: the lines of melody are there – Cheapside, Poultry, Carter Lane and so on all follow the same course they did 400 years ago – but the words, the houses and churches, livery halls and stables which gave them meaning have, with only a few exceptions, left not a rack behind. Groping for the words of this song is often as difficult in an elegant Georgian Square as it is in a shopping centre or traffic island, so, although I have tried where possible to offer walks which follow an engaging course I make no apology if some of them pass through some of London's more blighted districts.

And then there are the plays. The histories, of course, feature the great medieval centres to the east and west of the City – Westminster at one end and the Tower at the other – but little mention is given to specific sites in the great commercial centre in between. Only the Eastcheap and Clement's Inn of *Henry IV* seem to say anything direct about the texture of London life – a life evoked elsewhere with such particularity in the plays of, say, Jonson, Dekker or Middleton. And yet, and yet. London is also often indistinctly felt in Shakespeare – and not just in knowing, or perhaps inadvertent references such as the Bankside inn that Antonio seeks out in the suburbs of Illyria or the very London 'Bedlam beggars' dissembled by Edgar in the prehistoric Britain of *King Lear*. Hamlet's court owes more to Elizabethan Hampton Court than dark age Elsinore, Venice to the Royal Exchange than the Rialto, the brothels and corrupt administration of *Measure for Measure* to Bankside than Vienna. Lear in his madness exhorts an imaginary 'rascal beadle' not to lash the London whore; Cleopatra imagines 'some squeaking Cleopatra boy [her] greatness' as though the streets of Rome followed London's theatrical precedent. The City exists in the plays but is refracted by Shakespeare's imagination.

If the book was not to be limited to the area within the old City walls, a handful of its ancient suburbs – Southwark, Shoreditch, Clerkenwell, the Tower – and the royal precincts of Westminster, it had also to extend its period of interest. There is not much to detain anyone looking for relics of the Shakespearean period in modern Soho or Covent Garden, but of Shakespeare's long, active and increasingly complex afterlife – his later incarnations on the stage, the page and in the minds of the late 17th, and 18th, 19th and 20th centuries – there is a great deal. For the same reason I have included some of the major theatres – Drury Lane, Covent Garden, the Haymarket – several times as they play their parts in the successive centuries. Many of the walks are quite short, but in many cases the beginnings and ends are not far from each other and it is possible to combine two or three in an afternoon. There are also points of intersection, allowing walkers to pick up a different itinerary if they wish.

In 1628, the printer and bookseller Edward Blount, who took some part in the publication of Shakespeare's First Folio, wrote in the preface to his edition of *Micro-cosmographie*, a book of character types written by the witty cleric John Earle: 'If any faults have escaped the press (as few books can be printed without) impose them not on the author I entreat thee, but rather impute them to mine and the printer's oversight.' He took too much on himself; there are faults in the *Microcosmographie* all too imputable to the author, as there are also, no doubt, here.

> Jog on, jog on, the foot-path way,
> And merrily hent the stile-a:
> A merry heart goes all the day,
> Your sad tires in a mile-a.

Opposite: David Garrick's 'grateful temple to Shakespeare', built in the grounds of his villa at Hampton to house his collection of Shakespeare memorabilia.

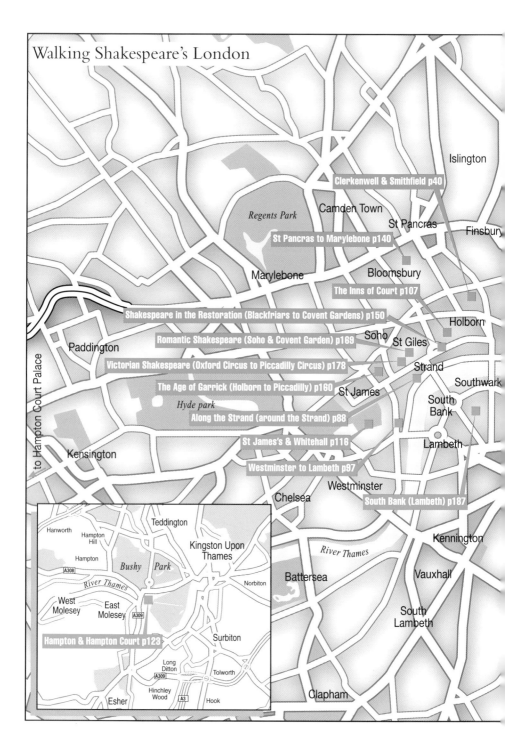

Walking Shakespeare's London

Islington

Clerkenwell & Smithfield p40

Camden Town

St Pancras

Finsbury

Regents Park

St Pancras to Marylebone p140

Bloomsbury

Marylebone

The Inns of Court p107

Shakespeare in the Restoration (Blackfriars to Covent Gardens) p150

Holborn

Paddington

Romantic Shakespeare (Soho & Covent Garden) p169

Soho

St Giles

Victorian Shakespeare (Oxford Circus to Piccadilly Circus) p178

Strand

to Hampton Court Palace

Southwark

The Age of Garrick (Holborn to Piccadilly) p160

St James

Hyde park

South Bank

Along the Strand (around the Strand) p88

Kensington

St James's & Whitehall p116

Lambeth

Westminster to Lambeth p97

Westminster

Chelsea

South Bank (Lambeth) p187

Kennington

Teddington

Hanworth

Hampton Hill

Kingston Upon Thames

River Thames

Hampton

Bushy Park

A308

River Thames

Norbiton

Battersea

Vauxhall

West Molesey

East Molesey

A309

South Lambeth

Hampton & Hampton Court p123

Surbiton

Long Ditton

A309

Tolworth

Esher

Hinchley Wood

A3

Hook

Clapham

Hackney

West Ham

Bow

Shoreditch

Shoreditch & Finsbury p12

Spitalfields

Mile End

Barbican & Cheapside p30

Around St Paul's p20

City

Stepney

Poplar

Blackfriars to Monument p50

Bishopsgate to London Bridge p59

The Tower and the Wharves p68

Wapping

Bankside p78

River Thames

The Borough

Rotherhithe

Bermondsey

Isle of Dogs

Walworth

Deptford & Greenwich p132

River Thames

Deptford

Camberwell   Peckham

Greenwich

0   1   2   3   4   5 km

0   1   2   3 miles

N

SHOREDITCH AND FINSBURY

Summary: Shakespeare's career probably began in the great public playhouses that stood in the fields of Shoreditch, once a suburb outside the walls of the City, an area rich in London's earliest theatre history. The route takes you through the 18th-century streets of Spitalfields to now-fashionable Shoreditch and St Leonard's Church, filled with names from London's theatrical past, to Finsbury, once the site of the city's most splendid playhouse. You also learn what celebrated duel was fought in the fields of what is now London's trendiest square.

Start:	Liverpool Street Station.
Finish:	Barbican Underground Station.
Length:	4 km (2½ miles).
Time:	2 hours.
Refreshments:	King's Stores, Sandys Row; Grapeshots and the Bolt Hole, Artillery Passage; Cafés in Spitalfields Market; The Pewter Platter, Folgate Street; New Inn, New Inn Yard; The Pool, The Bean, and The Barley Mow, all of Curtain Road; Artillery Arms, Bunhill Row.

Turn left out of the Bishopsgate side of the station; cross at the first set of lights and walk down Catherine Wheel Alley; turn left up Middlesex Street. When Shakespeare arrived in London, Hogge Lane, as it was known, was characterized by 'fair hedgerows of elm trees', with bridges and stiles which gave onto 'pleasant fields, very commodious for citizens therein to walk, shoot, and otherwise recreate and refresh their dull spirits in the sweet and wholesome air'. But by the early 1600s it had been built up on both sides, the fields turned into gardens.

Turn right down Widegate Street; cross Sandys Row and down Artillery Passage. Under these streets was Tassel Close, which served as an artillery yard where every Thursday gunners from the Tower of London came to

Opposite: St Leonard's Church, Shoreditch, the burial place of the actors Richard Burbage and William Sly, and of the clown Richard Tarlton, a 16th-century Eric Morecombe. Will Summers, Henry VIII's jester also lies here.

level 'certain brass pieces of great artillery against a butt of earth'. A map of the period shows people both firing guns and shooting arrows into targets here.

Turn left at the end of Artillery Lane and right up Gun Street; turn right at the end and over Brushfield Street. The local fields were rich in clay and were broken up for bricks, whose warm kilns were used as places to sleep by the homeless, a practice referred to in a play written by the subtle clown Robert Armin, who played the first Fool in *King Lear*:

> The winter nights be short
> And brickhill beds
> Does hide our heads
> As spittel fields report.

Shoreditch and St Mary Spital

The church at the end of Brushfield Street is the 18th-century Christ Church, Spitalfields. Spitalfields was the area east of the medieval priory and hospital of St Mary Spital, and in Shakespeare's time a rural district of fields and dirty lanes. London's contemporary historian, John Stow, records that in 1576, when the field was 'broken up for clay to make brick', a collection of urns was found 'full of ashes, and burnt bones of men, to wit, of the Romans that inhabited here'. Stow even reserved for himself an urn 'with the ashes and bones, and one pot of white earth very small, not exceeding the quantity of a quarter of a wine pint, made in the shape of a hare squatted on her legs...'

Take the central aisle through Charles II's Spitalfields Market; turn left through Elder Gardens on the other side of Lamb Street, right at the lane that bisects the gardens and left on Folgate Street; walk to Norton Folgate at the end.

The diverting and oft-distracted old gossip John Aubrey reports: 'Mr Beeston, who knows most of him fr[om]. Mr Lacy he lived in Shoreditch at Hoglane within 6 doors f[rom]-Norton Folgate.' The 'him' is taken to be Shakespeare and this stretch of Hog Lane is now Worship Street. Christopher Marlowe is also said to have lived on Norton Folgate, but it's not pleasant, so retrace your steps and turn left on Blossom Street.

Turn right on the horrible Fleur de Lis Street; turn left on Elder Street, left on Commercial Street and cross Shoreditch High Street. Shoreditch was a district of old ecclesiastical estates, and divided up between the priory of Holywell, the hospital of St Mary Spital, the Canons of St Paul's and the Bishop of London. The priory was dissolved by Henry VIII, and, as a 'liberty', was therefore outside the jurisdiction of the City, and so ripe

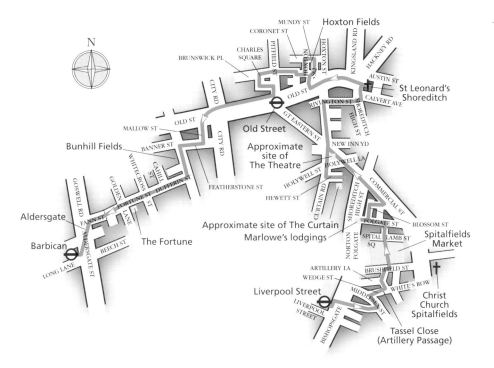

for theatrical, or some less reputable, development. According to Stow, there were fine houses along this street, but the district occasions one of his frequent laments about the greed and derisory social support that followed the dissolution of the monasteries. The houses once supplied by the hospital for the poor had become 'so decayed, that it was called Rotten Row' and sold to a rapacious draper called Russell, who imposed large rents, fines and made his bargains 'so hardly with all men, that both carpenter, bricklayer, and plasterer, were by that work undone...' Such was the property market in which Shakespeare and Marlowe may have lived.

The Theatre and The Curtain

Follow Great Eastern Street; turn left onto Holywell Lane and left on Curtain Road. At No 86 Curtain Road a plaque commemorates the Theatre, the first really significant purpose-built playhouse in London. (It is not now thought to have been the very first playhouse, which was a much cheaper and smaller affair called the Red Lion – not a tavern, but a farm in Stepney.) It was built by the actor and businessman James Burbage within the close of the old priory and was grand enough to be described by the Dutch visitor Johannes de Wit as an *amphitheatrum*.

The Theatre was a receiving house for a number of companies before Shakespeare's got an exclusive licence for the building in 1594. Afterwards, it became of central importance in Shakespeare's career. Many of his plays written after this date and before the Globe was built would have been composed with the Theatre in mind – including the great histories and comedies of his mid-career: *Richard II, 1* and *2 Henry IV* and *King John*; *Love's Labour's Lost, A Midsummer Night's Dream, Much Ado About Nothing* and *The Merchant of Venice*.

Not everyone approved. John Stockwood, in his Sermon at Paul's Cross, speaks with bitterness of the 'gorgeous playing place erected in the fields... a shew-place of all beastly and filthy matters'. William Fleetwood, London's Recorder, wrote in a report to Lord Burghley in 1584 of the disturbances that the Theatre seemed to draw to itself.

In 1597 Burbage fell out with his partner John Brayne and a dispute arose over the lease of the Theatre. It was closed, and described the next year as a 'dark silence and vast solitude'. Notoriously, in December 1598, the playhouse was dismantled, its timbers were carried over the Thames and used in the construction of the Globe. The Theatre and the Globe were, in a sense, one and the same.

Turn left again onto Hewett Street. A brown plaque on the building on the right before the gated yard at the end marks the approximate site of the Curtain Playhouse, which sprang up about a year after the Theatre (in 1577). It was built by a speculator called Henry Lanman and was in all probability quite similar to the Theatre (although there is precious little evidence about the appearance of either playhouse). The Curtain stood just outside old monastic turf, in the parish of St Leonard (of which more later) and, like the Theatre, probably had three galleries and a timber frame. In the period when the Theatre was empty, and before the company took up residence in the Globe, the Chamberlain's Men probably played at the Curtain. Also, it's likely that *Henry V* was first performed here and that the lines usually taken to be an apologetic description of The Globe – 'Can this cockpit hold / The vasty fields of France? Or may we cram / Within this wooden 'O...' is really a description of the Curtain. But the distinction is probably not very important, as both were large open-air theatres.

St Leonard's, Shoreditch

Return to Curtain Road, turn right and keep going, passing New Inn Yard on your right, at the end of which is King John Court. Pass Burbage House on your left and cross Rivington Street; turn right and at the end cross and turn left on Shoreditch High Street; on your right lies St Leonard's

Shoreditch, where you will find seats in the churchyard. St Leonard's has some of the richest theatrical associations of any church in London. With three important theatres nearby, one of them within the parish of this church, this is hardly surprising. Richard Burbage, Shoreditch man, the greatest actor in Shakespeare's company and the original of Hamlet, Lear and Othello, was buried here. He was the son of James Burbage, the builder of the Theatre, and his career almost exactly parallels Shakespeare's own. He probably took leading roles in all Shakespeare's plays at least from the opening of the Globe (in which he had a share with his brother Cuthbert) until he retired in about 1615. He was clearly a well-known performer, and there are many testaments to his genius for naturalism on the stage. An elegy to him runs:

> How to the person he did suit his face,
> Suit with his speech...
> Oft have I seen him leap into the grave,
> Suiting the person which he seem'd to have
> Of a sad lover with so true an eye,
> That there I would have sworn, he meant to die.

That may be his Hamlet leaping into the grave and there are several other echoes from Elsinore, the poet suggesting that Burbage has taken seriously Hamlet's advice to the players to 'suit the action to the word'.

William Sly is also buried here, another member of the Chamberlain's Men and one who ended up with shares in the company theatres, the Globe and the Blackfriars. His name appears on the list of players on the First Folio and he played in a number of Jonson's greatest plays, including *Every Man In* (and *Out*) *of His Humour* and *Volpone*. He appears as himself in a dramatic preamble to John Marston's *Malcontent*.

Almost as famous as Burbage was the clown Richard Tarlton, buried here in 1588. Blessed, apparently, with comic ugliness, Tarlton was the master of improvised comedy in the early Shakespearean period. He was also an all-round entertainer, the Elizabethan period's own variety performer. Fencing, singing, playing an instrument and dancing all featured in his repertoire.

Hoxton and Bunhill Fields

Cross the road at the crossing and turn left down Old Street; turn right into Hoxton Square. Hoxton was a pleasant suburb, quite rural and a favoured venue for afternoon jaunts, a resort, says Lovewit in Jonson's *Alchemist* for 'gallants, men and women, and all sorts, tagrag'. The herbalist John

Left: Queen Elizabeth I, by Marcus Gheeraerts. Here, the Virgin Queen is depicted as reigning over the map of England.

Gerard, when on a botanico-topographical walk, picked horseradish in Hoxton, 'in the field next unto a farme house leading to Kingsland'. Shakespeare, working locally, presumably knew that farm too.

On 22 September 1598, despite having a sword ten inches shorter, Ben Jonson killed the actor Gabriel Spencer in Hoxton Fields in a duel. When brought to trial at Old Bailey, Jonson confessed and claimed benefit of clergy – a privilege of exemption that extended to all 'clerks', or literate persons; his property was confiscated and his thumb branded. Gabriel Spencer's name appears on the First Folio in *3 Henry VI*. He, too, is buried at St Leonard's.

Cross the square at the bottom and turn right into Coronet Street; cross Pitfield Street onto Charles Square. Turn left at the far side of the square and right on Old Street. Cross Old Street by the subway, taking Exit 6; turn right down Mallow Street; right into Featherstone Street and left at the end down Bunhill Row.

To your left is what remains of Bunhill Fields. This was originally Bone Hill, and a place where over 1,000 cartloads of bones thrown out of the huge charnel house at St Paul's in 1549 were buried (although it apparently had the name before this grim deposit). The Duke of Somerset, Lord Protector in the reign of Edward VI, required the stone for his palace on the Strand. In the 16th century, Bunhill Fields, now a cemetery was, like Spitalfields, a place for young men to practise their archery.

The Fortune Playhouse

Turn right down Dufferin Street and cross Whitecross Street onto Fortune Street where you will find seats in the gardens. The third and latest theatre of the period was built in 1600 on Golden Lane. The Fortune, with money stumped up by the great tragedian Edward Alleyn and his impresario father-in-law Philip Henslowe, was probably built as a response to the decline of the Rose Theatre south of the river (which was ailing after the advent of the Globe). A detailed contract survives for the Fortune, drawn up between Henslowe and the master carpenter Peter Street, the man who had built the Globe earlier that year. It suggests the small world of the London theatre. The Fortune contract is the most detailed record of a theatrical building to have survived from Shakespeare's time and is full of references to the Globe Theatre – such and such a detail being required to be 'like the Globe'. Imitation is the sincerest form of flattery and it is easy to imagine the businesslike Henslowe taking in every detail of the Globe, neighbour to his Rose, and expressing a determination not to be outdone. It's chiefly from the Fortune contract that we get any sense of the stage at the Globe: 13 metres (43 feet) wide, extending to 'the middle of the yard'. Unlike the Globe, however, the Fortune was not circular, but square.

The Fortune was financially successful in spite of a mixed reputation, where petty theft and riot might alternate with visits from the ambassadors of Venice or Spain. In 1621, disaster struck: the theatre caught fire and, according to a contemporary diarist, all the 'apparels and playbooks [were] lost, whereby those companions are quite undone'. Alleyn himself was more matter-of-fact: 'this night at 12 of clock ye Fortune was burnt'. It was rebuilt in brick, and this time was round instead of square. It lasted until 1649 when it was dismantled.

Aldersgate

Cross Golden Lane and walk down Fann Street. At the corner of Fann and Aldersgate Streets you will find The Shakespeare, a pub decorated with a rollicking young ginger Bard shaking his plump calf at passers-by.

Turn left on Aldersgate Street. James I's triumphal entry to London in 1603 was commemorated on Aldersgate, one of the oldest gates to the city, pulled down in 1761. The great town houses of the Earl of Northumberland, rebellious to Henry IV, and the loyal Earl of Westmoreland stood here in the medieval period. Northumberland's house was seized by Henry IV and given to his queen, Jane, who turned it into her wardrobe. When Shakespeare was writing his history of that reign the house had been converted into a printing office. To your left is the Barbican Centre and to your right is Barbican Underground.

AROUND ST PAUL'S

Summary: The old St Paul's Cathedral was one of the largest medieval churches in Europe, until it was destroyed in the Great Fire of 1666. It dominated the skyline of Shakespeare's London, and was a centre of both religious and social life in the old City. It was also at the heart of London's book trade, where Shakespeare picked up the books that furnished him with source material for his work and where the first editions of his plays were bought and sold. This walk through some of the smaller streets of the City around its greatest building also takes in that fabled drinking-hole, the Mermaid Tavern, and the site, not far from the cathedral, of Shakespeare's point of entry into London from Stratford, and the grimmest prison within the city walls: Newgate.

Start:	St Paul's Underground Station.
Finish:	City Thameslink Station.
Length:	2.5 km (1½ miles).
Time:	1 hour. Allow another hour if you decide to go inside St Paul's.
Refreshments:	Hole in the Wall, Mitre Court; Viaduct Tavern, Newgate Street; the Rising Sun, De Gustibus (café), Carter Lane; the Cockpit, Ireland Yard (south of Carter Lane).

Leave the station at the Cheapside/Gresham Street exit; walk straight ahead and take the first left up Foster Lane. The street was lined with goldsmiths, jewellers and bookshops. One of the latter, at the sign of the 'Hart's Horn' belonged to Henry Walley, who published two editions of *Troilus and Cressida*. Walley was the most reluctant of all the publishers to sell his copyright to the publishers of Shakespeare's First Folio, when they were gathering the plays together. It is placed incongruously in the book, which suggests that it may have been introduced at the eleventh hour.

Herrick, Hilliard and the Mermaid Tavern
On the right you pass St Vedast Alias Foster. The poet Robert Herrick, the son of a Cheapside goldsmith, was baptized at the early 16th-century church that

Opposite: Wren's cathedral is built on the site of old St Paul's, one of the largest gothic buildings in Europe. In Shakespeare's day it performed many functions, not all of them religious.

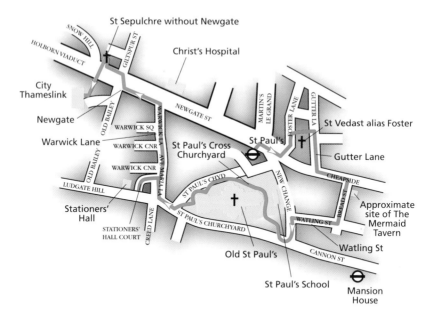

stood here in 1591. In Shakespeare's time Herrick was growing up under the shadow of his father's suicide and the unengaging prospect of a career as a goldsmith – a life he abandoned for Cambridge, the Church and poetry. He would probably have been numbered among those reluctant apprentices who took their afternoons off to visit London's playhouses. He caroused with the later generations of writers, musicians and theatrical men, those looking back on the great times at the Globe and elsewhere – Davenant and Carew – as well as the old Ben Jonson. On 19 December 1602, Herrick may have been in the congregation with John Manningham – the law student who left us the first record of a performance of *Twelfth Night* (see page 111) – to hear the sermon of 'one Clappam, a black fellow with a sour look but a good spirit'.

Turn right at Priest's Court and right at the end onto Gutter Lane. Nicholas Hilliard, the great miniaturist, and another goldsmith's son, lived here. Some of the greatest figures of the age were painted by Hilliard, including Queen Elizabeth, Drake and Raleigh and, it was suggested ingeniously by the scholar Leslie Hotson, Shakespeare – a theory since disproved. For Hilliard, the miniaturist's line must have no shadows, 'for the lyne without shadows showeth all to good judgment, but the shadowe without lyne showeth nothing'.

Turn down Goldsmith Street opposite Saddlers' Hall and right on to a dull stretch of Wood Street. You may want to find a seat under the large London plane tree at the defunct churchyard of St Peter Cheap to take in Cheapside at the end (see page 37). Cross Cheapside and turn down devastated Bread Street, site of a prison, the Wood Street Counter (or Compter) and, more famously, of the Mermaid Tavern. It is a place of literary myth, the meeting place of the Mermaid Club, said to have been founded by Sir Walter Raleigh. Luminaries of the age gathered here: Shakespeare, Jonson, Donne, Fletcher and Beaumont, whose couplets have become, ironically, his best-known literary effort:

> What things have we seen
> Done at the Mermaid!
> Heard words that have been
> So nimble, and so full of subtle flame,
> As if that every one from whence they came
> Had meant to put his whole wit in a jest,
> And had resolv'd to live a fool the rest
> Of his dull life...

Two hundred years later, John Keats took up the theme, promoting the pub over pastoral inspiration:

> Souls of poets dead and gone
> What Elysium have ye known,
> Happy field or mossy cavern
> Choicer than the Mermaid Tavern?

Unfortunately, Raleigh's club is a convivial 19th-century delusion, but it is true that Shakespeare knew the landlord – a certain William Johnson – who was witness to the signing of Shakespeare's mortgage for the property he bought at the Blackfriars in 1613. The club may be the stuff of folklore, but Shakespeare must have known the tavern and, living locally, was probably entertained here. It was owned by the Fishmongers' Company. In 1608, the year Shakespeare's company acquired their indoor playhouse in Blackfriars, John Milton was born on Bread Street, at the sign of the Spread Eagle.

Watling Street and St Paul's
Turn right onto Watling Street, which is an offshoot or perhaps a part of the Roman road that ran from Dover to St Albans and beyond. The street's antiquity merited it a mention in Michael Drayton's epic of British history *Polyolbion*, in which it 'doth hold her way / From Dover to the farth'st of fruitful Anglesey'. The 'swart and melancholy' Drayton, it should be said, though reputed to have been a friend of Shakespeare, Jonson and others, did not 'dominere in a pot-house'. Watling Street was full, says John Stow, of 'wealthy drapers, retailers of Woollen cloths, both broad and narrow, of all

sorts, more than in any one street of this city'. Stow also mentions the debased Tower Royal, once a wardrobe used by Philippa, Queen to Edward II, which stood crumbling here, and was used for stabling Queen Elizabeth's horses.

Cross New Change and turn left. A plaque here marks the old site of St Paul's School, which in Shakespeare's time taught 153 boys, nicknamed Paul's Pigeons. One of the great headmasters and champions of the English language, Richard Mulcaster, became 'High Master' here in old age. He was also headmaster of Merchant Taylors' School (see page 57).

Turn right at the end into Festival Gardens. Old St Paul's was a huge Gothic building, one of the largest in Europe. It had an immense tower and at one time a wooden spire surmounted by a weathercock in the shape of an eagle, in all some 30 metres (100 feet) higher than Wren's dome, and the highest spire ever built. The steeple was struck by lightning three years before Shakespeare was born and never replaced, but it was not forgotten in the literature of the time. Visitors could go up the tower for a penny, which they did, carving their names on the leads at the top. Even without its spire it was the most conspicuous building in the city and of Falstaffian proportions as Prince Hal recognized: 'This oily rascal is known as well as Paul's.'

There were numerous buildings outside: a chapter house; the bishops' palace with a great hall and garden; the dean's mansion, where John Donne, took up residence seven years after Shakespeare's death; the Jesus Bell Tower, a free-standing campanile with four bells; and the remains of a charnel house, demolished by Protector Somerset, who carted off the stone to use in his palace on the Strand.

There were lamps in the churchyard, the only publicly lit place in London.

Inside St Paul's

Inside, there were once tombs – the great courtier Sir Christopher Hatton's dwarfing those of his neighbours Sidney and Walsingham – but only one monument has survived intact from the great fire, John Donne's, which he designed himself. He can be found in the south transept of the cathedral in the attitude he assumed on his deathbed, when he 'disposed his hands and body into such a posture as required no alteration by those that came to shroud him'. Donne is the most famous Dean of St Paul's and was the greatest preacher of the age. His biographer, Isaac Walton, leaves an image of him 'weeping somtimes for his auditory, sometimes with them, always preaching to himselfe, like an angel from a cloud, though in none'.

As well as the monuments, there was a splendid clock with a man-in-the-moon and bells struck by a pair of jacks (figures that strike the bell on the outside of a clock), at which the dramatist Thomas Dekker stared, absorbed by 'the strangeness of [their] motion'. There were beautiful rose windows in the transepts, and there was a great organ, described by the travel writer Philip Hentzner as a thing 'which at evening prayer, accompanied with other instruments, is delightful'. Its great nave and aisles had played an important symbolic part in the history of the nation. The body of the deposed and murdered Richard II had lain in state here in 1400, as had that of Henry VI in 1471; his father Henry V prayed here before leaving for France in 1415, and returned to old St Paul's in triumph after Agincourt.

In common with all the other ecclesiastical estates in London, the cathedral suffered badly in the Reformation. The high altar and the great screen were demolished and the cathedral became half-secularized, its rood loft, font and tombs used as shop-counters. The nave, Paul's Walk, became a short cut between Paternoster Row to the north and Carter Lane to the south, and all types of goods: fish, bread, ale, meat and fruit, were lugged through, often on mules and horses. It became a promenading and meeting place for all kinds of people: lawyers met clients, gallants showed off their clothes, citizens exchanged news, servants were hired, bawds got pick-ups, foysts picked pockets and, 'cloaked rogues' malingered. Falstaff says he bought Bardolph at Paul's. One contemporary writer describes the noise 'like that of bees, a strange humming or buzz, mixed, of walking, tongues and feet'. Services somehow took place in the midst of this commotion.

One of London's children's acting companies – the Paul's Boys – performed in a small indoor playhouse located somewhere in the cathedral itself. They were drawn from the choir school, and not to be confused with St Paul's School itself. Acting occupied an important place in the school curricula, and the manager of the company got away with running the concern as a business by maintaining that the boys were being educated in the process. The Paul's Boys were in business for two periods: from 1575 to 1590, during which they offered some innovative plays by John Lyly (full of cross-dressing and mistaken identity), which had some influence on Shakespeare's comedies; and from about 1600 to 1608, when they premiered sexier, more violent fare from the likes of John Marston.

St Paul's Cross Churchyard and the book trade

Walk around the east end of the cathedral to the other side of the churchyard. St Paul's Cross stood here, a wooden pulpit, roofed with lead, from which many of the most distinguished English divines preached. It was also the centre of public news. Here, proclamations were read, marriages announced, persons excommunicated, victories declared. In 1577, just one year after the opening of London's first significant theatre, Thomas White pronounced syllogistically: 'The cause of plagues is sin, if you look to it well, and the cause of sin are plays: therefore the cause of plagues are plays.' In *Richard III*, the

Left: A sermon is delivered from a pulpit outside old St Paul's.

command is given that the indictment of Hastings should be read here.

This part of the churchyard was also the centre of London's retail book trade, and at the turn of the 16th century about 30 bookshops flourished here. While some were modest shops others were far more substantial buildings, sometimes as much as four storeys tall, but all had the distinctive signs that hung from London shops and businesses at the time. Here, it was possible to acquire the latest and the oldest books.

Shakespeare must have visited them, picking up perhaps some of those titles which became material for his plays: Holinshed's *Chronicles* for English history; Plutarch's *Lives* for Roman; romances by Greene, Lodge or Lyly; satires by Nashe; modern poetry by Spenser or Sidney and essays by Bacon; classical literature; old plays acted before his time; recent plays he might have missed; documentary accounts – such as the accounts of the expedition to the Bermudas and the colony in Virginia which influenced *The Tempest*; scientific works; treatises on melancholy; maps and works of geography.

He would also, and maybe with mixed feelings, have found copies of his own plays for sale here – perhaps pirated, probably always brought out under the auspices of his company, but never by himself. Individual plays were printed in quarto form, that is, about the size of a modern comic. They were usually sold unbound and printed in comparatively large quantities, the equivalent of a modern paperback. He would have had less equivocal feelings about setting eyes upon a copy of *Venus and Adonis*, his most popular published work during his lifetime, and one which he had written for publication. It ran through many editions, in some of which only a few copies have survived and those in poor condition, the books having been literally read to bits.

To your right, as you face the east end of the cathedral, was a row of about 16 shops, most of which published early or first editions of Shakespeare's plays. First came the Swan, run by Cuthbert Burby who published *Love's Labour's Lost* and the second quarto of *Romeo and Juliet*. A few doors down was the Green Dragon, owned by Thomas Hayes, the publisher of *The Merchant of Venice*. The shop was later owned by William Barrett, who in 1617 acquired rights to *Venus and Adonis* from John Harrison, who owned the White Greyhound, two shops down, and who also had the rights to *The Rape of Lucrece*. Richard Stonley, a retired civil servant, bought a copy of *Venus and Adonis* there for sixpence on 12 June 1593. He is the earliest recorded purchaser of a book by Shakespeare. The White Greyhound was later acquired, along with the rights to *Venus and Adonis*, by William Leake, who ran the Crane next door.

Not far from the Crane was Andrew Wise's shop, the Angel. Wise published *Richard II, Richard III*, the first and second parts of *Henry IV* and *Much Ado About Nothing* – the rights to the last two plays he shared with the proprietor of the Parrot next door.

On the other side, at the north door of the old cathedral, at the sign of the Gun, stood the shop of Edward White, where Shakespeare might have wistfully handled White's own edition of *Titus Andronicus*. Not far away was the Fleur-de-Lis, whose owner, Arthur Johnson, published a pirated version of *The Merry Wives of Windsor*. And last, the Spread Eagle, owned by Richard Bonian, who published the first quarto of *Troilus and Cressida* in 1609. The rights to *Troilus* were later acquired by the stubborn Walley of Foster Lane.

Towards the west end of the cathedral you will find the entrance to the crypt, the largest in Europe. You can visit the near end without having to pay, and there you will find a memorial to the memorials lost in the great fire and a small exhibition illustrating the history of the cathedral with pictures of old St Paul's. All but four of the outstanding collection of memorials in the crypt itself are later than the Elizabethan period.

Stationers' Hall
Turn left out of the crypt. Now is your chance to visit the cathedral. Otherwise,

cross the yard in front of the west end on the north side and go down Ludgate Hill. Turn right onto Ave Maria Lane, a street of 'text writers and bead-makers', and then take the first left, bringing you in front of Stationers' Hall. The Stationers' Company regulated the practices and protected the interests of everyone connected with the book trade: printers, publishers, binders and booksellers. One of its most important functions was to establish copyright. Once a title was written in the company's register book, copyright had been formally assigned, but to the publisher rather than the author. It could then be bought by or even mortgaged to another member of the Stationers' Company. The history of the early publication of Shakespeare's work can be traced in the Stationers' Register, from the poems, in whose publication he had a financial interest, to the quartos which appeared on the stalls at St Paul's Cross during his lifetime, to the great folios which appeared after his death.

The company catered for the interest of printers, not authors – and least of all playwrights. Copyright, although certainly expressed as an idea, did not exist in the modern sense. Shakespeare's plays were the property of his company, and for this reason it is often said that Shakespeare had no interest in the publication of his work. It is impossible to prove this one way or the other. What is unquestionably true is taht about half of Shakespeare's plays found their way in to print in various short ('bad') and long ('good') versions and that plays in general came to occupy an increasingly double existence during his lifetime: on the stage and on the page. The companies often followed up the publication of pirated plays by publishing improved versions of their own, advertising them as such on the title page as newly 'augmented' or 'corrected' or 'enlarged'. It's also possible that they came to believe that publishing was a good form of advertising, stimulating interest in 'old' plays brought back in to the repertory.

Christ's Hospital and Newgate

Turn left out of Stationers' Court and down Warwick Lane. The house of Richard Neville, 'Warwick the kingmaker', stood here, where he was waited upon, says Stow, by '600 men, all in red jackets'. This rather camp image sits oddly with the Warwick of Shakespeare's *Henry VI*, who has the son of Richard Duke of York crowned Edward IV, only to give the crown back to Henry VI: 'And who durst smile when Warwick bent his brow?' It ends badly for him, of course, on the battlefield at Barnet (of all places):

> My parks, my walks, my manors that I had,
> Even now forsake me, and of all my lands
> Is nothing left me but my body's length.
> Why, what is pomp, rule, reign, but earth and dust?

Keep going past Cutlers' Hall and turn left at the end. Before you, the blue plaques on Newgate Street mark the sites of the old Christ's Hospital and Greyfriars Monastery. The monastery was given to the hospital by Edward VI a few days before his death. It was intended for orphans, but 'many of them, taken from the dunghill, when they came to swete and cleane keping and to pure dyett, dyed downe righte'. The school which became attached to the hospital gradually took it over. The uniform of blue coats and yellow stockings was said to have been introduced to keep rats away from the boys' ankles. The cheerful poet and playwright George Peele went to school here, and his father was Clerk. He married well, which no doubt added to his good humour and allowed him to pursue his writing and acting with the Admiral's Men and to live a life of 'jests', some of which are preserved in print. His *Old Wive's Tale* is partly folk-tale, partly send-up of romantic drama.

Cross at the lights, the site of the old Newgate, one of the high-battlemented gates of the old City. On his way from Stratford, Shakespeare, having passed Shepherd's Bush and the gallows at Tyburn and walked down the Oxford road to Holborn must have entered London through the portcullis at Newgate, joining a stream of carts, wagons, oxen, horses, and pedestrians. The gate had long been used as a prison, and was by Shakespeare's time, and long after, the most important gaol in London and a by-word for prison life and culture. Obscene expressions were 'Newgate-terms', its inmates 'Newgate-birds'. John Marston, author of the bitter satire, *The Malcontent*, was imprisoned here in 1608 for writing a play, now lost, which was offensive to James I. Shakespeare alludes to those making their way to and from the prison in *1Henry IV*:

FALSTAFF: Must we all march?
BARDOLPH: Yea, two and two, Newgate-fashion.

Cross the handsome Giltspur Street, and enter the churchyard (continued rather messily round the back) of St Sepulchre without Newgate. Condemned prisoners led in 'Newgate-fashion' for execution at Tyburn were given a nosegay at St Sepulchre's. They later passed through Holborn (see page 42). The printer Thomas Purfoot kept a press near the church. He printed *Richard III* and *1 Henry IV* for one of the booksellers at St Paul's in 1622 – only a year before the publication of the First Folio. This was in Stow's time still 'a fair parish church in a fair churchyard'. You may want to look into the porch, the only remaining portion of the old church (1450).

The walk ends here, but you could extend it with a trip to the British Library (see page 140). City Thameslink provides a quick rail service to King's Cross.

BARBICAN AND CHEAPSIDE

Summary: You walk from the fields near Moorgate to the site of Shakespeare's unusual domestic circumstances in his lodgings near the Barbican, and on to London's surviving Guildhall and the traces of its great high street. This route takes in the City's most personal but little-known Shakespearean memorial, the birthplace of one of the playwright's greatest poet-critics and the old London headquarters of his most celebrated modern repertory company. This walk intersects with a number of other routes, allowing you to make the most of sites discussed elsewhere.

Start:	Moorgate Underground Station.
Finish:	Blackfriars Underground Station.
Length:	3 km (1¾ miles).
Time:	1½ hours.
Refreshments:	Numerous pubs and cafés on Carter Lane; the Cockpit, Ireland Yard.

Leave Moorgate Underground at the London Wall/Barbican Centre exit and turn left through Moorfields. The name suggests what this place north of the City wall once was: low-lying and marshy. It was drained in 1527 but remained for many years, according to a contemporary topographer, a 'noisome and offensive place, being a general lay-stall, a rotten moorish ground, crossed with deep stinking ditches'. During Shakespeare's career it went up in the world. In 1606 it was laid out with walks and became, like other semi-rural districts on the edge of the city, a popular resort for Londoners, somewhere to stroll and get a bit of fresh air away from the hectic half-timbered streets. Moorfields became a training-ground for the City militia. A pair of archers, rather dangerously placed in the midst of a lively scene of women bleaching linen, boys bearing baskets, cows, windmills and men driving swine, can clearly be seen on one of the surviving fragments of the delightful 'Copperplate' Map. The beggars from the Bedlam hospital on Bishopsgate and the duellists who also gathered here are not illustrated.

John Keats and St Giles without Cripplegate
You pass Keats Place and the John Keats at Moorgate pub, on whose sign the poet looks pert and uncomfortable. Keats was born at No 85. His letters are

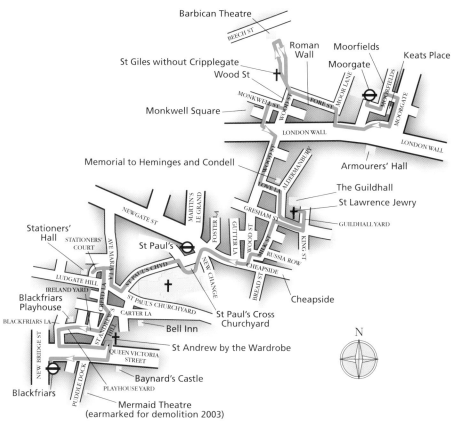

filled with references to Shakespeare. He based his famous creative idea of 'negative capability' on Shakespeare's imagination, 'that is, when a man is capable of being in uncertainties, mysteries, doubts, without any irritable reaching after fact and reason'. Shakespeare was also Keats's ideal of the 'poetical character', which 'is not itself – it has no self – it is everything and nothing – it has no character – ... it has as much delight in conceiving an Iago as an Imogen. What shocks the virtuous philosopher delights the chameleon poet... A poet is the most unpoetical of anything in existence, because he has no identity; he is continually in for, and filling, some other body.' It is a great passage on the playwright's inexhaustible sympathetic qualities and in retrospect seems a defining moment in the Romantic appreciation of Shakespeare. Jorge Luis Borges took from Keats the title and subject of his compelling parable about Shakespeare's imagination, 'Everything and Nothing'.

Turn right; make the most of stolid and bellicose Armourers' Hall on the other side of the road because the boxes and ziggurats of London Wall are a sustained essay in inhuman architecture. Turn right again as soon as you can onto Fore Street, which has the dubious distinction of having been hit by the first bomb dropped on the City in the Second World War. The pretty half-brick, half-stone tower ahead of you belongs to St Giles without Cripplegate. Through the piers supporting Salters' Hall to your left you can see a stretch of Roman wall, which once enclosed the City on both the land and river sides. By Shakespeare's time, the river sections, in earlier centuries only breached at Dowgate and Billingsgate, had been demolished, but the land sides were still substantial and well kept. The blazons of those sponsors – such as the great City companies – who had paid for its repair over the years were fixed to its sides. The gates which were let into it and whose names periodically make themselves known in the names of many of the City's larger streets – including Aldgate, Bishopsgate, Aldersgate, Newgate, Ludgate, Moorgate and Cripplegate – were shut at night. The mephitic old moat on the other side was notorious as a dumping ground for rubbish and dead dogs. By the mid-16th century London had burst its old wall and begun developing up the highways which still lead out of the City in various directions.

If you would like a closer look at St Giles without Cripplegate turn into the Barbican Centre at the end of Fore Street. The Great Fire spared St Giles, which is one of the few more or less medieval buildings still standing in the City. It has a sad association with Shakespeare's life, for it was here on 12 August 1607 that his nephew, Edward, the illegitimate son of his brother Edmund was buried. The parish interment records baldly state: 'Edward, son of Edward [sic] Shackspeere, player, base-born'. Edmund followed his elder brother into acting, but without his sibling's success. A few months later, at the age of 27, he was dead himself, and is buried in Southwark (see page 82). Some illustrious figures from the Shakespearean period are associated with St Giles. John Foxe, who wrote the *Book of Martyrs*, an endless gazetteer of English Protestant martyrdom and literally required reading in the Elizabethan period, was buried here in 1587. Oldcastle, the original of Shakespeare's Falstaff, and Cranmer, who features in *Henry VIII* (or *All Is True*), are entered in Foxe's distinguished roster. The cartographer John Speed, buried here in 1629, also had a hand in *Henry VIII*, supplying some of the historical background to Fletcher's contribution to that play. Speed's maps of Britain, which contributed to the country's sense of growing nationhood and imperial distinction, were presented as a 'performance' and gathered together under the title *The Theatre*

Opposite: Part of the old City wall near Barber Surgeon's Hall. In Shakespeare's day it bounded London from Blackfriars to the Tower and had seven gates: Ludgate, Newgate, Aldersgate, Cripplegate, Moorgate, Bishopsgate and Aldgate.

of the Empire of Great Britain. John Milton, born a few months after the first appearance of *Coriolanus*, was buried here in 1674. In a vile episode in 1793, his remains were exhumed, his hair tugged out, teeth bashed out for keepsakes and his carcass shown to the public for sixpence a glimpse.

The Barbican Theatre and The Mitre

Over the pond is the entrance to the Barbican Theatre. In 1982 the Royal Shakespeare Company moved into a purpose-built theatre here (their previous London home had been the Aldwych). For about 20 years, the Barbican Theatre itself took productions from the main stage in Stratford – the Royal Shakespeare Theatre – and the much smaller Pit took those from Stratford's Other Place. The RSC maintains its reputation as the world's most distinguished Shakespeare company. Strictly speaking, there is no permanent troupe – the longest contracts last 20 months – but the seasons are long and overlap, so there is a kind of loose long-term continuity and many actors return. It also employs the greatest number of actors in Britain, and has a huge technical staff. The RSC's artistic directors have included many of the most influential people in the British theatre. For all its technical excellence, there was never much love lost between the RSC and the Barbican Centre and in 2002, the RSC moved out. They now play in a number of venues in London.

Leave the Barbican the way you came in and turn right down Wood Street. The Mitre, a pub frequented by Jonson, and which he put into his wonderful comedy of London life *Bartholomew Fair*, stood here. Thomas Middleton knew the Mitre, too, and in his play *Five Gallants* includes praise for its 'neat attendance, diligent boys, and – push!' On the east side, north of Lad or Ladle Lane (now Gresham Street), stood the Compter or Counter, one of London's two debtors' prisons. It was a place as hateful to Falstaff 'as the reek of a lime-kiln'. It was facetiously compared to a university, where a man might pick up bad learning. Like other London prisons, the quality of accommodation depended on what prisoners could pay, and the place was divided up into three parts, suggestively described as the Master's side, the Knights' side, and the Hole. Like most Elizabethan gaols, the accommodation could be a good deal more expensive than a well-appointed inn.

Shakespeare's lodgings

Turn right into Monkwell Square. Ahead of you is Barber Surgeons' Hall, which occupied the same site in Shakespeare's time. The south-west corner of Monkwell Square occupies ground where once there met Silver and Muggle (or Monkwell) Streets. In and around 1604 Shakespeare lodged in a house here, the property of Christopher Mountjoy, a French Huguenot. A map of about 1550 shows the house, a large timbered property, with a shop on the ground floor. Silver Street was well known for its silversmiths and wig shops, and Mountjoy himself made a living as a tireman – that is, someone who made elaborate women's headgear. The case-book of the astrologer, physician and guru Simon Forman includes a reference to Mountjoy's wife, who consulted him and confessed her affair with one Henry Wood, a tradesman in Swan Alley, just off Bishopsgate. While engaged in the composition of, for instance, *Othello*, Shakespeare's domestic circumstances seem to have all the ingredients of an old farce, with the landlord engaged in his rather effeminate craft in the front room while his wife stole out to her lover at the back. They had a daughter, Mary, who kept shop with her father's three apprentices. One of these, Stephen Belott, later married her. The couple later fell out with old Mountjoy over the dowry and in 1612, Shakespeare was called in as a witness in the suit that followed. He proved a rather fallible one, apparently failing to remember anything useful about the arrangements that had been made for Mary Mountjoy's dowry.

Barber Surgeons' Hall to the Guildhall
The steps in that corner of the square lead up to the street and a path leads down to the gardens of the Barber Surgeons' Company and a pleasant herb garden. Plants grow out of the medieval additions to the City wall here as they once grew out of walls all over the City. In 1597 the herbalist John Gerard drew his readers' attention to the cinquefoile that grew upon 'bricke and stone wals about London, especially upon the bricke wall in Liver Lane' and the whiteblow that 'groweth plentifully upon the back wall in Chancery Lane, belonging to the Earl of Southampton'.

If you want to visit the excellent Tudor and early Stuart galleries at the Museum of London, turn right on London Wall and return to this spot afterwards, otherwise, turn left on London Wall and right on Wood Street past the tower of St Alban Wood Street. The churchyard that once lay here was used by the barber surgeons for to bury dissected felons. Turn left onto Love Lane, which commemorates the prostitutes who worked here in the 16th century.

Turn left into the gardens at the corner of Love Lane and Aldermanbury where you will find the memorial to Heminges and Condell. While living at Silver Street, Shakespeare could easily visit his friends and colleagues John Heminges and William Condell, who, as well as being members of Shakespeare's troupe, the King's Men, were respectively sidesman and churchwarden at the church of St Mary Aldermanbury that once stood here. The memorial here commemorates the great and, it seems, really selfless commission they performed for Shakespeare after his death: compiling the First Folio of his plays, 'without ambition either of self-profit or fame, only to keep the memory of so worthy a friend and fellow alive as was our

Left: A letter from Shakespeare's patron, Henry Wriothesley, Earl of Southampton, to Sir Julius Caesar in 1603.

Shakespeare'. Heminges and Condell, actors and men of the theatre, knew very well how remote the chances were of a play's survival after it had dropped out of the repertoire. Had they not published the First Folio some 16 plays would have been lost for good and many more would have survived only in the often-inferior quarto texts available on the stalls at St Paul's Cross (see page 26). The editors sought literary prestige for Shakespeare, sorting the plays, somewhat controversially, according to genre: history, comedy or tragedy, and dividing them up into acts and scenes. When it came out in 1623, the First Folio was a large and expensive book that sold for about £1 and was worth looking after. About 240 copies from the original print-run of 1,000 survive.

Turn right on Aldermanbury; on your left is the Guildhall, most of which was built in the reigns of Henry IV (who was Shakespeare's Bolingbroke) and Henry V. In Shakespeare's time, it was the centre of civic government in London. It was also used occasionally for important trials, including that of Henry Garnet, a Jesuit implicated in the Gunpowder Plot, in 1606. Although it survived the Great Fire, it has been changed a bit. The playful porch, designed in idiosyncratic Asiatic style, was added in the 18th century by Nathaniel Dance. There were also statues on the outside of the building, celebrated in some doggerel verse:

> Jesus Christ aloft doth stand,
> Law and Learning on either hand,
> Discipline in the devil's neck,
> And hard by her are three direct;
> There Justice, Fortitude and Temperance stand:
> Where find ye the like in all this land?

In *Richard III* Gloucester dispatches Buckingham here to address the citizens, 'infer the bastardy of Edward's children' and 'urge his hateful luxury'. Buckingham embarks on this smear campaign, but it is not well received by the citizens in the hall:

> They spake not a word,
> But, like dumb statues or breathing stones,
> Stared each on other and looked deadly pale –

Turn left on Gresham Street and left into Guildhall Yard. Leave Guildhall Yard via the church of St Lawrence Jewry. Thomas More delivered a series of lectures in the church that stood here before the Great Fire, to which 'resorted all the chief learned of the City of London'. In a poignant moment in *Sir Thomas More*, in which Shakespeare had a hand, More reminds his executioner: 'You were a patient auditor of mine when I read the Divinity Lecture at St Lawrence's.'

Cheapside
Turn right on Gresham Street and left on Milk Street, one of the market streets which runs into Cheapside and where a plaque marks the house where Sir Thomas More was born. Turn right on Cheapside, the chief market place ('chepe') and high street of Shakespeare's London. The names of the streets that run into it recall the things that were sold: Bread, Wood, Milk, Honey, Poultry. Fish was sold on Friday Street, hardware on Ironmonger Lane, and doves and pigeons at Dove Court off Grocers' Hall Court. There was little that could not be procured here. Between Bread Street and Bow Church to the east was Goldsmith's Row, subject of a reminiscent song in Dekker's *Eastward Ho!*

> Farewell, Cheapside! Farewell, sweet trade
> Of goldsmiths all, that ne'er shall fade.

Beyond the church were the mercers and drapers in whose pattern books could be found, as John Donne's fourth satire affirms, any 'wardrobe's inventory'. Beyond these, at the end of Bucklersbury, were the grocers and druggists, for herbs, drugs, tobacco and sweetmeats. And of course, wherever there was money, there were pickpockets and prostitutes – as the ironic title of Middleton's *A Chaste Maid in Cheapside* implies.

Cheapside was the City's widest street and pageants took place here, which the Queen witnessed from a terrace on old Bow Church. On his ceremonial return journeys from Westminster, the Lord Mayor disembarked at Paul's Wharf and processed down Cheapside to the Guildhall, his boatmen carrying their boats and silver oars upon their shoulders. In these pageants, three structures in the middle of Cheapside had parts to play. There was the little, or 'pissing' conduit, extravagantly decked and made to run with wine at coronations. Opposite Wood Street stood old Cheapside Cross built, like Charing Cross, by Edward I to honour the resting place of his queen's funeral bier. Gilded and adorned with saints, it was for hundreds of years one of the best-known and best-loved monuments in London. In 1596 the figure of the virgin on the top was replaced by a naked Diana, out of whose breasts water spouted. Rosalind alludes to it in *As You Like It* when she says she will 'weep for nothing, like Diana in the fountain'. It became at last an object of puritanical hatred, and a large crowd came to see it pulled down in 1643. Opposite Milk Street was the Standard, a square pillar with a conduit, statues round the sides and a figure of Fame at the top. It also had a grimmer function, presiding over executions and book-burnings.

Many apprentices learned their trades here, an occasionally rebellious lot who might be brought out for trouble with the cry of 'Clubs!' Their day ended when the curfew was rung from Bow Church and woe betide the clerk if this office was not punctually observed:

Clerk of Bow bell with thy yellow locks
For thy late ringing thy head shall have knocks.

Cheapside is the likely location for an impressive attack on bigotry against the intervention of 'strangers' – that is, foreign exiles – in London's trade in that fragment of *Sir Thomas More* believed to be by Shakespeare.

New Change to Baynard's Castle

Turn left at the lights at the end of Cheapside. For this section of the walk you will need to refer to other passages in the book. Cross New Change and turn right through St Paul's Churchyard, which was the centre of the London book trade (see page 25). Turn down Ludgate Hill and right up Ave Maria Lane; turn left into Stationers' Hall Court, where printers and publishers registered their books, including Shakespeare's plays (see page 27). Retrace your steps and cross Ludgate Hill and turn down Creed Lane; cross Carter Lane, passing the site of the Bell Inn (see page 55) and down St Andrew's Hill; turn right down Ireland Yard, past the Cockpit pub and on to Playhouse Yard, which was the site of the Blackfriars Playhouse (see page 50). Turn left at the end down Blackfriars Lane and right at the bottom. On the other side of the road, Puddle Dock leads down to the Mermaid Theatre. When it opened in 1959, the Mermaid was the first new theatre in the City of London for 300 years. It was founded by the actor Bernard Miles and, in honour of its Elizabethan inheritance, given a stage designed by the illustrator and theatre historian C. Walter Hodges. At the time of writing it is earmarked for demolition.

To the left of Puddle Dock stood Baynard's Castle, an ancient place built by Ralph Barnard, who came over with William the Conqueror. It passed in and out of Crown hands until it was burned down in the Great Fire. It was bestowed upon the Fitzwalter family. His daughter Matilda refused the advances of King John, for which insult the castle was burned down and she was sent to the Tower and fed a poisoned poached egg. The Fitzwater in *Richard II* lived here. More memorably, in *Richard III* it is here that Gloucester sets himself up and advances his villainous plans of usurpation. The citizens are brought to Baynard's Castle to admire the 'pious' Duke, who enters 'aloft, between two bishops':

Two props of virtue for a Christian prince
To stay him from the fall of vanity;
And see, a book of prayer in his hand –
True ornaments to know a holy man...

Henry VIII converted the castle to a palace and put up the King of Castile here when he was driven to England by a storm. In Shakespeare's day, its keepers were the Pembroke family, who entertained Elizabeth here with dinner and fireworks. Shakespeare, who after 1608 was working nearby, must have known it well.

Keep going until you reach the churchyard of St Andrew by the Wardrobe. Take a seat here, if you wish. Just off St Andrew's Hill to your right stood the gatehouse to the Blackfriars, the only property in London that Shakespeare ever owned (see page 54).

Retrace your steps down Queen Victoria Street for Blackfriars Station.

CLERKENWELL AND SMITHFIELD

Summary: Now a ruinously expensive and fashionable neighbourhood of quiet Victorian streets, old pubs, new clubs and attractive closes and squares, Clerkenwell in the 16th century still bore the vestiges of its rich priory, occupied by a mixture of bureaucrats and low lifes. Shakespeare's plays were first licensed for performance here, and the office still survives. Still standing, too, are bits of the Charterhouse, another illustrious monastic estate, and one of the last portions of a 16th-century suburban London street, both passed *en route* to the site of London's greatest fair, forever associated with Shakespeare's friend and rival, the dramatist Ben Jonson.

Start:	Chancery Lane Underground Station.
Finish:	Barbican Underground Station.
Length:	3 km (1¾ miles).
Time:	1½ hours.
Refreshments:	Ye Olde Mitre, 1 Ely Court (off Ely Place); The Three Kings, Clerkenwell Close; cafés in Clerkenwell Green; Rising Sun, Rising Sun Court; Hand and Shears and Ye Old Red Cow, Cloth Fair; Barley Mow, Barley Mow Passage; Jerusalem Tavern, Britton Street (off route); Fox and Anchor, Charterhouse Street.

Leave Chancery Lane Underground at Exit 1. To your left, at the corner of Chancery Lane, is the site of Southampton House, London residence of Shakespeare's patron Henry Wriothesley (see page 114). To your right is Staple Inn. So little of Shakespeare's London survives that it's worth having a look at this. A survivor of the Great Fire and (just) World War II, it is fairly typical of the kind of half-timbered building which would have lined the streets of 16th- and 17th-century London. The City's houses were commonly three or four storeys high, at least one storey higher than most provincial buildings. According to the traveller Fynes Morrison, London houses were 'built all

Opposite: St John's Gate, Clerkenwell, originally part of the medieval priory. In Shakespeare's day it served as an office for the Master of the Revels, the royal servant responsible for licensing plays for public performance.

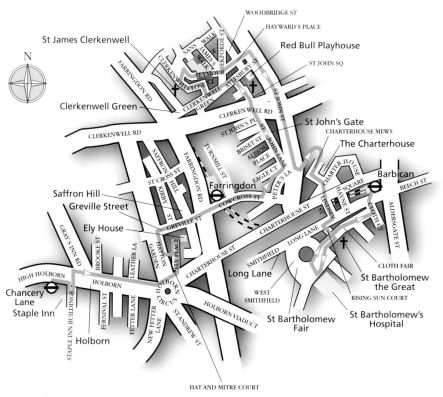

inward, that the whole room towards the streets may be reserved for shops of tradesmen, make no show outwardly, so as in truth all the magnificence of London building is hidden from the view of strangers at the first sight.' In the Elizabethan period Staple Inn was a kind of preparatory school for students wishing to be called to the Bar by the Inns of Court.

Holborn and Ely House

Turn left out of Staple Inn, cross the road at the lights opposite the inn and turn right down Holborn. The street takes its name from Holebourne, a tributary of the Fleet River (which Holborn once crossed). A major highway into the City, and lined with taverns in the 16th century, it was probably the route Shakespeare first took into London from Stratford. The George and Blue Boar, the Castle, the Old Bell, the Sun, the Bear and the Black Bull have all gone now, and the street's character has changed even more than that of the Strand. At one time, at the entrance to Ely Place, the street descended sharply to a stone bridge that crossed over the Fleet River, where Farringdon Street now runs. Prisoners from the Tower and Newgate, bound for execution at

Tyburn, were led up Holborn or 'Heavy Hill', as this stretch was then nicknamed. With Inns of Court (Gray's, Lincoln's) and of Chancery (Barnard's, Staple, Furnival's, Thavie's) on both sides, Holborn was a lawyers' quarter, lined with large houses and gardens. Both Sir Thomas More and Sir Francis Bacon lived here, as well as the herbalist John Gerard, who brought back exotics from the New World and elsewhere in the Old World and planted them in his physic garden.

Turn left at Ely Place, which marks the site of Ely House, the late 14th-century palace of the Bishops of Ely and its 16ha (40-acre) estate (now Hatton Garden). 'Large and commodious' were the rooms thereof, says Stow, and a venue for 'divers great and solemn feasts'. One of these, from the 23rd year of the reign of Henry VIII, boasted an immense menu, including 24 'beefs', 100 fat muttons, 51 great veals, ten dozen Kentish capons and 37 dozen pigeons.

It is a place of strong Shakespearean connections. John of Gaunt, who leased it from the bishop after his palace at the Savoy was smashed up during the Peasants' Revolt, lived and died here. When Gaunt dies in *Richard II* the king wastes no time in dispatching his favourite to seize his estate:

Go, Bushy, to the Earl of Wiltshire straight.
Bid him repair to us to Ely House
To see this business.

The house also featues in *Richard III*, when Richard with characteristic insolence sends the Bishop to fetch strawberries: 'When I wandered I saw good strawberries in your garden there; I beseech you, send for some of them.' Ely House was demolished in the 18th century with the exception of the late 13th-century chapel of St Etheldreda. The Spanish ambassador Gondomar lived at Ely Place in the 1620s, and Catholics were permitted to worship here; since the 1870s it has been a Catholic chapel.

Turn right out of the church, right again down Ely Court and past Ye Olde Mitre, dating from least 1546 (the mitre referred to is that of Ely). Turn right at Hatton Garden. In Shakespeare's day, Ely House was leased by Elizabeth's favourite, Chancellor Sir Christopher Hatton, for an annual rent of £10, ten loads of hay and a rose picked at midsummer. In the 1580s, when the see of Ely was unoccupied, Hatton built himself a house in the orchard of the bishops' palace. He was a patron of the poet, Spenser, and backed the voyages of Drake and Frobisher. Hatton's house went to his nephew on his death, and then to that nephew's widow, Elizabeth and her second husband, Edward Coke, the forceful lawyer and rival to Francis Bacon. Coke was a principled and ruthless prosecutor at many of the show trials of the age: Essex, Raleigh and the Gunpowder Plotters.

Greville Street and Fulke Greville

Turn right onto Greville Street, which remembers the politician, patron, poet and intimate of Sir Philip Sidney, Sir Fulke Greville, 1st Lord Brooke. Greville was one of the great political survivors, whose career dipped and rose according to the fortunes of the parties he had allied himself with at Court. Among the more prominent, often ruthless figures who jockeyed for power in the Elizabethan and Jacobean Courts, Fulke Greville was patient and long-suffering. In some ways he recalls John Donne, seeking to reconcile the paradoxes of love and religion in poetry that, like Donne, he was content simply to circulate among his friends. As well as poetry (chiefly sonnets) Greville wrote 'closet' dramas (plays for private performance). One of these, *Antony and Cleopatra* on the subject of 'irregular passions in forsaking Empire to follow sensuality', he destroyed when he feared it would annoy a government recently disturbed by Essex's rebellion (see page 95). Greville's house occupied this street, and here he was murdered by his manservant at the age of 74; Greville, with characteristic dispassionateness, forgave this act on his deathbed. The servant, who had felt aggrieved at decisions Greville had made about his will, subsequently committed suicide. The biographer Park Honan has suggested that the Earl of Southampton, Shakespeare's patron, came to know of Shakespeare through the young Fulke Greville, because they were both presented at Court at the same time. Fulke Greville's father was honorary recorder of Stratford-upon-Avon and probably came across Shakespeare's father.

Cross Saffron Hill. The gardens of the Bishop of Ely were famous for their fruits and for saffron, first introduced into Cambridgeshire and the see of Ely in the 14th century. Saffron was widely used to flavour the not-altogether-fresh meat which faced Londoners at the supper table, and wild saffron grew freely in London gardens.

St John's Gate and Museum

Cross Clerkenwell Road onto Cowcross Street (not a cattle crossing, but once the site of a cross); turn left down White Horse Alley and bear right through the large courtyard; turn left past the handsome brick building with the bull's head and turn left up St John's Lane (not Street) to St John's Gate and Museum.

Only the gatehouse of the Priory of St John of Jerusalem remains. Once one of the greatest religious foundations in medieval London, it was the home of the Knights Hospitallers, and also served as a hospice and house of refuge to travellers (who paid the Knights in the news they brought). According to the antiquarian William Camden, the priory 'resembled a palace, had a very faire church, and a tower steeple raised to great height with so fine workmanship that it was a singular beauty and ornament in the City'. At the dissolution of the monasteries the buildings were broken up and sold; Henry VIII used the 'faire church' to store his 'toils and tents' for hunting. Shakespeare could have known its great tower only by repute, for this great adornment of the north London skyline was blown up by Protector Somerset, who wanted the stone for his palace on the Strand.

The gatehouse, once lapped in lead and surrounded by gardens, orchards and fishponds, eventually became the Office of the Revels. The Master of the Revels was responsible for the licensing of plays for public performance. The official reason for the existence of playing companies in the Shakespearean period was to provide entertainment for the Court; public performance was tolerated by the sovereign because it meant the players were always ready to perform at the royal behest. Edmund Tilney held this office for most of Shakespeare's career. Shakespeare would hand over the play to his company, who would present it to Tilney with a fee to obtain a licence for its performance. If the Master found material within it offensive to Church or state it would not receive a licence or (more likely) would receive a licence with certain conditions attached. Tilney's hand can be detected in the scores which strike out parts of a passage from *Sir Thomas More*, the only extended specimen of Shakespeare's handwriting, held in the British Library. It is a matter of scholarly debate as to whether the Master was regarded as an agency of prohibition or consultation: as someone to get round or as someone whose help was required to keep the players out of trouble. It was not the Master, after all, who would prosecute them if they got on the wrong side of the law or offended the powerful. Possibly he was both.

Philostrate, in *A Midsummer Night's Dream*, is Theseus' Master of the Revels. He cautions the duke against the play offered by Quince, Bottom and the rest, but for critical rather than political reasons:

> No, my noble lord
> It is not for you. I have heard it over,
> And it is nothing, nothing in the world.

The lines are sometimes given to Egeus. The Master of the Revels was not responsible for overseeing the publication of plays; this lay with the Star Chamber and the Stationers' Company (see page 27).

Clerkenwell Green and the Red Bull
Cross Clerkenwell Road and then cross over St John's Square. St John's Church incorporates a crypt and parts of the nave of the original priory. Pass Albemarle Street on your right and walk up Jerusalem Passage at the top of the square; Clerkenwell Green is to your left. Clerkenwell Green was the

centre of a suburban village, inhabited by the nobility and prosperous City merchants. The 'Clerken' refers to the parish clerks or scholars who, in the Middle Ages, Stow records, 'were accustomed there yearly to assemble and to play some large history of holy Scripture'. The 'well' refers to one of the numerous springs in the locality, which although dammed up by Shakespeare's time, still survived in name: Skinners well, Fags well, Tode well, Loder's well, Rede well. An annual wrestling match took place here, and it was attended by people from all over the country. It seems to have gone into social decline in the Shakespearean period, however, by which time it had a reputation for theft and prostitution.

Turn up Clerkenwell Close. This became the site of Clerkenwell's own 'Bridewell' (by then a by-word for prisons) in 1616. It was an overflow prison for the Bridewell itself (see page 150). Walk up the steps into the church of St James Clerkenwell. The church was once at the centre of a Benedictine nunnery most of which, like the neighbouring priory, was demolished after the dissolution of the monasteries in 1539 and the land given over to the building of 'many fair houses'. Sir John Oldcastle, the original of Shakespeare's Falstaff, lived near here.

You should be able to walk through the churchyard via the gate to your left at the bottom of the steps; pass through the first gate, walk up Hayward's Place and over the top of Woodbridge Street. Between here and St John Street stood the Red Bull, one of the longest lasting and rougher theatres of Shakespeare's time. It was an inn-yard playhouse and, according to its detractors, its audience was composed of 'cutt throats and other lewd and ill disposed persons'. It perpetuated the rather wilder, more exaggerated acting style associated with Edward Alleyn, the 'tradition' of the Rose and the Fortune (though this is a matter of dispute). In 1610 a production of *Richard III* performed by boys was probably given at the Red Bull with a droll prologue by Thomas Heywood, its hugely prolific resident playwright: 'If any wonder by what magic charm Richard the third is shrunk up like his arm...'

In 1627, Shakespeare's old company brought the Red Bull to book for giving unauthorized performances of plays by Shakespeare, who by then had been published in Folio and was *en route* to classic status. The theatre's reputation for mischief lasted throughout the Commonwealth period when the company smuggled in illicit 'drolls' (playlets knocked together from bits of old plays, usually comedies, some of them Shakespeare's). It is ironic that the theatre most conspicuously disrespectful of the licence to perform Shakespeare's plays was later the only one to keep them on the stage. After the Restoration in 1660, Charles II's favourite, Thomas Killigrew, operated under royal licence here, and so it became the only open-air theatre to survive the theatrical holocaust of England's Commonwealth period.

The Charterhouse and Bartholomew Fair

Cross St John Street at the zebra and turn right; keep going over Clerkenwell Road, passing Hat and Mitre Court on your left; turn left at the end on to Charterhouse Street; bear left into Charterhouse Square. The Charterhouse, once the most important Carthusian monastery in England, has no specific Shakespearean association except that it is a survivor of the Great Fire. It has an illustrious and sometimes bloody history: the prior, John Haughton, who committed the grave error of inviting Thomas Cromwell here to discuss the dubiousness of Henry VIII's supremacy over the Church, ended up at Tyburn, hanged, drawn and quartered.

Like Clerkenwell, only the gatehouse and parts of the chapel remain. The Charterhouse subsequently passed through a number of great families, including the Howards and the Percys. Elizabeth stayed here before her coronation and again three years later, two visits which ruined its then owner Lord North, who was obliged to put on extravagant shows. In Shakespeare's time it was, for a period, back with the Howard family. Thomas Howard, the Earl of Suffolk, named it Howard House. James I stayed here on his arrival in London in 1603; he made Thomas Howard his Lord Chamberlain and created 133 new knights in the Great Chamber – a room once described as the finest surviving Elizabethan interior in London before a bomb did for it in 1941. In 1611 Thomas Sutton, the coal magnate and reputedly the wealthiest commoner in England, acquired the Charterhouse and turned it into a hospital for aged men and a school for children of poor parents. The character of Jonson's legendary miser Volpone is allegedly based on Sutton. Perhaps he had taken the imputation of calculating meanness to heart.

Cross the bottom of Charterhouse Square and turn right and then left on Lindsey Street. Long Lane was then the home of pawnbrokers and second-hand clothes dealers. It gets a mention in *The Taming of the Shrew*, where Petruccio, when considering his poor clothes and those of his wife, and with Shakespeare's habitual disregard for topography, requests that his horses be brought 'unto Long Lane end': a piece of Smithfield in Padua. In 1634, one Cromes, a pawnbroker of Long Lane, was imprisoned for lending the players at Salisbury Court an ecclesiastical vestment with the name of Jesus upon it (see page 154).

Cross Long Lane at the zebra crossing and turn right; turn left at Rising Sun Court onto Cloth Fair; ahead you will see a church porch with striking flush-work; turn right and right again and pass under the half-timbered gatehouse into the churchyard of St Bartholomew the Great. The church, spared by the Great Fire, would have been ancient in Shakespeare's day. It was originally a priory founded in 1123 by Rahere, jester to Henry I and a reformed character.

At the dissolution, the nave of the priory church was kept for parishioners and the remainder of the priory was sold to Sir Richard Rich in 1544 and used for storage and as workshops.

The large square outside the churchyard was the site of Bartholomew Fair, held annually on 24 August and the most famous in England. What began as a cloth fair became a great carnival, with puppet plays, drummers, freak shows, ballad singers and wrestling matches. Amongst the frequenters of the fair – its 'Bartholomew Birds' – thrived Autolycus types, picking pockets, ripping off the crowds and perhaps employing 'Bartholomew terms' – the slang of the fair. The chief emphasis was on eating (traditionally roast pig) and drinking, usually to excess. Jonson's most generous play *Bartholomew Fair* gives probably the greatest and most vivid picture of London life of the time. At the play's heart is Dame Ursula, the pig woman, 'all fire and fat', whose pork works on the appetites of all who come across her. Shakespeare doesn't pass over the fair: Falstaff is described by Doll Tearsheet as a 'tidy Bartholomew boar pig', while in *Henry V* Burgundy notices the notorious clouds of flies which buzz around the heads of the cattle driven up from the country: 'For maids, well-summered and warm kept, are like flies at Bartholomew-tide: blind though they have their eyes'.

St Bartholomew's Hospital and Cloth Fair

Go back through the gatehouse into West Smithfield, site of the fair. To your left you will see the Henry VIII gatehouse to St Bartholomew's Hospital. Pass through the arch; on your left is St Bartholomew the Less, another survivor of the Great Fire, also founded by Rahere and built as a chapel to the hospital. Inigo Jones, Jonson's collaborator and the greatest architect and scenic artist of the period, was christened here in 1573. Pass through the archway onto the main courtyard of St Bartholomew's Hospital. Rahere was also responsible for the foundation of this hospital, the oldest in London. Henry VIII was negligent towards the hospital after the dissolution; it was subsequently 'granted' to the City, whose citizens bailed it out. In Shakespeare's day it was maintained by a board of City governors presided over by the Lord Mayor. The unfortunate Portuguese Jew Roderigo Lopez, later physician to Queen Elizabeth, was chief physician here for 12 years. In 1594 he was accused of attempting to poison the Queen at the instigation of Philip II and executed, unquestionably the victim of latent anti-Semitic feeling. It has been suggested that Lopez was a model for Shylock; it's possible that Graziano's unpalatable rant against the wolf 'hanged for human slaughter' may make reference to a recent and notorious case. (The Latin for wolf is *lupus* – Lopez.) William Harvey was appointed house physician at the hospital in 1609. During Shakespeare's last years in London Harvey would have been working here on his theory of the circulation of the blood, first propounded in 1615.

Blood, before William Harvey discovered its circulation, was thought to be the refined end-product of our food and drink; if it was overproduced its excess might erupt in disease and would therefore have to be 'let'.

In Shakespeare's day, medical ideas were still based on those of ancient Greece. The body's humours goverened its health and corresponded to the elements of the earth – earth, air, fire and water: blood (hot and moist), phlegm (cold and moist), black bile (cold and dry), yellow bile (cold and moist). The opposition between these humours determined the body's health, and the object was to keep the right balance or temperature throughout life (as one or other humour gained the ascendance). To be 'distempered', as Henry IV complains of his kingdom, was not to be ill, but to be in the right condition to admit illness, as Warwick explains:

It is but a body yet distempered
Which to his former strength may be restored
With good advice and little medicine.

The physician's job was seen to correct distempers by restoring the body's balance, by administering herbs, change of diet or air and, perhaps most commonly, bloodletting.

Before any knowledge of bacilli, bad air was quite reasonably believed to be at the root of many illnesses. This is not lost on Caliban:

All the infections that the sun sucks up
From bogs, fens, flats on Prosper fall ...

Good air – the smell of pomanders – or the breath of the young and healthy were seen as a cure for air-borne disease, as Orsino says of Olivia in *Twelfth Night*: 'Methought she purged the air of pestilence.' Diseases were also thought, correctly in some cases, to be caught from other people and during times of plague the playhouses and similar places of resort were closed down.

Retrace your steps to the square and up Cloth Fair to your right. Until Elizabeth's reign, Bartholomew Fair was England's leading cloth fair, attracting merchants from all over Europe. This street was home to drapers and clothiers, and until recent years was one of the last bits of medieval London. Only its low, narrow character and the over-restored front of no 41 suggest anything of the Middle Ages now. Inigo Jones, whose father was in the trade, was born in this street.

Cloth Fair becomes Middle Street; turn left, right and left again for Barbican Undergound.

BLACKFRIARS TO MONUMENT

Summary: Some of the City's most attractive old streets wind around Blackfriars, site of Shakespeare's exclusive indoor playhouse and, after the Globe, the most important theatrical site in Elizabethan London. The district also recalls a great monastic estate, and the drastic effects of the Reformation, evident throughout the City in Shakespeare's time. The route then seeks out the site from which the only surviving letter to Shakespeare was written; passes the locations of a school and the lodgings of a number of his literary contemporaries; unearths one of London's most bizarre relics; and ends with Sir Christopher Wren's great memorial to the City Shakespeare knew.

Start:	Blackfriars Underground Station.
Finish:	Monument Underground Station.
Length:	2 km (1¼ miles).
Time:	1 hour.
Refreshments:	The Old Wine Shades, Martin Lane (1663); The Bell, Bush Lane; The Cockpit, Ireland Yard; Olde Bell Tavern, St Bride's Avenue; The Black Friar, Queen Victoria Street; cafés and restaurants on Carter Lane.

Leave the Underground at Exit 8; turn left down Watergate ahead and down Kingscote Street; cross Tudor Street onto Bridewell Place; turn left at New Bridge Street and left again onto Bride Lane, past the Bridewell Institute, left on St Bride's Avenue and into the churchyard of St Bride's (see page 154). Turn right at the end of St Bride's Avenue and right again off Ludgate Circus. From the time of Richard II, like many old gatehouses, the medieval Ludgate was used as a prison. It was rebuilt in 1586, and in Shakespeare's day was embellished with statues of Queen Elizabeth, King Lud and his two sons. This little group of statuary now adorns St Dunstan Fleet Street. On the opposite side of Ludgate Hill, towards St Paul's, stood the large Bell Savage Inn, well known in Shakespeare's time as a major venue for prize sword fights.

Blackfriars Monastery and Playhouse
Cross New Bridge Street at the lights and head down Pilgrim Street. Turn right onto Ludgate Broadway, where a plaque marks the site of the Blackfriars

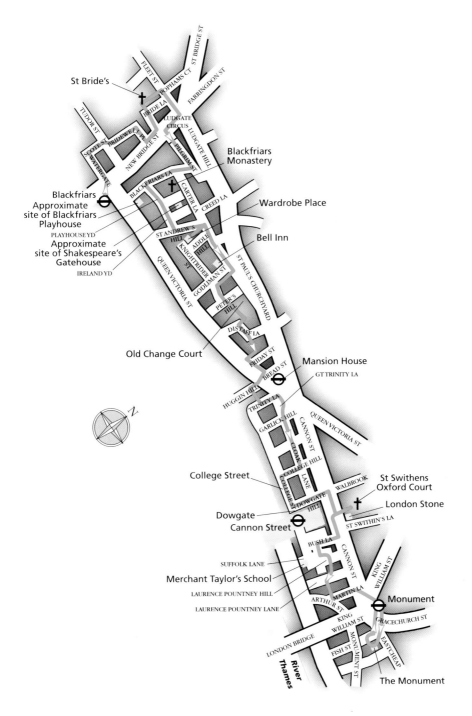

St Bride's

FLEET ST

POPHAMS CT

ST BRIDE ST

BRIDE LA

FARRINGDON ST

LUDGATE
CIRCUS

TUDOR ST

SCOTE' ST

BRIDEWELL

WATERGATE

NEW BRIDGE ST

PILGRIM ST

LUDGATE HILL

Blackfriars
Monastery

BLACKFRIARS LA

CARTER LA

CREED LA

Wardrobe Place

Blackfriars
Approximate
site of Blackfriars
Playhouse

PLAYHOUSE YD

Approximate
site of Shakespeare's
Gatehouse

IRELAND YD

ST ANDREW'S
HILL

ADDLE
HILL

KNIGHTRIDER ST

GODLIMAN ST

QUEEN VICTORIA ST

ST PAUL'S CHURCHYARD

Bell Inn

PETER'S
HILL

DISTAFF LA

Old Change Court

FRIDAY ST

BREAD ST

Mansion House

GT TRINITY LA

HUGGIN HILL

TRINITY LA

GARLICK HILL

CANNON ST

QUEEN VICTORIA ST

CLOAK
LANE

COLLEGE HILL

College Street

COLLEGE ST

DOWGATE HILL

WALBROOK

St Swithens
Oxford Court

London Stone

Dowgate

Cannon Street

ST SWITHIN'S LA

BUSH LA

CANNON ST

KING
WILLIAM ST

SUFFOLK LANE

Merchant Taylor's School

LAURENCE POUNTNEY HILL

LAURENCE POUNTNEY LANE

ARTHUR ST

MARTIN LA

Monument

GRACECHURCH ST

KING
WILLIAM ST

MONUMENT ST

EASTCHEAP

LONDON BRIDGE

FISH ST

River
Thames

The Monument

N

Monastery, one of the most magnificent religious institutions in medieval London (and in 1522 sufficiently dignified to put up the Emperor Charles V). Henry VIII dissolved the Blackfriars in 1538, and many of its buildings were pulled down. What survived was converted into expensive residential apartments, convenient for courtiers at Whitehall, Westminster and the Tower, and even Hampton Court and Greenwich. The right of sanctuary, however, remained within the precincts of the old monastery, which, like some other ecclesiastical estates, was a 'liberty', and so outside the jurisdiction of the City authorities. It was the ideal neighbourhood for a playhouse.

Keep going, passing Apothecaries' Hall on your left. At the end turn left onto Playhouse Yard. Shakespeare's Blackfriars Playhouse stood here; with that of the Globe, this is the most important site in English theatre history. There's a lot to take in about the playhouse, so turn left up Church Entry and take a seat. You are sitting in the nave of the old Blackfriars church, a wreck in Shakespeare's time, 'bare ruined choirs / Where late the sweet birds sang'.

In the same year that James Burbage opened the Theatre (the first substantial purpose-built playhouse in Shoreditch), the impresario Richard Farrant leased the upper refectory of the old monastery at Blackfriars for the performance of plays. Farrant and his successors ran a company of boy actors here, keeping on the right side of their respectable neighbours by catering to an elite audience and maintaining a cunning pretence that the playhouse was used for 'rehearsal' rather than performance. The company lasted for eight years. Twelve years later, James Burbage, anticipating the end of his theatre lease in Shoreditch, bought the property for £600. The illustrious site inside the City must have seemed the perfect place for a small, exclusive theatre, charging admission prices much higher than might be looked for from an open-air theatre. The local residents objected – but then James Burbage died.

The Chamberlain's Men gave up the idea, deciding to concentrate their resources on a large public open-air playhouse. They dismantled the Theatre, brought the timbers over the river and re-erected it as the Globe. To cut their losses, Burbage's sons Richard (the actor) and Cuthbert leased out the refectory, once again to a boys' company, and for ten years or so the theatre carried on more or less as it had before. But in 1608 the boys overstepped the mark by staging a play by Chapman which was rude about the French ambassador. James I insisted that the company be wound up and a second opportunity presented itself to Shakespeare's troupe; now enjoying royal patronage and called the King's Men, the time was right for them to return to the Blackfriars. Richard Burbage formed a syndicate with Shakespeare and

Opposite: Christopher Wren's monument to the Great Fire of 1666, in which most of the city Shakespeare had known was burned down.

others, including Heminges and Condell (later to edit the First Folio), and in 1608 they bought the playhouse. But there was further delay, this time an outbreak of the plague. At last, in the winter of 1609, the theatre opened for the first time and Shakespeare's company had a permanent venue in which to perform in the winter months.

The Winter's Tale and *Cymbeline* were probably written with the Blackfriars rather than the Globe in mind (though both were played in both theatres). Some of the special qualities of the late plays can be explained by the company's acquisition of the Blackfriars: their intimate style, their rather different pace and structure. Music, chiefly woodwind rather than brass, played a more important part at the Blackfriars than at the Globe: the musicians who played there had a high reputation, performing before and after the performance, and during the intervals which were introduced between each act (an innovation later brought to the Globe). The audience, paying much more than at the Globe, was correspondingly better off; unlike the open-air theatres, the best places were near the stage rather than in one of the three galleries. The most expensive place of all was on a stool on the stage itself.

The last show came down on the Blackfriars, as at the Globe, in 1642. In 1655 the playhouse was pulled down. No visual evidence has survived to give us an idea of what it looked like, but it was the Blackfriars and not the Globe which was the ancestor of the theatres of the Restoration – and beyond.

Shakespeare's gatehouse and the King's wardrobe

Retrace your steps to Playhouse Yard and turn left into Ireland Yard, where the Cockpit pub marks the approximate site of Shakespeare's gatehouse. On 10 March 1613, Shakespeare bought the old priory gatehouse from Henry Walker, 'citizen and minstrel' for £140. It was the only London property he ever owned, and he never lived there. The day after he bought it, he mortgaged the gatehouse back to Walker (presumably to raise the money), and later let it to one John Robinson. Shakespeare put up all the money, but had three trustees to guarantee the loan: John Heminges, the actor and later editor of the First Folio; John Jackson, believed to be a man from Hull and in the shipping business; and William Johnson, the landlord of the Mermaid Tavern. Shakespeare's decision has fed speculation. By holding the property in trust it would effectively place it outside the reach of his widow. Was this itself an incentive, suggesting marital discord? Or was it merely a consequence of the business arrangement? Was there anything in his choice of a property which had once been believed to be a headquarters of Catholic intrigue? Probably nothing. The mortgage deed for the gatehouse (pulled down in the late 18th century) is on display at the British Library.

Turn left up St Andrew's Hill and right on Carter Lane. Down a passage on your right you'll find the lovely Wardrobe Place. This was the site of the King's wardrobe, established by Edward III to hold not just his clothing but also the garments for the entire royal family for great state occasions. James I, rather rashly it seems, sold many of the old clothes to the Earl of Dunbar 'by whom they were sold, re-sold, and re-sold...some gaining vast estates thereby'. The wardrobe was destroyed in the Great Fire.

As clothes were so expensive in the 16th and 17th centuries, the costumes owned by a playing company were usually, along with the plays themselves, its most valuable asset – sometimes worth more than the theatre in which it worked. There was little in the way of scenery, so costume was used lavishly and played an important part in the drama. There was a lively second-hand clothes trade in London (see page 47), and servants sometimes sold sets of clothes bequeathed to them by their employers to the theatre companies. In fact, the Elizabethan 'sumptuary laws', not repealed until 1604, made it illegal for persons below a certain rank to wear clothes of the upper classes – except on the stage. A drawing of a scene from *Titus Andronicus*, the only depiction of a Shakespearean production of the time, shows the actors wearing contemporary Elizabethan dress with a few sashes and belts to suggest ancient Rome. Little attempt was – or could be – made at historical accuracy.

The Bell Inn and Old Change Court

Cross Addle Hill, at the bottom of which Valentine Sims first printed Thomas Dekker's masterpiece *The Shoemaker's Holiday* 'at the signe of the White Swanne'. On your right, past Deans Court, a plaque marks the site of the Bell Inn. The only surviving letter to Shakespeare was written from here by Richard Quiney, a Stratford alderman and Shakespeare's son-in-law (he was Shakespeare's daughter Judith's husband). Quiney was in London to petition for a new charter and tax relief for Stratford following some serious fires and a period of bad trade. He got stuck in London for four months, had run up debts and turned to his 'loving good friend and countryman Mr William Shakespeare' for a loan of £30, a large sum. The letter was found among Quiney's papers after his death, and so was presumably never delivered. We do not know whether Shakespeare lent the money, but Quiney's suit was successful and his expenses were reimbursed by the Exchequer.

At the top of Sermon Lane stood The Paul's Head, next door to which were the premises of the booksellers Thomas Millington and John Busby, where the first quarto of *Henry V* was first sold in 1600. Turn down Sermon Lane, left on Knightrider Street onto Distaff Lane; have a seat at Old Change Court.

The poet Lord Herbert of Cherbury, 'black' Lord Herbert, the archetypal courtier and Renaissance writer, dwelled 'in a house among gardens near the Old Exchange'. As well as poetry, which he considered an adornment, Herbert was a skilled musician, fencer, horseman and dedicated duellist, and believed duelling to be the best way to settle wars. Temperamentally, he was the ideal courtier, tolerant and concerned always with 'decencye or seemlynesse'.

His toleration extended to religion, for which he wrote one of the first comparative histories, and to morality, believing sin to be an hereditary physical defect. He was the brother of George Herbert, the great devotional poet, a friend of Jonson, and a civilized young contemporary of Shakespeare.

Dowgate Hill and Robert Greene

Bear right around St Nicolas Cole Abbey, down Old Fish Street Hill and turn left on the horrendous stretch of Queen Victoria Street; cross at the double zebra and make for Huggin Hill (where somebody kept hogs). Huggin Court will take you to Little Trinity Lane; turn left past Painters' Hall and right down Great Trinity Lane; over Garlick Hill (where garlic was sold). Continue down St Thomas Apostle and over Cloak Lane (probably named after the sewer – *cloaca* in Latin – which ran down the lane and debouched into the River Walbrook). Turn right down College Hill, which commemorates Dick Wittington's college, and included an almshouse and five priests charged to pray for his soul at St Michael Paternoster Royal. In Shakespeare's day only the almshouse remained. Walk around St Michael Paternoster Royal at the bottom and past the Innholders' Company on College Street; turn left up Dowgate Hill, home of the Dyers', Skinners' and Tallow Chandlers' Companies.

Dowgate was one of the old water gates which opened onto the Thames at the bottom of this lane; the hill flooded in heavy rain. John Stow recalls a sad event on 4 September 1574, when follow-

ing a 'storm of rain' the water 'ran with such a swift course towards the common shores, that a lad of eighteen years old, minding to have leapt over the channel... was taken with the stream' and drowned.

The poet Robert Greene died penuriously at the house of a shoemaker in Dowgate in 1592, and here made his famous jibe at Shakespeare, warning others against the 'upstart crow, beautified with our feathers, that with his tiger's heart wrapped in a player's hide, supposes he is as well able to bombast out a

Left: 'Give me an ounce of civit, good apothecary.' An apothecary's shop.

blank verse with the best of you'. The passage appears in his otherwise bitter-ly repentant *Groatsworth of Wit*. Greene was a dissolute character. His early work was unfavourably compared with Marlowe's, and he was spectacularly unsuccessful in getting a patron. Yet Greene showed great literary promise. He was versatile, excelling in romances; he was, in a sense, popular – his *Pandosto* was the basis of *The Winter's Tale*. He had some success as a playwright, writ-ing the innovative romantic comedy *Friar Bacon and Friar Bungay*, which had considerable influence over Shakespeare's comedies. But he remains the most conspicuous literary failure of the age.

A more successful life was led by John Willis, rector of the long-vanished St Mary Bothaw on Dowgate Hill, who in 1602 (the year of *Troilus and Cressida*) published *The Art of Stenography*, the first usable system for shorthand.

London Stone to the Monument

Cross the road and turn right up Cannon Street; have a seat in St Swithens' Oxford Court, where the daughter of Owen Glendower, husband of the rebellious Mortimer in *1 Henry IV*, is buried. Opposite Cannon Street Station, and against the building adjoining St Swithens' Gardens (the green-and-grey-marbled OCBC Bank) behind a white railing crouches the unremarkable-looking London Stone. It may be a Roman milestone, perhaps one from which all measurements in Roman Britain were taken; it may be a chunk from the Roman governor's palace whose remains may lie under Cannon Street Station. It has been cherished for centuries. In Shakespeare's day it was 'fixed in the ground very deep, fastened with bars of iron, and otherwise so strongly set, that if carts do run against it through negligence, the wheels be broken, and the stone itself unshaken'. In *Henry VI*, Jack Cade strikes his staff on London Stone and declares:

> Now is Mortimer Lord of this City, and here, sitting upon London Stone,
> I charge and command that the Pissing Conduit run nothing but claret
> wine this first year of our reign.

A popular initiative. The pissing conduit stood on Cheapside and ran with wine at coronations.

Cross Cannon Street and down Bush Lane opposite, turn left on Gopher Lane and left up Suffolk Lane. The Duke of Suffolk had a house here in the 15th century, bought by the Merchant Taylors' Company in 1561 and turned into a school. The school's first headmaster, Richard Mulcaster, had some advanced views on education, championing English and believing girls to be as entitled to a good education as boys. His enlightened views were not lost upon his pupil Edmund Spenser, whose first published poem *The*

Shepheardes Calendar was written in part to demonstrate that the English language is as capable of producing a great poet as are Latin or Greek. Bits of his epic masterpiece, *The Fairie Queene*, crop up throughout Shakespeare's work: images, and tales such as the story of Claudio and Hero in *Much Ado About Nothing* and certain details of Cordelia and Lear.

Thomas Lodge, author of the hit romance *Rosalynde*, Shakespeare's source for *As You Like It*, was also an old boy of Merchant Taylors', as was the dramatist Thomas Kyd. After leaving the school, Kyd dropped out of his scrivener's apprenticeship and by 1590 had joined the service of the Earl of Essex as a secret agent. In 1593 he was arrested on suspicion of inciting xenophobia in the capital. The Privy Council searched his lodgings, and found an incriminating essay questioning the doctrine of the Trinity. Kyd blamed his old flat-mate Christopher Marlowe. Marlowe was exonerated; Kyd was tortured and died soon after his release from prison. Between these disasters, Kyd wrote a lost play called *Hamlet* (presumed to be in part the basis of Shakespeare's, and now known as the 'ur-*Hamlet*'), and *The Spanish Tragedy*, the most popular and influential tragedy of its time and, even allowing for the influence of the Roman playwright Seneca, an amazingly original play that provided not just Shakespeare but many later dramatists with a model. Here is Heironimo, the first revenge hero and Lorenzo, the first Machiavellian villain; here are the soliloquy, the dumb show and the play-within-the-play. The 'antic disposition' that Hamlet (and Edgar) would later put on features first in *The Spanish Tragedy*; and so do the ghost demanding retribution, the mad wife/lover who kills herself and the familiar catalogue of grim ironies and shock tactics – such as the horrid image of the son left hanging in an arbour, a 'place made for pleasure, not for death'.

Turn right down Laurence Pountney Hill, left at the end, left up Martin Lane and right at the end on Cannon Street. Cross the main road by subway, taking the Monument exit at the far end of the station.

Wren's Monument is to your right, built in 'perpetual remembrance' of the devastation wrought by the Great Fire (and by implication the phoenix-like recovery of the City). Climb the 311 steps to the top and you will get an impression of the progress of the fire, which consumed 162ha (400 acres) within the City walls and 25.5ha (63 acres) outside them, destroying 87 churches, 44 livery halls and 13,200 houses. Of the London Shakespeare knew, only the north-east corner was spared, the wind carrying the fire more or less westwards from this point, and it is largely in that district that a few of those buildings which stood within the walls of the Tudor City survive (see the next walk). Monument Underground Station lies opposite.

BISHOPSGATE TO LONDON BRIDGE

Summary: The Great Fire of London missed some of the streets covered in the first part of this walk, and later generations have spared a handful of buildings which Shakespeare would have known – one of them his own parish church, in the heart of affluent Bishopsgate, another well known to John Stow, London's Elizabethan historian. Behind the modern façades passed on this route sometimes stirs the financial life of the Tudor city, remembered in names and, occasionally, institutions. Beyond these, the walk crosses the river over the ghost of a bridge once famous throughout Europe, into Southwark, the chief entertainment district of Elizabethan London. The walk provides the option to join the Bankside walk at page 80.

Start:	Liverpool Street Station.
Finish:	London Bridge Station, with possible extension to Southwark.
Length:	2.5 or 4 km (1½ or 2½ miles), depending on whether you decide to join the Bankside walk at the end.
Time:	1–2½ hours.
Refreshments:	The George and Vulture, George Yard; Simpson's Tavern, 38½ Cornhill, off Ball Court, EC3.

Turn left out of the Liverpool Street exit, passing the site of the old Bethlehem Hospital or Bedlam on your left, now occupied by the Great Eastern Hotel. Originally a priory – of St Mary of Bethlehem – the Bethlehem was converted to a hospital, later specifically for the mentally ill. Henry VIII sold it to the city at the dissolution of the monasteries. The name became synonymous with 'distracted persons'. Bedlam was frequented on Sundays as a resort for the wealthy to divert themselves by watching the 'sports' of the unfortunate inmates. Perhaps curiosity drew Shakespeare here. It must have drawn the playwright Thomas Dekker, because there is a scene in his *Honest Whore* where the various kinds or madness of a Bedlam in 'Milan' are exhibited for the entertainment of the company. Bedlam features on a number of occasions in Shakespeare's history plays, but most memorably in *King Lear*. Dissembling Edmund deceives his brother Edgar with 'villainous melancholy, with a sigh like Tom o'Bedlam'. It is Edgar, though, who leaves the strongest impression, in his impersonation of a 'Bedlam beggar', and his image of their vagrant lives:

The country gives me proof and precedent
Of Bedlam beggars who with roaring voices
Strike in their numbed and mortified bare arms
Pins, wooden pricks, nails, sprigs of rosemary,
And with this horrible object from low farms,
Poor pelting villages, sheep-cotes and mills
Sometime with lunatic bans, sometime with prayers
Enforce their charity.

The patients were sent out to beg with a metal badge stuck to their arms.

St Botolph without Bishopsgate

Turn right down White Hart Yard and along Alderman's Walk; turn right into the church (or churchyard) of St Botolph without Bishopsgate. Stephen Gosson, a formidable polemicist against the Elizabethan theatre was rector here. He smilingly attacked the theatre from all angles: its vaingloriousness, its hypocrisy, its encouragement of vice: 'In our assemblies at plays in London, you shall see such heaving, and shoving, such itching and shouldering to sit by women: such care for their garments, that they be not trod on...such pillows to their backs, that they take no hurt...such giving them pippins to pass the time...such toying, such smiling, such winking...' Gosson's *School of Abuses* was dedicated to Sir Philip Sidney, and provoked Sidney to write his *Defense of Poesie*. Gosson was a contradictory character, and his attack on the theatre a remarkable *volte face*, for he had been a playwright in his youth, the author of *Catiline's Conspiracy*, that 'pig of mine own sow'. He also remained a friend of the great actor Edward Alleyn, who was baptized here. He was a bit of a humorist, as much amused as disgusted by the playhouses. All his plays are lost. Ben Jonson's infant son is buried here.

Farewell, thou child of my right hand, and joy;
My sin was too much hope of thee, lov'd boy,
Rest in soft peace, and, ask'd, say here doth lie
Ben Jonson his best piece of poetry.

Cross Bishopsgate, named after one of the ancient gates which let into the old city. The Bishop of London levied a tax of one piece of wood for every cartload brought through the bridge, hence the name. It still stood in Shakespeare's

Opposite: Shakespeare's parish church: St Helen's Bishopgate, spared by the Great Fire and sometimes called the Westminster Abbey of the City for the quality of its tombs.

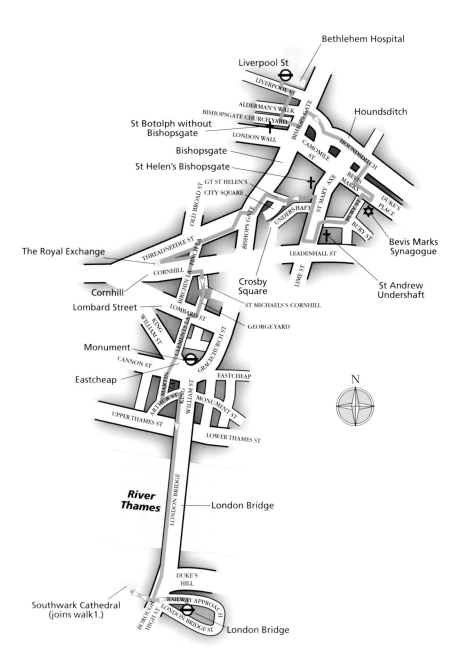

Bethlehem Hospital

Liverpool St

LIVERPOOL ST

Houndsditch

ALDERMAN'S WALK

BISHOPSGATE CHURCHYARD

St Botolph without Bishopsgate

BISHOPS GATE

LONDON WALL

CAMOMILE ST

HOUNDSDITCH

Bishopsgate

St Helen's Bishopsgate

BEVIS MARKS

GT ST HELEN'S

CITY SQUARE

OLD BROAD ST

ST MARY AXE

DUKE'S PLACE

BISHOPS GATE

UNDERSHAFT

FINCH LA

BURY ST

Bevis Marks Synagogue

The Royal Exchange

THREADNEEDLE ST

LEADENHALL ST

BURY ST

CORNHILL

BIRCHIN LA

LIME ST

St Andrew Undershaft

Cornhill

Crosby Square

Lombard Street

LOMBARD ST

ST MICHAELS'S CORNHILL

WILLIAM ST

KING

CLEMENTS LA

GRACECHURCH ST

GEORGE YARD

Monument

CANNON ST

EASTCHEAP

Eastcheap

ARTHUR ST

KING WILLIAM ST

MARTIN

MONUMENT ST

N

UPPER THAMES ST

LOWER THAMES ST

River Thames

LONDON BRIDGE

London Bridge

DUKE'S HILL

Southwark Cathedral (joins walk1.)

RAILWAY APPROACH

BOROUGH HIGH ST

LONDON BRIDGE ST

London Bridge

time, enriched by a prominent gargoyle with a large and gaping mouth, something not lost on contemporary playwrights. In *The Seven Deadly Sins* of Thomas Dekker, Sloth enters the city through Bishopsgate with 'a most sleepy and still triumph'. Bishopsgate Street was the main thoroughfare between London Bridge and Shoreditch, an affluent neighbourhood with 'divers fair inns, large for receipt of travellers' and before the emergence of any of the purpose-built theatres, troupes performed at one of these, the Bull, in the 1560s. As a route between the Rose Playhouse, south of the river, and the Theatre and the Curtain to the north, Shakespeare must have known it well. Part of the street and the district to the east escaped the Great Fire, so there are a few surviving medieval buildings in the area which Shakespeare would have known – and well, as we shall see.

Houndsditch to John Stow's church

Walk straight down Houndsditch, which covers the moat which once ran around the outer walls of the City. That accounts for the 'ditch'. The 'hounds' may commemorate the site of the old kennels where the dogs were kept for the city hunt, or, as Stow says, where 'dead dogges were there laid or cast'. Whatever the case, dogs, dead or living, were but memory in Shakespeare's time, the moat having by then been filled in and paved over.

Turn right on Goring Street; cross Bevis Marks and turn left; just beyond the end of Bury Street you will find on your left the Bevis Marks Synagogue, built on the site of the house of the Abbots of Bury St Edmunds. The synagogue was not here in the Shakespearean period, although there were a few – perhaps 100 – Jews resident in London, nearly all of Spanish or Portuguese origin. They practised their faith in secret – or at least very discreetly. The closest thing to a Jewish institution in the city was the converts' house – or *Domus Conversorum* – on Chancery Lane, where some poor Jews who had converted to Christianity might be found. There were a very few prominent Jews in England – including the Bohemian mineralogist Gaunse, who voyaged with Raleigh, and the unfortunate royal physician Lopez, executed for allegedly plotting against the Queen (see page 48).

Turn left down Bury Street, left on Brown's Buildings; turn left at St Mary Axe, where at the end you will find St Andrew Undershaft. The church survived the Great Fire, appropriately, because it is the church of John Stow, the writer to whom we owe much of what we know about Shakespeare's London and who was buried here in 1605. Stow was one of a number of writers – Camden, Carew and Lambarde are others – who dedicated long periods of their lives to surveying the material legacies of their native land. Antiquarianism is usually perceived as a sedentary pursuit, but Stow and his peers, with their 'surveys' and 'perambulations', pursued their task with a sense of real urgency. His project was to preserve a record of the institutions and treasures of a city that had been almost swept away by rapacious peers and men on the make, particularly during the short and destructive reign of Edward VI, a process rejoiced over by the radical reformers of the time, who wanted to reject all the 'duncery' of the past. Libraries, schools, charities, hospitals had collapsed with the institutions that had fostered them. Stow sought to redress the balance by stressing the continuity of those institutions, and to restore the city's consciousness of its own history.

This church was not spared the fanaticism of the time. One zealous curate, preaching at St Paul's Cross, incited a mob to bring down the 'shaft' or maypole which hung under the eaves of the houses on Shaft Alley 'from the hooks whereon it had rested two-and-thirty years' and sawed it to bits. 'Thus,' Stow relates angrily, 'was his idol, as he termed it, mangled and afterwards burned.' The same curate also denounced the bailiff of Romford, who was hanged, protesting his innocence, on Stow's very doorstep. Such incidents encouraged Stow to pursue that passionate transcription of his native city.

Great St Helen's

Retrace your steps up St Mary Axe, bearing left for St Helen's Bishopsgate, visible at the bottom of Undershaft. St Helen's is a rare survivor of the Great Fire. The strange shape is attributable to its having two naves, one for the parishioners and one for the Benedictine nuns who lived here. In Shakespeare's day, it was a parish church, though surrounded by buildings vacated by the nuns and taken over by the Leathersellers' Company. It was also for a time Shakespeare's parish church and he presumably worshipped here. We know this because on 15 November 1597 the tax collectors for the Ward of Bishopsgate noted that of the 73 rateable residents of the parish of St Helen's, William Shackspere, failed to pay 5s on taxable goods worth £5. For this and subsequent delinquencies, Shakespeare's name was entered in the back-tax accounts for London. We do not know where in the parish he lived.

Gresham, the financier and builder of the Elizabethan Royal Exchange, is buried here. He failed to build the steeple he promised the parishioners in recompense for the size of his sombre monument in the church. St Helen's is known as the Westminster Abbey of the City for the quantity and splendour of its monuments. A window commemorates Shakespeare's local residence.

Crosby House and the Royal Exchange

Leaving St Helen's you pass on your left the uninteresting Crosby Square, once the site of Crosby House. When Shakespeare lived nearby, the Lord Mayor entertained here. Previously, it had been the residence of the Countess of Pembroke, sister to Sir Philip Sidney and dedicatee of his *Arcadia*. Before the

Right: 'Neither a borrower nor a lender be.' From John Blaxton's pamphlet The English Usurer *warning about the dangers of using money-lenders.*

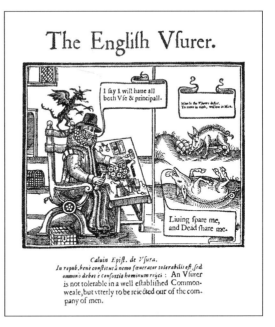

The Englifh Vfurer.

I fay I will haue all both Vfe & principall.

Liuing fpare me, and Dead fhare me.

Caluin Epift. de Vfura.
In repub.benè conftitutâ nemo fœnerator tolerabilis eft,fed omnino debet e Confortio hominum reijci : An Vfurer is not tolerable in a well eftablifhed Commonweale,but vtterly to be reiected out of the company of men.

countess, Sir Thomas More lived here, and some forty years before him it had been let to Richard, Duke of Gloucester, Shakespeare's Richard III. The Lady Anne is invited to repair to Crosby House, and so are the murderers of the princes in the Tower 'when [they] have done'. Richard tells his brutal henchman Catesby that he will be found with Buckingham at Crosby House. The building, reputedly the highest house in London, was dismantled in 1910 and re-erected in Chelsea.

Turn left at the end onto Bishopsgate; cross at the lights and head for Threadneedle Street; turn left onto Finch Lane; turn right down Royal Exchange Avenue, at the end of which stands the Royal Exchange. This building replaces the 16th-century one destroyed by fire in the 1830s. It was one of the most splendid buildings in Shakespeare's London, initiated by Sir Thomas Gresham in imitation of the Bourse at Antwerp and built as a gesture to demonstrate London's commercial pre-eminence in northern Europe. It was a sumptuous four-storey Renaissance building with a large courtyard resting on marble pillars. Its primary functions were to receive bullion, distribute new coinage and exchange foreign currency, but it was also London's first shopping mall and contained over 100 shops, largely luxurious. It was a byword for fashion and novelty and a meeting place for business and pleasure, not to mention rogues. It now houses couturiers.

Turn right out of the Royal Exchange and cross Cornhill, site of the old corn market. The street was well provided with disciplinary facilities: a pair of stocks, a pillory for cheating dealers and the Tun, a gaol for nocturnal malefactors. There was also a standard and conduit for water pumped up from the Thames. Stow saw young men tilting at a 'quinten' or swinging target on Cornhill and 'he that hit not the broad end of the quinten was of all men laughed to scorn, and he that hit it full, if he rid not the faster, had a sound blow in his neck with a bag full of sand hung on the other end'.

Turn left and right down Ball Court. Turn left at the end into the churchyard of St Michael Cornhill, where there are some seats; turn right out of the churchyard into George Yard (squeezed in the corner is the George and Vulture, which declares itself 1600, though it's a cross between 18th-century and mid-Victorian now); walk past the St Edmund King and Martyr and over Lombard Street, a place of bankers, foreign agents and money-lenders. In Shakespeare's time their business meetings had moved to the newly appointed Royal Exchange. Alexander Pope was born on Lombard Street (see page 162). Mercers also lived here, including Sir Thomas Gresham – it is his grasshopper which hangs over the pavement. Falstaff haunts a tavern in Lombard Street, as Mistress Quickly, bringing her action, complains:

> A comes continuantly to Pie Corner – saving your manhoods – to buy a saddle, and he is invited to dinner to the Lubber's Head in Lombard Street, to Master Smooth's the silkman. I pray you, since my exion is entered, and my case so openly known to the world, let him be brought in to his answer. A hundred mark is a long one for a poor lone woman to bear; and I have borne, and borne, and borne, and have been fobbed off, and fobbed off, and fobbed off, from this day to that day, that it is a shame to be thought on.

Eastcheap and London Bridge

Walk down St Clement's Lane, passing St Clement Eastcheap at the end. King William Street, built in the 1830s as an approach to London Bridge, now effaces any trace of Eastcheap, one of London's chief meat markets. The district abounded with taverns in Shakespeare's time and the statue of William IV marks the probable site of the Boar's Head, the legendary tavern of Falstaff and Hal. It was both invention and fact, for a Boar's Head stood here in the 16th century, but not in the 15th, when the fat knight would have done his carousing. Shakespeare allowed himself some poetic licence, for with the fish market to the south, the meat market to the west and the hay and corn market to the north it would have been well situated for the gourmandizing of that great bed-presser, that horse-back breaker, that huge hill of flesh. Some of Shakespeare's greatest scenes are imagined here:

PRINCE HARRY:	Do thou stand for my father, and examine me upon the particulars of my life.
SIR JOHN:	Shall I? Content. This chair shall be my state, this

	dagger my sceptre, and this cushion my crown. *He sits.*
PRINCE HARRY:	Thy state is taken for a joint-stool, thy golden sceptre for a leaden dagger, and thy precious rich crown for a pitiful bald crown.
SIR JOHN:	Well, an the fire of grace be not quite out of thee, now thou shalt be moved. Give me a cup of sack to make my eyes look red, that it may be thought I have wept; for I must speak in passion, and I will do it in King Cambyses' vein.

Cross King William Street and walk down Martin Lane, turning left at the Old Wine Shades, left up Arthur Street and right to the approach to London Bridge; under the left-hand side of the bridge is Old Billingsgate Market (see page 75). Walk over London Bridge. This drab utility, perhaps the dullest bridge over the Thames, suggests nothing of its wonderful predecessor, which was one of the architectural splendours of the city: 'a work very rare,' wrote Stow, 'it seemeth rather a continual street than a bridge', and all the more prodigious for the stand it took against 'the incessant assaults of the river'. It was then the only bridge which crossed the Thames, some 480 metres (800 feet) long, built of stone with splendid and substantial houses built all its length. Most were shops, selling goldsmiths' work, jewellery and, a speciality of the bridge, pins. The tradesmen who dwelt in the storeys above their shops must have been heavy sleepers, for 'the incessant assaults of the river' created a great noise through the lozenge-shaped piers or 'starlings' that supported the structure. At the north end, the German engineer Pieter Morice installed two waterwheels to pump water from the Thames into the city. He demonstrated the efficacy of his machine by shooting a jet of water over the steeple of St Magnus Church. In the middle was the chapel of St Thomas à Becket, once a jewel of the early Gothic style, but in Shakespeare's time given over to commercial use. Approaching the bridge from the south the foot passenger was greeted by a collection of grinning, shrunken faces that stared down from the heads of the executed, stuck on the end of poles. In 1598, the year *1 Henry IV* went to press, the German traveller Paul Hentzner counted over 30 heads stuck over the gatehouse to the bridge *pour encourager les autres*. It was celebrated in songs and eulogies of the city. Although much altered after fires in the 17th century, it survived until the 19th, when it was pulled down, an incalculable loss to London's riverscape.

Turn right at the end of the bridge for London Bridge Station or turn left for Southwark Cathedral and join the Bankside walk at page 80.

THE TOWER AND THE WHARVES

Summary: No London building looms more conspicuously and with more foreboding in Shakespeare's history plays than the Tower, much of which appears as it would have in the 1590s. This walk encircles this vast medieval fortress, once standing in its own 'liberty' outside the City walls, and catches echoes from *Richard III* and *Henry VI* as well as from Shakespeare's more recent and contemporary history. The second half of the route follows a course along the 16th-century riverside, the hub of London's international trade and transport.

Start:	Tower Hill Underground Station or Fenchurch Street Station.
Finish:	Mansion House.
Length:	2.5 km (1½ miles).
Time:	1½ hours. Allow an additional 3–4 hours if you want to see the inside of the Tower
Refreshments:	Some snack bars around the Tower; various places at St Katharine's Docks, east of the Tower.

Turn left out of Fenchurch Street Station into Cooper's Row. Leaving Tower Hill Underground, follow the signs for the Tower. As you go down the steps towards the underpass, a statue of Trajan stands before a large portion of the City wall. Further on stands a medieval postern which formed part of the wall. For more on London Wall see page 32. Turning right, you get a good view of the ramparts of the Tower from the first corner, where a panel describes the position of the various towers within the fortress.

The Tower of London

The Tower of London occupied an important, miscellaneous, almost incongruous place in Shakespeare's London. John Stow, trying to come to grips with it, seems relieved to wind up his account with a brisk summary: 'The Tower is a citadel to defend or command the city; a royal palace for assemblies or treaties; a prison of state for the most dangerous offenders; the

Opposite: The Liberty of the Tower: palace, prison, fortress, garrison, mint, treasury, archive, church and zoo.

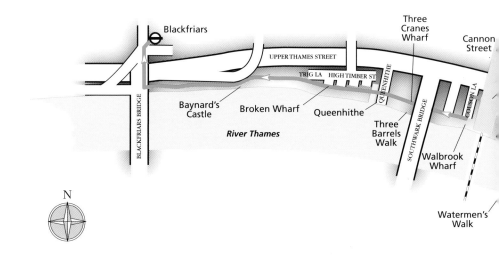

only place of coinage for all England at this time; the armoury for warlike provision; the treasury of the ornaments and jewels of the crown; and general conserver of the most records of the king's courts of justice at Westminster.' He might have added zoo, place of worship and torture chamber. The place must have seemed almost a state in itself, London's grim Vatican. It went some way towards this in another sense, for it was at the heart of the Tower Liberties, an estate, like those of London's dissolved monasteries, which lay outside the authority of the City.

The Tower in Shakespeare's time

By Shakespeare's time, the Tower presented much the same appearance as it does now, except that the royal palace south of the White Tower was pulled down by Oliver Cromwell. And the moat, whose water was drawn from the Thames, is now a smooth green lawn. Princess Elizabeth was a prisoner here, kept in the Bell Tower from March to May 1554 at the pleasure of her sister Mary to encourage her to convert to Rome. She took her daily exercise between the Bell and Beauchamp Towers. She did not convert, of course, and returned to the Tower a few years later to set off for her coronation.

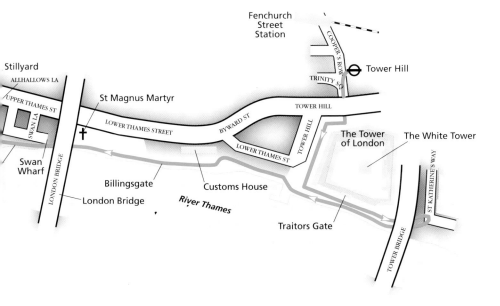

Under the threat of the Armada, many Roman Catholic priests and noblemen were imprisoned here, including Henry Percy, Earl of Northumberland, who was murdered in the Bloody Tower. Robert Devereux, Earl of Essex was imprisoned at the Tower after his ineffectual rebellion of 1601 (when he seditiously commissioned a revival of *Richard II*). The Earl of Southampton, Shakespeare's patron, was also brought here for his part in the Essex rebellion, and allowed to bring his cat. Essex had the privilege of being executed at Tower Green rather than on a scaffold at Tower Hill. Devereux Tower honours its guest.

Elizabeth was almost as displeased with Sir Walter Raleigh, who was briefly imprisoned in the Tower in 1592 for seducing Elizabeth Throckmorton, one of the Queen's ladies-in-waiting. Raleigh was back in the Tower in 1603, kept here on a charge trumped up on behalf of James I, who disliked and feared him. James' object was largely to keep him out of the way, for Raleigh lived comfortably with his wife and sons in the upper floors of the Bloody Tower for 13 years, conducting experiments in a lean-to chemical laboratory and writing, at Prince Henry's instigation, his melancholy *History of the World*: 'For whatsoever is cast behind us, is just nothing and what is to come, deceitful hope hath it'. The Tower is often present in Shakespeare's history plays, a fit setting for the nation's real, usually dark history. Richard II never makes it to 'Julius Caesar's ill-erected Tower' (a grammar school myth), and is despatched to Pomfret Castle at the last minute, but the historic (dead) Richard lay in state for one night in the chapel here.

A number of scenes in *Henry VI* are set at the Tower. The rebel Jack Cade exhorts his followers to burn it down. Warwick the kingmaker released Henry VI from the Wakefield Tower after six years, but he was sent back for a second time, where he met Richard of Gloucester:

KING HENRY:	Teeth hadst thou in thy head when thou wast born,
	To signify thou cam'st to bite the world;
	And if the rest be true which I have heard
	Thou cam'st –
RICHARD:	I'll hear no more. Die, prophet, in thy speech.
	He stabs him.
	For this, amongst the rest, was I ordained.
KING HENRY:	Ay, and for much more slaughter after this.
	He dies.

It was a true word spoken, for the Tower really comes into its own in *Richard III*. Clarence from his cell allegedly in the Bowyer Tower recounts his famous dream of drowning:

> ...often did I strive
> To yield the ghost, but still the envious flood
> Stopped-in my soul and would not let it forth
> To find the empty, vast, and wand'ring air...

Richard's hired killers enter later in the scene. One of them stabs Clarence and, notoriously, drags him offstage and drowns him, in grotesque fulfilment of the prophecy in his dream, 'in the malmsey butt within'. Later in *Richard III*, the boy Edward V is led to the Tower:

> I do not like the Tower of any place.
> Did Julius Caesar build that place, my lord?

Buckingham, the plausible tour guide replies (inaccurately):

> He did, my gracious lord, begin that place,
> Which, since, succeeding ages have re-edified.

There follows soon after the 'most arch deed of piteous massacre', the murder of the Princes, Edward V and his brother the Duke of York, as they lay 'girdling one another / Within their alabaster innocent arms'.

The Princes in the Tower and Middle Tower
The real princes were allegedly found dead in the Garden Tower a month after Richard's coronation. They were buried in the Wakefield Tower, and later removed to a consecrated place, probably near St John's Chapel, under whose stairs two small skeletons were found in the late 17th century. Charles II had these remains interred in Westminster Abbey.

Unless you want to go inside the Tower, turn left when you reach the river; on your left is the Middle Tower, which James I occupied as a palace. He was much taken with his royal menagerie, which was situated between here and the outer gate on the south-west side. Here, not counting the *de rigeur* bears and dogs, lived some eleven lions, two leopards, two mountain cats, three eagles, two owls and a jackal. The king made the most of their sportive potential. He had a viewing gallery built above the Lion Tower, from which he enjoyed watching lions fight mastiffs and other pleasant shows. Animal fights were a regular event until a Tower bear killed a child. As punishment it was thrown in with the lions. To James' disgust, they shrank from it. Like the Westminster tombs, the Tower lions were one of the sights of Shakespeare's London.

Byward Tower and Traitors' Gate
Keeping on the left-hand side of the road, walk past the Byward Tower; opposite lie the Queens' Stairs and Postern Gate; a little further on lies Traitors' Gate. The recent history of the Tower had been violent. The generation before Shakespeare's would remember the imprisonment of Thomas More and Bishop Fisher, later executed for refusing to take the Oath of Supremacy. Thomas Cromwell, Henry VIII's strategist and enforcer, was imprisoned and then beheaded on Tower Hill. Anne Boleyn was tried in the Great Hall and executed here. Similar fates met Catherine Howard and, only a few days before the king's own death, the Earl of Surrey, one of the chief courtier-poets of the age. Surrey's father, the Duke of Norfolk, only escaped execution because the king died on the day he was due on the block. During and after the brief reign of Henry's son Edward VI, Somerset, the Lord Protector, was imprisoned and executed here for conspiring against his successor the Duke of Northumberland. Northumberland himself met the same end at the hands of Queen Mary when he tried to hold on to power after Edward's death. Mary also imprisoned the Bishops Cranmer and Latimer at the Tower.

Happier associations might also have been spoken of, if not quite remembered. Henry VIII's coronation, one of great splendour, left from the Tower.

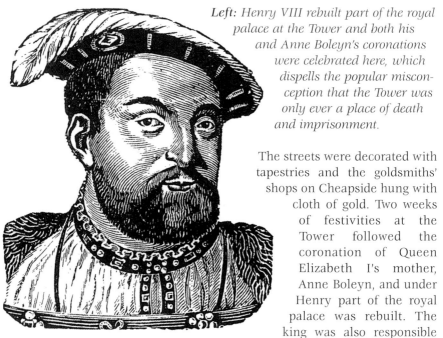

Left: Henry VIII rebuilt part of the royal palace at the Tower and both his and Anne Boleyn's coronations were celebrated here, which dispells the popular misconception that the Tower was only ever a place of death and imprisonment.

The streets were decorated with tapestries and the goldsmiths' shops on Cheapside hung with cloth of gold. Two weeks of festivities at the Tower followed the coronation of Queen Elizabeth I's mother, Anne Boleyn, and under Henry part of the royal palace was rebuilt. The king was also responsible for the building of the half-timbered houses which still stand on Tower Green.

The White Tower and the Cradle Tower

The terrible scene in *Richard III* is placed in the chamber in the White Tower. It begins with a nervous exchange over the arrangements for Richard's coronation, proceeds to the dismissal of the Bishop of Ely to fetch strawberries from his palace in Holborn, the mock paralysis of Gloucester's arm 'like a blasted sapling withered up' and ends with the summary indictment of Hastings:

CATESBY: Come, come, dispatch: the Duke would be at dinner.
Make a short shrift. He longs to see your head.

It is perhaps only a minute's walk from the council chamber to Tower Green – and the block.

Next is the Cradle Tower, from which John Gerard escaped, not the herbalist but the Jesuit priest, by means of a rope over the moat. Up the steps on the other side of the bridge you get a view of the eastern walls of the Tower (trying not to look at the abominable Thistle Tower Hotel) and may catch a last echo from *Richard III*. Richard and Buckingham appear to the Lord Mayor on top of the Tower walls 'in rotten armour, marvellous ill-favoured' and brag about their dissembling powers.

'Tut' says Buckingham,
I can counterfeit the deep tragedian
Tremble and start at wagging of a straw
Speak, and look back, and pry on every side,
Intending deep suspicion; ghastly looks
Are at my service, like enforced smiles...

It is a rare description, or perhaps send-up, of one 16th-century acting style.

Billingsgate to St Magnus Martyr

Retrace your steps and take the riverside path out of the Tower precincts, past the gift shop, and turn left down Three Quays Walk. On your right is the Custom House. There was an Elizabethan predecessor a little east of this site which was destroyed in the Great Fire. Next comes Billingsgate, a large wharf which received not just fish but also 'shell-fishes, salt, oranges, onions and other fruits and roots, wheat, rye, and grain of divers sorts'. Billingsgate, being downriver from the bridge, was also a usual landing place for travellers from abroad or from the lower reaches of the Thames and in about 1600 there were 150 households of 'strangers', most from the Netherlands, in Billingsgate ward where thirty years before there had been hardly three.

To your right is St Magnus Martyr, one of the oldest churches in London. The corner of the church was an important meeting-place, where notices were read and malefactors punished. The rebellious Jack Cade, as you might expect, takes exception to the place, crying in *2 Henry VI*: 'Up Fish Street! Down St Magnus's Corner! Kill and knock down! Throw them into Thames!' The churchyard once formed part of the approach to London Bridge, and preserves bits of the old bridge and a Roman wharf.

Along the Thames to Cannon Street

After London Bridge (for which see page 68) comes Swan Wharf. Swans were once a common and majestic sight on the Thames. According to the journal of the German visitor Paul Hentzner: 'They live in great security, nobody daring to molest, much less kill, any of them, under penalty of a large fine.' Anyone caught stealing a swan's egg would be imprisoned for one year and fined at the monarch's pleasure and the stealing or snaring of a swan was even more severely punished. Henry VIII ordered that no one who owned swans could appoint a new swanherd without a royal licence and instituted the marking of cygnets with nicks on their beaks. Any swan without a mark was deemed to belong to the Crown. Elizabeth supported this with her 'Order of Swannes' of 1570. Their uses extended beyond decoration; they were a delicacy at royal feasts and their feathers were used in the palace upholstery.

To your right is Fishmongers' Hall; on the south side of the river you can see the tower of Southwark Cathedral and St Mary Overy Dock (see page 80). On your right lies Swan Lane and after Oystergate Walk, Watermen's Walk. The river was London's chief thoroughfare, and filled with boats of every kind. The people working on the Thames – those unloading freight from larger boats and bringing it to the quays (lightermen) and those carrying passengers up, down and across the river (watermen) – formed an important part of the social and economic life of Elizabethan London.

The river afforded the cheapest, quickest and pleasantest way of getting about the city. In Elizabethan London about 3,000 watermen plied their trade between Westminster and London Bridge and advertised their services with cries of 'Oars', 'Eastward Ho!' and 'Westward Ho!' – hence the titles of the comedies by Jonson and Dekker. Their trade was regulated at first by the City corporation, later by the Watermens' Company, which was founded in 1555. (Their pretty 18th-century hall is on St Mary at Hill just north of here – not far, but a busy road lies in your way.) They were opposed to any developments which hindered their prosperity: the growth of hackney carriages, schemes for new bridges or legislation against theatres. Conveying people to the playhouses on Bankside – the Globe, the Rose and the Swan – and the bear-baiting arenas constituted a major part of their business. They suffered great hardship in times of plague and in severe winters when the Thames froze over, as it sometimes did above London Bridge.

Walk through the dark passage which leads under Cannon Street rail bridge. This was the site of the Stillyard, where the merchants of the Hanseatic League had their headquarters and, operating like an independent province, they held themselves aloof from all unnecessary contact with Londoners, elected their own councillors in their own guildhall and issued their own currency. Rhenish wine was drunk deeply from stone bottles, but women were forbidden, and it was not permitted to play games with Englishmen in case quarrels arose. Perhaps it was not surprising that the place suffered from anti-alien attacks and that during the 16th century the Hanseatic merchants gradually lost their privileges. They were expelled from the country in 1598 and the Stillyard became a naval storehouse. Some returned in the Jacobean period, but the place preserved few of its old associations except for the drinking of Rhenish, a custom apparently provoked by ingesting neats' tongues and other thirst-inciting titbits. Claudius would have felt at home.

> The King doth wake tonight and takes his rouse,
> Keeps wassail, and the swagg'ring upspring reels;
> And as he drains his draughts of Rhenish down,
> The kettle-drum and the trumpet thus bray out
> The triumph of his pledge.

Walbrook Wharf to Baynard's Castle

Next comes Walbrook Wharf. The river Walbrook rose in Finsbury, flowed through Shoreditch, passing near the Curtain Theatre, through the City west of the street which bears its name and debouched here into the Thames. Unlike the Fleet, in Shakespeare's day it was completely hidden, its course more or less forgotten. Three Cranes Wharf is named after the three great timber cranes operated by the Vintners' Company which once lifted barrels of Bordeaux from the wide lighters here. Shakespeare must have seen the ships come in, for he has Doll Tearsheet say of Falstaff: 'There's a whole merchant's venture of Bordeaux stuff in him, you have not seen a hulk better stuffed in the hold.' There was a tavern named after these cranes, allegedly a resort of wits and thieves. The Fruiterers' Company was based a little further along. They inspected all the fruit which entered London and assessed its duty. Follow Fruiterers' Passage under Southwark Bridge to Three Barrels Walk, whose name honours the Vintners' Company. Their hall has stood on the site west of the bridge since 1446. On the south side of the river you can see the reconstructed Globe Theatre (see page 86).

Queenhithe, revenues from which went to the medieval queens, was a landing-place for all kinds of goods arriving by sea. As ships got bigger and could not pass through the little drawbridge that opened at London Bridge, choosing instead to use the wharf at Billingsgate, business declined at Queenhithe. Some plays of Shakespeare's period repeat the legend of Queen Eleanor who, lying about her part in the murder of a Lady Mayoress, was reputed to have sunk into the ground at Charing Cross and risen again here. Stow records the memory of a sort of floating mill moored at Queenhithe.

High Timber Street is named after the wharf where timber was loaded and stored. This was also the trade of Broken Wharf, so-called because of its ruinous condition. Paul's Walk passes along what was once the front of Baynard's Castle (see page 38).

There are signs for Blackfriars Underground at Blackfriars Bridge.

BANKSIDE

Summary: Shakespeare's life and career is most intensely felt in Southwark, once London's chief entertainment district, and home to numerous playhouses, animal-baiting rings, inns and brothels. Southwark, too, had its great fire (in 1676), but the outline of the medieval (now largely Victorian) streets and vestiges of the 16th- and 17th-century Borough survive, and some of what was lost has been reconstructed – notably the Globe Theatre, which, if you can, you should allow time to visit. Bankside is the indispensable walk for those interested in Shakespeare's theatrical life.

Start:	Borough Underground Station.
Finish:	Southwark Underground Station.
Length:	2.5 km (1½ miles).
Time:	2 hours. Allow an additional half-hour for the cathedral and 2 hours for Shakespeare's Globe.
Refreshments:	The George Inn; the Market Porter, the Wheatsheaf, Stoney Street; the Anchor, Bankside; the Globe, Bedale Street; the Chapter House Restaurant, Southwark Cathedral; Shakespeare's Globe Café; the Rose and Crown, Paris Garden.

Shakespeare worked in Southwark for the longest and most successful part of his career. And, from the evidence provided by a tax return of 6 October 1600, we know he lived locally for a while, too. Turn left out of the Underground and cross Borough High Street. Tabard Street, beyond the church, is the first and most famous of several lanes which run off this side of the street and recall the names of inns which lined the route out of London to Kent: Queen's Head Yard, Talbot Yard, George Inn Yard, White Hart Yard, King's Head Yard. The street was, according to Thomas Dekker, 'a continued ale house with not a shop to be seen between'. In Shakespeare's day Borough High Street was the main road to and from the south and a terminus for coaches, when London Bridge was too narrow to admit them into the city.

The Tabard and the George

Here stood the Tabard Inn, whence Chaucer's fellow-travellers set out on their pilgrimage to Canterbury. The inn went downhill after Chaucer's time, but by the late 16th century, when Shakespeare could have made his pilgrimage to it, the building had been repaired and enlarged. Shakespeare must have thought a lot of Chaucer, for he returns to him a number of times throughout his

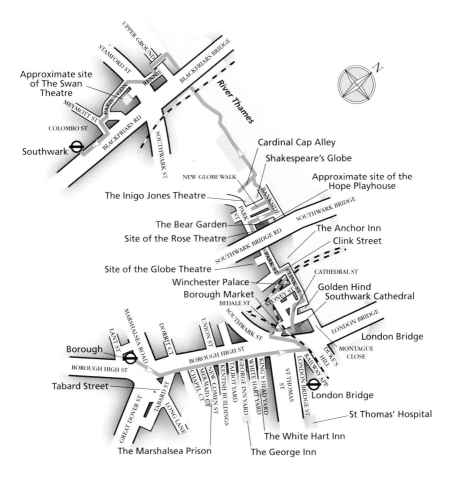

career. *Troilus and Cressida* follows the narrative of Chaucer's *Troilus and Criseyde*. There are traces of Chaucer throughout Shakespeare, but the most influential of *The Canterbury Tales* was *The Knight's Tale*, clearly the basis of the tale of Palamon and Arcite in *The Two Noble Kinsmen* (written by Shakespeare in collaboration with John Fletcher).

The George, in another yard to your right, stands on the site of an inn extant in 1542 and probably earlier. This building dates from 1676, the year of Southwark's great fire, and once surrounded three sides of the courtyard. It is the last galleried inn in London, and the only one to give any idea of the kind of establishment used by troupes in the city (and throughout England, when the players went on tour). Before purpose-built theatres such as the Globe were constructed, inns such as this were commonly used for performances.

Once the players had erected their portable stage, the galleries round the edge and the yard itself offered a ready-made auditorium. At least, that is the usual interpretation. It is possible, though, that inn performances took place indoors, in the kind of large chamber not really available to the public anywhere else. After 1594 most theatre companies, including, no doubt, the companies in which Shakespeare worked in the early years of his career, moved from the big open-air theatres in the summer to inns in the winter, which probably makes an indoor playing space more likely. Two permanent theatres – the Boar's Head in Whitechapel and the Red Bull in Clerkenwell (see page 46) – were essentially inn yards adapted for performance. After 1600, the Privy Council banned all inn performances in London.

Borough Market and Southwark Cathedral

Continuing down Borough High Street you pass on your right St Thomas Street, where the original St Thomas's Hospital once stood. The hospital, which Shakespeare would have known, was ancient even then, having been founded in 1106. In Shakespeare's day, before any knowledge of bacilli, bad air was believed to be the root of many illnesses. Good air – the smell of pomanders or the breath of the young and healthy – was seen as a cure for air-borne disease, as Orsino says of Olivia in *Twelfth Night*: 'Methought she purged the air of pestilence' and as Venus says of Adonis: 'The plague is banished by thy breath.'

Continue in the same direction up Borough High Street. The road once continued into the old London Bridge, described on page 67. Cross the road at the lights, turn left and go through the entrance to Borough Market, probably the oldest fruit and vegetable market in London, dating back to at least 1276. In the 16th century, the market place was beside the leather market and the long-vanished church of St Margaret, a few yards to the south of here.

Turn right through the market, cross Bedale Street, walk under the railway bridge and past the back of the Globe pub. In front of you stands Southwark Cathedral, once the parish church of St Saviour's and St Mary Overie ('over the water'). The church was within the see of Winchester. At the dissolution of the priory in 1539, the buildings were surrendered to Henry VIII. The nave was reconstructed in the 19th century and the tower, with its four pinnacles, was rebuilt in 1689, but the rest of the church was much as Shakespeare must have known it. From a previous tower, the lovely panoramas of John Norden and, later, of Wenceslaus Hollar, whence we get the most reliable visual record of

Opposite: The Globe Theatre was reconstructed after decades of fundraising and research driven by actor and director Sam Wanamaker. It now provides performances in the summer, a year-round educational programme and the world's largest exhibition devoted to Shakespeare and the theatre of his time.

the Globe and its neighbouring theatres, were drawn. Entrance to the cathedral is at the south door, to your left.

Turn right on entering the aisle. There is a monument to Shakespeare in the south aisle created by Henry McCarthy in 1912. Above it is a memorial window designed by Christopher Webb in 1954, which replaces a window smashed in World War II. A birthday service is held at the cathedral annually in Shakespeare's honour, and a piece of rosemary (for remembrance) is placed in the playwright's hand. On the other side of the aisle is a memorial to Sam Wanamaker, who led the project to reconstruct the Globe Theatre on Bankside, of whom more later. In the south transept you will find carved a cardinal's hat and coat of arms. When he was still Bishop of Winchester, Cardinal Beaufort – who dies guilt-stricken in *Henry VI* – restored St Saviour's after a fire in 1393.

In the north aisle lies the colourful monument to John Gower. The poetry of Chaucer's contemporary was popular reading in Elizabethan and Jacobean England, and Shakespeare, who, as a parishioner of St Saviour's, would have known this effigy, drew occasionally upon his work – particularly *Confessio Amatis*, the bottom volume of the stack of books which supports Gower's head here, parts of which are paraphrased in *Pericles*. In acknowledgement of this, Gower plays the part of Chorus in the play:

> To sing a song that old was sung,
> From ancient ashes Gower is come,
> Assuming man's infirmities,
> To glad your ear, and please your eyes.

John Fletcher, Shakespeare's collaborator on *Henry VIII* and successor as playwright to the King's Men, is buried here, and so is his successor, John Massinger. On 31 December 1607, at the heart of the Great Frost, when the river was frozen over, one 'Edmund Shakespeare, a player' was buried at St Saviour's 'with a forenoon knell of the great bell'. The cost of these and other, more expensive, obsequies was 20s, a sum almost certainly borne by his brother William. Edmund was 27, and the only other member of Shakespeare's family to follow his elder brother into the theatrical profession.

Turn right out in the cathedral yard, through the gate and right down Cathedral Street. Ahead of you in the little St Mary Overie dock stands the reconstruction of the *Golden Hind*. In Shakespeare's time Drake's famous ship was moored at Deptford (see page 135).

Liberty of the Clink

Continue in the same direction down Clink Street. The Liberty of the Clink was the estate associated with the manor of the Bishop of Winchester. As an old monastic 'liberty' it lay outside the jurisdiction of the City of London, which accounts in large part for Southwark's status as a district devoted to pleasure. Most of the bishop's property was leased-out for rent, much of it to brothel-keepers.

One of the ratepayers in 1600 was Shakespeare, whose rates debt of 13s. 4d was transferred in 1600 to the Bishopric of Winchester. He probably lived in the district from 1600 to about 1604. We don't know where.

To your left lie the remains of the great hall of Winchester Palace, the London residence of the Bishops of Winchester for 500 years and in Shakespeare's day a 'very fair house, well repaired'. The Palace had a long river frontage and was attached to a 10-acre park.

The Globe

Turn left and then right on Park Street. On your left, before you come to the road bridge, you will find a plaque and a series of panels which illustrate the remains of the Globe Theatre, most of which lie under the approach to Southwark Bridge. Approximately 5 per cent of the foundations of the first (and second) Globe have been excavated, enough to tell us that it was a 20-sided polygonal building – important information in the quest to rebuild the first Globe some 180 metres (200 yards) from this spot.

About 15 of Shakespeare's plays had their first, or very early performances at the Globe, including many of his greatest, but in spite of its illustrious history, there is an air of the second-best and almost the desperate about the decision of the Chamberlain's Men to build the theatre. The first Globe was constructed in early 1599 and recycled some of the timbers which had been used in the Burbage family's Theatre in Shoreditch, pulled down after a disagreement between Shakespeare's company and the freeholder over the terms of the lease (see page 16). What's more, all the evidence suggests that what the company really wanted was to work in an exclusive, indoor playhouse at Blackfriars which was not available to them (see page 52). The decision had significant personal implications for Shakespeare, for the financial straits in which the company found itself gave its in-house playwright and four of his fellow actors the opportunity to invest a one-eighth share in the theatre. This investment provided Shakespeare with a decent income for the rest of his career – a financial security highly unusual for 16th- and 17th-century playwrights, who were often in the hands of more or less rapacious impresarios.

The Globe was open-air, with a diameter of between 24 and 30 metres (80–100 feet). It had three galleries and a yard into the middle of which a stage was thrust. Both the stage and auditorium, although made of oak and plaster, were quite richly decorated, the pillars painted to look like marble. The stage itself had a canopy or 'heaven' above, probably supported by substantial pillars, which in about 1610 was fitted with machinery to let gods and others descend. Hamlet in his great prose speech in Act 2, Scene 2, in describing the world, also evokes these 'heavens':

> this goodly frame, the earth, seems to me a sterile promontory; this most excellent canopy the air, look you, this brave o'erhanging firmament, this majestical roof fretted with golden fire

Under the stage was the 'hell', from which, for example, the ghost of old Hamlet cried, 'Swear'. The Globe was a microcosm, the action taking place on the platform – or earth – between heaven and hell. Otherwise, the stage was quite bare. There was no scenery to speak of, each location being suggested – in Shakespeare's case powerfully, if ambiguously – by language alone. The Globe, like the other open-air playhouses of the period, relied to a very great extent on the essential imaginative resources of the theatre: language, movement, gesture. All the parts, as in every Elizabethan theatre, were played by men and boys.

The Globe could accommodate an audience of about 3,000 people, offering gallery seating for 2,000 at 2 or 3 pence a place and standing room for 1,000 in the yard. Hamlet took a dim view of the standing audience:

> O! It offends me to the soul to hear a robustious periwig-pated fellow tear a passion to tatters, to very rags, to split the ears of the groundlings, who for the most part are capable of nothing but inexplicable dumb-shows and noise.

A 'groundling' was a kind of fish whose mouth was dragged along the river bottom, and which, in looking up, gaped. The audience was composed of people from all walks of life, from the nobility who took one of the lords' or gentlemen's rooms (or even, on occasion, sat on the stage), to citizens and their wives, who sat in the galleries, to apprentices and tradesmen of all kinds, prostitutes, petty criminals and pickpockets, who, for the most part, stood in the yard. Plays took place daily in the afternoon at 2pm.

The theatre was burned to the ground on 29 June 1613, when a bit of burning wadding flew out of a prop cannon and onto the thatched roof at what must have been the discharge of 'chambers' in *Henry VIII*. No one was hurt in the fire, save one who 'with a provident wit put his trousers out with bottle ale'. A year later it had been rebuilt on the same foundations, but this time with a tiled roof and 'far fairer' than before. It is the second Globe which is depicted in Wenceslaus Hollar's famous 'Long View' and gives us the best idea of the

Right: William Hornby's verse pamphlet against drink was the work of a reformed drunkard. It also shares James I's disapproval of tobacco. Arguments about the pros and cons of smoking (a very expensive habit) were dramatized by Ben Jonson in Every Man in his Humour.

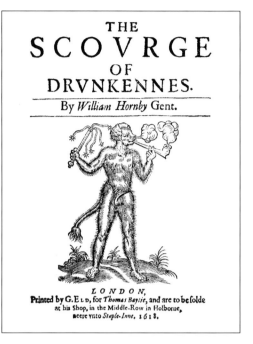

THE
SCOVRGE
OF
DRVNKENNES.

By *William Hornby* Gent.

LONDON,
Printed by G. E l d, for *Thomas Baylie*, and are to be folde
at his Shop, in the Middle-Row in Holborne,
neere vnto *Staple-Inns.* 1 6 1 8.

appearance of the theatre. The King's Men continued to offer plays by Shakespeare and his successors at the second Globe until the playhouses were closed by the Puritan administration in 1642. It was pulled down in 1644 to make way for tenements.

The Rose Theatre

Over the road and on the other side of the railway bridge a large office block covers the remains of the Rose Theatre, another open-air playhouse and the first to be built on Bankside. Marlowe's plays were first performed here, the great parts which vented his famous 'mighty line' and 'high astounding terms' – Tamburlaine and Doctor Faustus – being taken by the great tragedian Edward Alleyn, the leading man in the Admiral's Men and probably the most successful actor of the period. Alleyn also took the part of Hieronimo in Thomas Kyd's sensationally successful *Spanish Tragedy* here (see page 58). The Rose was run by Alleyn's father-in-law, the entrepreneur Philip Henslowe, whose 'diary' or account book, which still survives in the library at Dulwich College, gives us the best idea of the day-to-day running of any of the Elizabethan playhouses. Here are itemized the props and costumes, the fees paid to playwrights and actors, the theatre revenues and maintenance costs. It also gives some idea of the mind-boggling repertory system the theatres operated: a different play every day, drawn from a repertory of anything up to 40 plays, depending on how many playbooks the company owned. The Admiral's Men had relatively few, and so in the 1590s had to add a new play to their repertory every fortnight. Many of those listed by Henslowe were never printed and have been lost. A new play which failed on its first performance might never appear again; others would have perhaps a dozen performances over a season lasting up to about six months. It must have been tough on the leading players, who might at any time be required to keep parts from several plays in their head at once. Two early Shakespearean titles are just discernible through the erratic spelling of Henslowe's 'diary', 'tittus & ondronicus' and 'harey the vj' (*1 Henry VI*), which is how we know that they, too, were performed at the Rose.

The Rose was a 14-sided polygon, rather irregular, with a fairly narrow tapered stage and a thatched roof. It was also smaller than the Globe, in spite of alterations made to enlarge its yard some five years after it was built. In 1600 Henslowe and Alleyn sank their money into the construction of another, larger and more up-to-date theatre, the Fortune in Finsbury (see page 19), and by 1606 the Rose had been demolished. The site was excavated in 1989.

Bear Gardens and Shakespeare's Globe

Turn right down Bear Gardens. Near here stood the Bear Garden. Animal-baiting shows were popular before the playhouses were erected on Bankside. Bears imported from Russia and Germany, as well as bulls, were kept for baiting by dogs. The little lanes of kennels which housed the dogs are visible on maps of the period. Like the theatres, the Bear Garden was frequented by all kinds of people, and like the theatre companies, the bears and dogs entertained by royal command, sometimes in the royal palaces. The animal baiting rings were similar to the playhouses: round, with galleries and a yard.

The Hope Playhouse, which Philip Henslowe built in 1613, stood on this street. It attempted to offer both animal baiting and drama. Jonson's *Bartholomew Fair* was first performed here (see page 48), but the prologue to the play makes it clear that the smell and mess which attended the animal-baiting lingered. It was eventually used exclusively for animal-baiting.

Turn left at the end of Bear Gardens. On your left you will come to Shakespeare's Globe. The new Globe, thanks to the uncompromising vision of Sam Wanamaker and the team of scholars, architects and craftsmen he built around him, is the best estimate we currently – perhaps will ever – have of Shakespeare's theatre on Bankside. In spite of the important place theatregoing had in Shakespeare's time, Londoners seem to have taken this pleasure very much for granted and almost nobody – not even London's conscientious Elizabethan chronicler John Stow – took any trouble to record what the theatres looked like. But the little that has come down to us – building contracts, maps, panoramas and sketches, hints provided by the plays themselves and surviving 16th- and 17th-century buildings – has stood up to generations of intense scrutiny and debate. The result is a masterpiece of authentic timber-frame craftsmanship, using 'green' (that is, untreated) oak, lime plaster reinforced with goat hair, bricks created to an Elizabethan recipe and Norfolk reed thatch. The stage is sumptuously gilded, marbled and painted.

The theatre is at the heart of a range of activities, including an exhibition dedicated to all aspects of Shakespeare's theatre, a wide programme of educational activities and, between May and September, performances of plays. A theatre company, created every spring, has offered seasons of plays chiefly by Shakespeare and his contemporaries since the theatre's official opening in 1997. There is no substitute for a visit to Shakespeare's Globe, whether in or out of the performance season.

Around the corner, at the south-east corner of the site, on New Globe Walk, you will find the brick shell of the little Inigo Jones Theatre. Plans for this theatre were drawn up by Inigo Jones in either 1616 (for the Cockpit in Drury Lane) or 1638 (for a theatre proposed but never built by William Davenant in Fleet Street). It is the only surviving design of an indoor theatre of Shakespeare's period, and although probably not very like the playhouse used by Shakespeare's company in Blackfriars (see page 50), is the nearest thing to it. When finished, it will offer a complementary winter playing venue for the summer season Globe.

Cardinal Cap Alley and the bishops' brothels
Continue along Bankside. Just beyond Shakespeare's Globe you reach Cardinal Cap Alley, which runs between two early 18th-century houses. The Cardinal Cap is the last name which remains of the brothels which once ran along Bankside, presenting a colourful iconography on the front of the buildings on the river. Far from being prohibited, prostitution was encouraged and regulated by the bishops. The brothels, or 'stewhouses', provided a tidy income to the see, and the local prostitutes were known as 'Winchester geese'. Bankside had the highest concentration of prostitution in London, and trade was encouraged by the other local attractions: the taverns, theatres and animal-baiting rings.

The reprimand that Gloucester brings against the Bishop of Winchester in *1 Henry VI* was very near home – 'Thou that giv'st whores indulgences to sin' – and most of Shakespeare's plays somewhere touch upon prostitution. The venereal disease which carries off Doll Tearsheet would also have killed many of those who lay in the unconsecrated graveyard for prostitutes on Bankside.

Continue on Bankside, past Tate Modern, the Founder's Arms pub and under Blackfriars Bridge. Turn left up Marigold Alley, cross Upper Ground, and go down Rennie Street ahead of you; cross Stamford Street, turn right and then immediately left down Paris Garden, which marks the end of old Bankside (see page 193). Turn left at the end on Meymott Street and right on Blackfriars Road. Southwark Underground station is on your right.

ALONG THE STRAND

Summary: The Strand was once London's Grand Canal, and this walk around the busy thoroughfare which joins Westminster to the City follows a route which in Shakespeare's day was lined with the riverside palaces once owned by great bishops, and later many of the famous names of 16th- and 17th-century England. For the rich and powerful, the Strand was *the* address at which to live. The walk passes the site of Essex House, in which the feckless and over-reaching Earl was besieged, and the haunts of the young Falstaff and Justice Shallow, ending with a visit to a charming and little-visited Jacobean interior which commemorates one of the great might-have-beens of 17th-century England.

Start:	Embankment Underground Station.
Finish:	Chancery Lane Underground Station.
Length:	1.5 km (1½ miles).
Time:	1½ hours, plus an extra hour for visits to the National Portrait Gallery and Prince Henry's Room.
Refreshments:	The Ship and Shovell, Craven Passage; the Sherlock Holmes, Northumberland Street; numerous on the Strand and Fleet Street; the Seven Stars on Carey Street (off Bell Yard).

Turn left out of Embankment Underground and walk up Villiers Street; turn right under the Arches Shopping Centre, down Craven passage and over Craven Street; turn right at the Sherlock Holmes pub on to Northumberland Street. The street runs over the site of Northumberland House. When Shakespeare arrived in London, this would have been an old convent its buildings converted into tenements, later a building site, and later still, the residence of the Earl of Northampton. John Hall, Shakespeare's son-in-law and physician, rode from Stratford to Ludlow to minister to the Earl after he contracted pleurisy chasing his hounds on a wet day. Only later did it pass to the Northumberland family, Shakespeare's Percys.

Opposite: The Queen's Chapel of the Savoy, much restored but the only surviving fragment of the once gigantic Palace of the Savoy and home to John of Gaunt.

Charing Cross and St Martin in the Fields

At the end turn right onto the Strand up to the forecourt of Charing Cross Station, where the Charing Cross stands. This is a Victorian reconstruction of one of the crosses built by Edward I in memory of his queen, Eleanor of Castile. By the early 17th century it had become ruinous and in 1608 the humane playwright and pamphleteer Thomas Dekker lamented the decay of 'that ancient and oldest son of mine with his limbs broken to pieces, his reverend head cut off, the ribs of his body bruised, his arms lopped away, his back almost cleft in sunder'. Nevertheless, it survived another 40 years, and was only taken down in the Commonwealth period. Shakespeare must have known it well, but makes only one reference to it when he has the Carrier at Rochester complain that he's got 'a gammon of bacon and two races [roots] of ginger, to be delivered as far as Charing Cross' (*1 Henry IV*).

Cross the Strand and Duncannon Street; walk past the back of St Martin in the Fields, once in open country, but not quite in the fields even in Shakespeare's time: a map of about 1560 shows the recently rebuilt church with a walled yard abutting to the north 'Convent Garden'.

Only to the north-west, on the other side of St Martin's Lane and in the district now covered by Leicester Square, do the maps describe St Martin's Field, with its cattle grazing and women drying linen on the grass. It was an area that was ripe for development and St Martin's Lane grew into a fashionable residential street during Shakespeare's career, its parish church enriched between 1606 and 1609 by Prince Henry, son and heir to James I (of whom, more later).

Francis Bacon was christened at St Martin's in 1561 (see page 115). Nicholas Hilliard, the miniaturist and creator of some of the most romantic images of the Elizabethan age, is buried here (see page 22). Also buried at St Martin's is Nicholas Stone, one of the most accomplished Elizabethan sculptors. His tombs and monuments give a few clues to some of the stagecraft conventions – its clothing, expression and gesture – of the time. Theodore Mayerne, the great French physician to James I, who wrote the treatise on Prince Henry's typhoid, also lies here, in that prince's adopted church. Mayerne made deep studies of the plague (a necessary undertaking in a city so often afflicted) and was one of the first physicians to apply chemical principles, in particular mercury, to medicine.

Turn left along the church, cross St Martin's Place – the entrance to the National Portrait Gallery is on your right. There is a great collection of Tudor and Stuart portraits on the first floor, some depicting figures mentioned on this walk.

On leaving the gallery cross St Martin's Place and go down William IV Street; cross the Strand and walk down George Court.

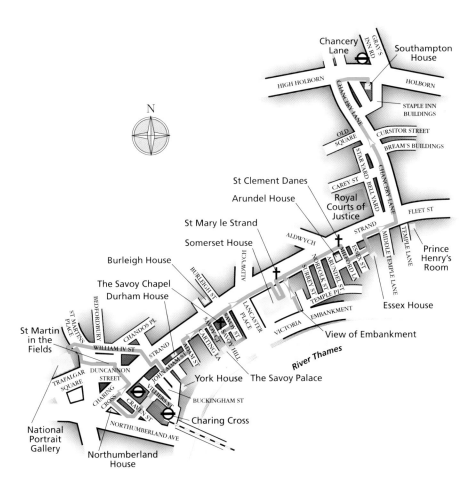

From York House to the Savoy

York Buildings in front of you occupies part of the site of York House. Francis Bacon was born at York House and the Earl of Essex was called to account here by the Queen after his failure to engage the rebellious Earl of Tyrone in Ireland, of which more later. Turn left up John Adam Street, passing Durham House on your left. The Bishops of Durham had their London base in a palace here. At the Reformation, it passed to the Crown. Elizabeth made great use of it, bestowing it upon those who went in and out of her favour: Robert Dudley, Earl of Leicester had it first. It then passed to Sir Henry Sidney, from him to the Earl of Essex, who was in turn succeeded by Sir Walter Raleigh in 1583, who kept a splendid apartment here for 20 years with a turret-study

91

Left: Raleigh, one of the greatest men of his age, was disliked by James I, who sent him to the Tower.

overlooking the river. It was at Durham House that Raleigh, experimenting with the new drug, tobacco, received a soaking from a servant who thought he'd caught fire when he exhaled. Shakespeare was polishing off *Timon of Athens* when James I, not caring for Raleigh, threw him out of Durham House and restored it to the bishops. Then the unengaging William Cecil, and the state's most powerful minister, enlarged neighbouring Salisbury House by encroachment into Durham House. Four years later, when Shakespeare was working on *Pericles*, further encroachment was made by the New Exchange, which obliterated the stables on the Strand side of the house.

Turn left up Adam Street and right on to the Strand, passing the top of Ivybridge Lane, the second of two bridges which crossed the numerous brooks which ran over the Strand, draining the fields to the north. Indeed, open fields occupied most of the north side of the Strand in Elizabeth's time, but a few buildings would have caught Shakespeare's eye. Lord Burleigh, Elizabeth's Secretary of State, lived in a vast house which stretched from Exeter Street to Burleigh Street, a place now occupied by the Strand Palace Hotel. Elizabeth called him 'my spirit'. She visited him when he was laid up with gout and in his last illness fed him 'with her own princely hand' at his bedside. It was Burleigh who requested that Shakespeare change the name 'Oldcastle' in *2 Henry IV*. This may have been at the instigation of his son Robert, whose father-in-law, the Puritanical Lord Cobham, had taken exception to the portrayal of his ancestor, a Protestant martyr, as a glutton, drinker and coward. Shakespeare changed the name to Falstaff.

On the south side turn into the courtyard of the Savoy Hotel, a stylish art deco assemblage. In the 14th century, chiefly after the improvements made by the 1st Duke of Lancaster, the Palace of the Savoy was one of the greatest houses in England. With its long crenellated walls, great chapel, cloisters, stables, gardens, fish ponds and river gate, 'there was,' says Stow, 'none in the realm to be compared in beauty and stateliness'. This grandeur did not last. It passed to John of Gaunt, who had married the duke's daughter. Wat Tyler and his rebels attacked the palace in 1381. The hated Gaunt escaped, but his physician and serjeant at arms were killed. The mob 'bruised' its treasure in mortars, smashed up the plate and threw the lot in the Thames, the people 'more malicious than covetous'. They inadvertently blew up the great hall. It became uninhabitable and Gaunt took up residence in Ely House where Shakespeare's Duke delivers his famous panegyric on England in *Richard II* (see page 42).

Turn right at Savoy Street; the accidental square formed by the back of the Savoy buildings and the sides of the offices reveals a surprising survival of medieval London, the Queen's Chapel of the Savoy. By Shakespeare's time the Savoy was a rather run-down hospital, having been converted, endowed, suppressed, re-endowed and corrupted by various administrations. It was still suffering from the management of one Thomas Thurland in the 1570s, who 'borrowed' hospital funds and had sex with hospital staff. By the 1580s the hospital had become a doss-house for 'vagbonds', and its precincts, which enjoyed the privilege of sanctuary, 'the chief nursery of evil men'. The Savoy Chapel was one of three originally attached to the hospital and lavishly endowed by Henry VII. Although much altered and partly rebuilt, it is the only survivor of a building from the Shakespearean period on the Strand.

Retrace your steps back to the Strand. Lancaster Place remembers the possession of the Savoy by the Duchy of Lancaster. Beyond the bridge, turn into the courtyard of Somerset House. The first Somerset House – the building Shakespeare would have known – bears no resemblance to this, William Chambers' 18th-century masterpiece. The original was built by the Duke of Somerset, Lord Protector to the young Edward VI, between 1547 and 1550. It was the first Renaissance palace in England and one of the most arrogant architectural statements of Tudor London. The Inns of the Bishops of Worcester and Chester and the parish church were pulled down to make room for it and the great Priory of St John in Clerkenwell (see page 44) and the cloisters and ossuary of old St Paul's broken up to provide its building material. The bones from St Paul's were removed to Bunhill Fields (see page 18). Although it would not have looked very classical to our eyes, it would have looked so to the Elizabethans, and very modern. Its architecture supported the self-image of the Elizabethan ruling class which saw itself as equivalent to the patricians of Rome.

After Somerset's execution in 1552, the house was given to the Princess Elizabeth. She later divided it up into grace-and-favour apartments and lodgings for foreign ambassadors. She also gave part of it back to Somerset's family, the Seymours, and stayed there occasionally herself. In 1604 Shakespeare's company was put at the disposal of the new Spanish ambassador and his entourage here for eighteen days, and played before them. In the same year, John Gerard, the King's chief gardener at Theobalds, his Hertfordshire palace, was granted a 0.8ha (2-acre) site at Somerset House on condition that he provided herbs, flowers and fruit for the Queen. Inigo Jones had an apartment here, and while Anne of Denmark was in residence and Jones still on good terms with Ben Jonson, Somerset House was a venue for some of the most splendid masques of the Jacobean period (see page 121). In 1606, when Christian IV of Denmark came to stay with his sister and after debauched scenes at the palace, it was renamed Denmark House.

River views and Arundel House

Turn left out of the courtyard and right along King's College; at the end, the terrace affords fine views of the river in winter (the trees obscure the view in summer). Along the Embankment to the west on this side, there would have been a view of the gardens and water-gates of the Savoy, Durham, York and Northampton Houses. Beyond that could be seen the gardens and assortment of buildings which constituted Whitehall Palace, and then the lower buildings which ran between Whitehall and Westminster, the long roofline of Westminster Hall (now behind the Victorian palace) and the nave (but not the towers) of the Abbey. To the east lay the 'bricky towers' and great trees of the Temple, the old buildings of the Whitefriars, recently developed by Robert Cecil as a site for Salisbury House, and lastly, the old palace of Bridewell, by then a workhouse, orphanage and prison (see page 150). On the south side, Lambeth Palace, still held by the Archbishop of Canterbury, gave way to marsh, fields and stiles; only beyond the current South Bank Centre, at the manor of Paris Garden and the inns and brothels in its environs, would substantial buildings detain the eye.

Retrace your steps past King's to the Strand, turning right, past the little Baroque church of St Mary le Strand. There was no church here in Shakespeare's day, its site and stone being too useful for Protector Somerset, who used both in the building of his palace. He never rebuilt the church, leaving the parishioners to worship at the Savoy Chapel. James Gibbs started from scratch in 1714.

Cross Surrey Street and dismal, brutalised Arundel Street. Arundel House stood here. Thomas Howard, the Earl of Arundel, once a consumptive, ugly youth, dubbed by Essex the 'winter pear', lived here from 1607. He built his house in an Italianate style, under the supervision of Inigo Jones. Arundel was the leading connoisseur of the age, amassing a great collection of classical art. He went as ambassador to Bohemia in 1632, bringing back with him the engraver Wenceslaus Hollar, who had an apartment at Arundel House and executed one of his views of London from the top of the house. Hollar has left the most beautiful and accurate image of mid-17th-century London, including the only really reliable image of the Globe Theatre.

St Clement Danes and Essex House

Wren's church of St Clement Danes replaces an older building, though not one destroyed in the Great Fire; it had simply fallen into decay. Near here was Clement's Well, which in Shakespeare's time was curbed and paved and always full of water. On the other side of the road stood Clement's Inn, one of the Inns of Chancery, once filled with lawyers and law students, and which stood in relation to the Inns of Court rather in the same way that the Oxbridge colleges still stand in relation to their respective universities. Stow mentions disturbances that were caused in the neighbourhood by 'the unthrifts of the inns of chancery', the roisterings of Falstaff and Shallow perhaps, who were both alumni of the Inn and could hear the bell of St Clement's: 'We have heard the chimes at midnight, Master Shallow'.

Turn right down Milford Lane and left at the Cheshire Cheese pub on Little Essex Street. Monastic and ecclesiastical property lay also under Essex House, residence of the Queen's successive favourites Robert Dudley, Earl of Leicester from 1563 and of his nephew Robert Devereux, Earl of Essex, from 1588. Edmund Spenser's *Prothalamion*, describes it as the 'stately place wherein doth lodge a noble peer, great England's glory and the world's wide wonder'. The Chorus in *Henry V* sustains the adulation of Essex, in its anticipation of the return from Ireland of that 'general of our gracious Empress... Bringing rebellion broached on his sword'. But the Earl made a poor showing, and proved himself incompetent, lethargic and self-indulgent and the Queen stripped him of his titles and offices. The unstable Essex was piqued and five months later plotted to seize Whitehall Palace and force the Queen to dismiss her ministers. The scheme was discovered and precipitated a disastrous rising by Essex and his faction.

One of these, the improbably named Sir Gelly Meyrick, was sent to hire the Chamberlain's Men to perform a play depicting the deposition and murder of a king – *Richard II* of course, a stale thing 'so old and so long out of use' that the company feared that they would 'have small or no company at it'. But Sir Gelly was not swayed. 'So earnest he was' wrote Frances Bacon in his report on the case 'to satisfy his eyes with the sight of that tragedy which he thought soon after his lord should bring from the stage to the state.' A command performance was presented at the Globe but the day after the whole business came to nothing. Essex's uprising concluded in tragi-comedy, with the Earl surrounded at his house, forced to surrender, tried and executed. What seems surprising is that Shakespeare and his fellow actors did not get into trouble. Some two weeks later, on the very night of Essex's execution on Tower Green, the Chamberlain's Men played at Court. All the same, Elizabeth was far from unaffected: 'I am Richard II, know ye not that?'.

Prince Henry's Room

Keep going into Devereux Street, turn left at the pub and rejoin the Strand at the George; turn right. On your left, opposite Chancery Lane, stands Prince Henry's Room. In the 1590s the house was an inn named the Hand. It was rebuilt and renamed the Prince's Arms in 1610, probably because Henry, the eldest son of James I, became Prince of Wales that year, an event which was also marked by jousts and masques (in which the prince himself performed) devised and enriched by his protegés Ben Jonson and Inigo Jones. He was an intelligent and promising heir, a great patron (in addition to Jonson and Jones he also supported George Chapman and Edward Alleyn's playing company), a major art collector and an aggressive Protestant who vigorously supported the wedding of his sister Elizabeth to the Elector Palatine, later King of Bohemia. In 1612, at the age of 17, Henry suddenly died having apparently contracted typhoid swimming in the Thames at Windsor. His death was a blow to national spirits and 'numberless were the elegiac offerings to his memory'. *The Winter's Tale*, performed as part of the celebrations for his sister Elizabeth's wedding, with its depiction of the death of the boy prince Mamillius and the marriage of his sister Perdita to a future king of Bohemia, seems, in retrospect, to assume a poignant topicality. One part of the inn, a handsome oak-panelled room survives.

At the top of Chancery Lane stood Southampton House and now stands Chancery Lane Underground Station.

WESTMINSTER TO LAMBETH

Summary: Three great institutions, the Palace, Abbey and School of Westminster, are included in this route through the concentrated heart of royal London. Shakespeare would have known those parts of each which have survived from the Elizabethan period, some of which find a place in his history plays, while others evoke periods in the lives of many famous contemporaries. Elizabethan and Jacobean Westminster had its louche side, too, anticipating the extended tail-end of this walk through the long-vanished marshes of Lambeth. This route can be preceded by the walk on page 116.

Start:	Westminster Underground Station.
Finish:	Lambeth North Underground Station.
Length:	2 km (1¼ miles).
Time:	1½ hours. Allow 2 hours for visits to the Abbey and the Jewel Tower. Refreshments: Cafés are occasionally open in the Jewel Tower and the Abbey cloisters; the Westminster Arms, Storeys Gate.

Quite distinct from the commercial and more populous City, and the heart of royal London, Westminster occupies an important place in Shakespeare's history plays. It had also by Shakespeare's time long established itself as the centre of the nation's administration. Turn right out of the Westminster Underground exit at Portcullis House; cross the road, keeping Big Ben on your left and past New Palace Yard.

Westminster Hall

The long, comparatively low building on your left is Westminster Hall, the most substantial survivor of the old Palace of Westminster, the predecessor of the Houses of Parliament. Built by William Rufus, the son of the Conqueror, and refurbished by Richard II in 1397 (when it was given its stupendous hammerbeam roof), the hall was ancient in Shakespeare's day. It was intended as the banqueting hall of the palace, but became the centre of administrative life in the kingdom, accommodating parliaments and important councils. During the Shakespearean period it was also used as a court, with the King's Bench, which dealt with common law, on one side and the Court of Chancery on the other. It was therefore the venue for great state trials. In 1417, the proto-

Protestant martyr Sir John Oldcastle, the name Shakespeare originally and unfortunately gave to Falstaff, was condemned here (see page 93).

The Hall had also seen more recent trials and in Shakespeare's early career there would have been some old folk who still remembered Sir Thomas More's in 1535, Anne Boleyn's in 1536 or Protector Somerset's in 1552. Shakespeare himself might have witnessed some notorious ones: perhaps that of the Earl of Essex in 1601, with Sir Francis Bacon leading the prosecution (see page 96); or, more likely, that of his patron Henry Wriothesley, the Earl of Southampton, for being of the Essex party (he got off with a comparatively light sentence). He could also have seen Guy Fawkes tried here in 1606 for attempting to blow up Parliament.

In the 17th century there were numerous shops and stalls selling books, trinkets and keepsakes in the hall and grave trials shared the room with petty commerce. Morose, the noise-hating anti-hero of Ben Jonson's great comedy *Epicoene*, complains that it is one of the noisiest places in London. Low characters mingled outside with the litigants and lawyers. In a not-very-well-known play of the period called *A Knack to Know a Knave* a shifty character declares himself to have been 'a post-knight in Westminster this 12 year'. This 'office' involved hanging about the courts and making oneself available to give false evidence, or do any other dirty work for those bringing cases to court.

Avert your gaze from the statue of Oliver Cromwell, under whom all legitimate theatrical activity in England came to an abrupt stop in 1642. Who can say how long the days of the public theatres such as the Globe would have continued if they had not been suppressed by the Puritan administration? Certainly, the conditions under which the playhouses were revived at the Restoration created a very different kind of theatre from that which had flourished before the Commonwealth and in which Shakespeare had worked in the early years of the century.

The Palace of Westminster

Keep going past the Houses of Parliament, until you reach Victoria Tower Gardens, a convenient place to take a seat and consider the Palace of Westminster. This was the chief residence of the kings of England between Edward the Confessor and Henry VIII and occupied part of the site of the present Houses of Parliament. It was damaged by fire in 1512 and deserted by Henry VIII, who transferred his court to the palace of the disgraced Wolsey in 1530. This was York House, which Henry renamed 'Whitehall'. Shakespeare would have known the buildings which survived that fire. A fountain or conduit played in the area now occupied by New Palace Yard; nearby was also a bell-tower with an ancient clock and a high gate. The chief survivors of the fire, though, aside from the Hall were the Painted Chamber, the Star Chamber

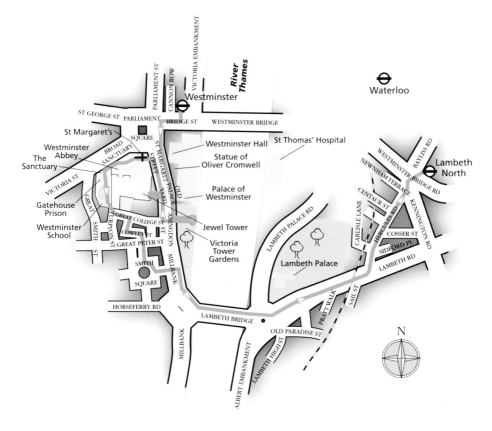

and St Stephen's Chapel. St Stephen's, which had been a royal private chapel on two storeys, filled with exquisite stained glass, was secularized and became the House of Commons, the members sitting in the choir stalls on the north and south walls, similar to the present arrangement. Its crypt and cloisters were used for storing parliamentary papers. Hard against the river was the notorious Star Chamber, under whose ceiling of golden stars the King's Council operated – a tyrannous and arbitrary institution that could exact any punishment short of the death penalty without recourse to common law. Its activities became very severe under James and Charles. In 1834 another disastrous fire swept everything away except the hall, the crypt of the chapel and the Jewel Tower. Many of the scenes in Shakespeare's English history plays located 'in the palace' or which ask for a throne, or which, while calling for royal characters, do not specify anywhere else, supposedly take place at Westminster.

Return to Abingdon Street, turn right and cross the road at the traffic lights, and then go left down the little path which leads to the blunt, once-moated fragment, the 14th-century Jewel Tower. Another survivor from the old palace, this was the depository for clothes, furs, jewels and plate from the time of Edward III. It is open to the public, but you will pass quiet places to sit at the front and rear of the moat if you do not care to go in. The tower contains pictures of the old palace and Westminster Hall, an exhibition on the history of Parliament, including panels illustrating the operation of Tudor parliaments and an account of the Gunpowder Plot. There is an instructive schematic map of the old palace in the courtyard.

Walk straight ahead out of the tower and left up the steps at the end. On your left is Henry VII's chapel, which was intended to honour his murdered uncle, Henry VI, for whom Henry VII had sought canonization. There is a touching, almost sacramental relationship between uncle and nephew in *3 Henry VI:*

King Henry lays his hand on Richmond's head.
                    If secret powers
Suggest but truth to my divining thoughts,
This pretty lad will prove our country's bliss.

The papal fee was too high for his uncle's sainthood, however, and the parsimonious King decided instead on a chapel in honour of the Virgin Mary – and himself: he is buried under a great monument by the Italian sculptor Torrigiano.

Keep walking and turn left again at the lane which leads past the late 15th- and early 16th-century church of St Margaret's Westminster. Protector Somerset, with characteristic arrogance, set his eye on the stones of St Margaret's for his palace on the Strand and was only prevented from taking them by the parishioners, who fought off his builders. The 16th-century east window was intended for Westminster Abbey as a celebration of the betrothal of Catherine of Aragon to Prince Arthur, eldest son of Henry VII; but by the time it was finished Arthur was dead and Catherine had married his brother, Henry. Under a cloak of pious rectitude Henry later used this earlier marriage as a get-out clause to rid himself of Catherine, who had failed to give him a son. Henry's intentions were clear to his contemporaries, but Shakespeare and his collaborator John Fletcher, who sustain a lofty mythologizing regard for Henry in *Henry VIII or All is True,* intend us to take the king's position at face value. The window was installed at Waltham Abbey instead, which is where it would have been in Shakespeare's time. It was brought here in the 18th century.

Opposite: Westminster Abbey, whose monuments were on every 16th-century tourist's itinerary. Its towers were added in the 18th century but the body of the church is more or less as Shakespeare would have known it.

Westminster Abbey

To your left stands Westminster Abbey, which in the 16th century would have looked much as it does now. The chief difference would have been the lack of towers at the west end: these, designed by Nicholas Hawksmoor, were not added until the 18th century. The abbey features on a number of occasions in the history plays. Ann Boleyn's coronation in Henry VIII is reported by a gentleman who has been:

> Among the crowd i' th'Abbey, where a finger
> Could not be wedged in more. I am stifled
> With the mere rankness of their joy.

The Duchess of Gloucester's fantasy of becoming queen in *2 Henry VI* naturally takes place in the 'cathedral church of Westminster / And in that chair where kings and queens are crowned'. It is the Abbot of Westminster whom Shakespeare in *Richard II* casts as the leader of a faction against Bolingbroke (later Henry IV) and for whose pains the 'grand conspirator...with clog of conscience and sour melancholy' yields up 'his body to the grave'. And it is near here that the young King Henry V, fresh from his coronation at the Abbey, banishes his fat old acquaintance Falstaff.

Continue along the side of the abbey and around to the west end. Near here there once stood the Abbot's – later the Dean's – house. It contained a famous parlour, around whose fireplace there ran three inscriptions: 'O pray for the peace of Jerusalem'; 'Build thou the walls of Jerusalem'; and 'Jerusalem which is above is free.' This was the Jerusalem Chamber, the room in which Henry IV first falls ill and later dies:

> It hath been prophesied to me many years
> I should not die but in Jerusalem,
> Which vainly I'd supposed the Holy Land;
> But bear me to that chamber; there I'll lie;
> In that Jerusalem shall Harry die.

You should be able to get into the abbey through the doors in the north side. It is filled with tombs containing the originals of the royal characters in Shakespeare's history plays. Edward the Confessor, 'pious Edward', the remote 'holy' sovereign in *Macbeth*, lies in a chapel behind the High Altar. The tomb of Edward III, subject of a play recently attributed at least in part to Shakespeare, was erected by his grandson Richard II. Richard himself and his queen, Anne of Bohemia, share the same tomb. The abbey also contains a famous portrait of Richard, the first 'realistic' depiction of an English monarch.

At the eastern end of St Edward's Chapel, behind the High Alter, lies Henry V, his tomb richly embellished with scenes from his life. The embalmed body of Henry's queen, Catherine of Valois – the 'angel' Kate whom Henry haltingly woos after Agincourt – lay in an open tomb until in the 1770s it was placed under a memorial to the Duke of Buckingham. Some – not many – believe Shakespeare wrote the anonymous play *Edmund Crouchback*, who is buried here too, the youngest son of Henry III. 'Innocents' corner' houses, among others, the tomb of two children believed to be Edward V and his brother the Duke of York – the Princes in the Tower, whom Shakespeare imagined 'girdling one another / Within their alabaster innocent arms' before their Uncle Richard had them smothered.

Closer to Shakespeare's time, there were the tombs of Anne of Cleves (too ugly for Henry's taste), Edward VI and Mary Tudor; and from his own time, those of Mary, Queen of Scots, and Elizabeth I. By the end of the 16th century, the abbey tombs were already tourist attractions. Thomas Dekker, in his satiric manual for a London visitor, *The Gull's Hornbook*, alludes to a country gent who 'brings his wife up to see the tombs at Westminster, the lions in the Tower' – two essentials on any 17th-century tourist itinerary. John Donne, later to become Dean of St Paul's, alludes to the abbey guides in one of his *Satires*:

> at Westminster...
> The man that keeps the abbey tombs,
> And for his price doth with whoever comes
> Of all our Harrys and our Edwards talk.

Chaucer, who was buried in the Abbey in 1400, set the trend for Poets' Corner. Edmund Spenser, England's Renaissance poet *par excellence*, followed him in 1598; writers are said to have thrown unpublished work of their own into his grave by way of tribute. His monument was not raised until 1619. Shakespeare's friend and great contemporary, Ben Jonson, is remembered with lapidary brevity: 'O rare Ben Jonson'. He is buried upright, also for economy's sake. Michael Drayton, who co-wrote the play *Sir John Oldcastle*, a dramatic effort to rehabilitate the good name of the original of Shakespeare's Falstaff, also lies in Poets' Corner. He is better known for his *Polyolbilon*, a vast poem on the history and mythology of Britain. According to John Ward, a vicar of Stratford, 'Shakespeare, Drayton, and Ben Jonson had a merry meeting and, it seems, drank too hard, for Shakespeare died of a fever there contracted.' Drayton was occasionally in Warwickshire; Jonson, it seems, never.

Although Spenser had to wait over 20 years for his monument, Shakespeare's was not raised for 124. Widely reproduced, it was executed by the Dutch sculptor Peter Scheemakers to a design by the Palladian architect

William Kent. Its fundraising committee included Alexander Pope. The Bard leans in a distinctly 18th-century attitude against a plinth decorated with (appropriately for the Abbey) bas-reliefs of English monarchs.

The Sanctuary

If the abbey is closed, walk to the west end and cross the Sanctuary. The spacious square and the wide thoroughfare which now leads off Broad Sanctuary (Victoria Street) give a poor idea of how the area must have looked in Elizabethan times, which was rather one of narrow streets and courts. In fact, Westminster, particularly during certain times of the year, could be a distinctly unsavoury place, littered, in all probability, with the offal, urine and faeces which decorated the lanes of the city. When the Court was absent, those who depended upon it for a living were forced to get by however they could, criminally if necessary. Victims were found among the pilgrims who came to visit the shrine of Edward the Confessor in the Abbey.

The problem was exacerbated by the custom of sanctuary which still operated in its precincts. There were other sanctuaries in London – including Whitefriars south of Fleet Street, the Palace of the Savoy off the Strand, the Mint in Southwark, and St Martin's le Grand in the City – but Westminster was the best known and most used. In the early years of Elizabeth's reign any criminal except those guilty of sacrilege or treason had the right to sanctuary here. The Queen later restricted the right to debtors; James abolished it altogether in 1623.

In Shakespeare's grimmest history play, *3 Henry VI,* Lady Gray, later Elizabeth, Queen to Edward IV, laments the capture of her husband by Warwick and Clarence, and makes for the Sanctuary 'to save at least the heir of Edward's right' – that is, her unborn child. The historical Queen built the chapel of St Erasmus next to the abbey's Lady Chapel out of gratitude for the sanctuary Westminster had provided. This was perhaps premature. That unborn child was to be Prince Edward in the next play in the sequence – *Richard III.* Once again the queen, this time learning of the imprisonment of Lord Rivers and Lord Gray, seeks sanctuary at Westminster, taking with her not Edward but his little brother, Richard, the Duke of York. It is a last resort and a later exchange between the Lord Cardinal and Buckingham, that incarnation of medieval *realpolitik,* makes it plain that there will be no sanctuary. 'You are too senseless-obstinate' says Buckingham.

Too ceremonious and traditional
Oft have I heard of 'sanctuary men',
But 'sanctuary children' ne'er till now.

The cardinal's scruples are swept aside, the duke is fetched and in course despatched with his brother Edward to the Tower.

The Victorian offices here were built on the site of the Gatehouse Prison, which, rather ironically, looked over the Sanctuary. In October 1618, Sir Walter Raleigh, had a night here to reflect on his extraordinary life before it was brought to an end on the block. Then in his late sixties, he had recently returned from a trip to the Orinoco during which, falling sick, he had been obliged to leave affairs to his juniors. A Spanish town was recklessly sacked, and on the expedition's return to London the Spanish ambassador called for Raleigh's execution. King James, who had always hated Raleigh, was accommodating, and one of the greatest personalities of the age – soldier, explorer, courtier, intellectual and poet – was condemned. We can imagine breaking forth the stoical and melancholy spirit that had always lain under the pale satins and pearl eardrops.

> Even such is time which takes in trust
> Our youth, our joys, and all we have,
> And pays us but with age and dust;

He is reported to have written this here, the night before his execution, after which Lady Raleigh bore off and embalmed his head. The rest of his body is buried in St Margaret's.

Westminster School to Lambeth

Pass through the arch to the left into Dean's Yard, the heart of Westminster School. Shakespeare would have known the school, which after its dissolution by Henry VIII had been re-founded by Queen Elizabeth in 1560. It had a reputation for drama: plays were regularly performed here, an annual Latin play was instituted, which continues, and the school even provided companies of boys who occasionally performed at Court. Nicholas Udall, author of the first published English comedy, the no-longer-very-funny *Ralph Roister Doister* (1541), was headmaster here. He had been a schoolmaster at Eton, where he was strict to the point of sadism, giving out 53 strokes to one of his pupils for a 'fault but small, or none at all'. He was dismissed from Eton for sexually abusing his pupils and came to Westminster late in his dubious career. He is buried in St Margaret's.

An altogether more attractive and distinguished headmaster was the great historian and antiquarian William Camden. Camden considered Shakespeare a 'pregnant wit' and explores the variants and antecedents of the name 'Shakespeare' in his *Remains of a Greater Work Concerning Britain*, coming up with *Breake-speare*, *Shotbolt*, *String-shield* and *Wagstaff* amongst others. Ben

Jonson was a boy at Westminster and always spoke fondly of his old headmaster. Camden instilled in Jonson a love of classical learning which must have sustained him after he left the school and was apprenticed by his stepfather into bricklaying, a trade Jonson detested (see page 112).

Walk through the short passage at the far side of Deans Yard and turn left on Great College Street. Turn right on Barton Street, bearing round Cowley Street and right on Lord North Street. At Smith Square, turn left, walking round Thomas Archer's great Baroque church; turn left on Dean Stanley Street and, at the end, right on Millbank. Cross the road and over Lambeth Bridge.

The bridge is a continuation of Horseferry Road, which led to a landing stage for what was exactly that: a ferry for conveying horses over the river. The alternative was a ride to London Bridge, on the far side of the City. Ahead of you, to the left, stands Lambeth Palace. The only buildings of importance in Lambeth in the 16th century (and before) were the palaces of the great Kent clerics, the Archbishop of Canterbury and the Bishop of Rochester. Rochester House, which was given to the Bishop of Carlisle by Henry VIII, is long gone, but the second Lambeth Palace, with its 13th-century chapel, 15th-century Lollards Tower and early 16th-century gatehouse still stands. Ironically, it's perhaps the only building in central London which gives any idea of the great ecclesiastical 'inns' which once ran along the Strand, and which were taken over by the nobility in the 16th century.

At the roundabout at the end, head for Lambeth Road. Turn left on Hercules Road after the railway. You pass Carlisle Road to your left, which recalls the estate owned by the Bishop of Carlisle. Lambeth in Shakespeare's day was a low swampy tract of open country, its lanes the haunt of thieves and prostitutes – the 'maids of Lambeth Marsh'. Subtle, the confidence trickster in Jonson's *Alchemist*, has a client who is a 'bawd of Lambeth' and when the district gets a mention in the plays of the period, it is usually with this reputation in mind.

Turn left at the end of Hercules Road for Lambeth North Underground Station.

THE INNS OF COURT

Summary: The Inns of Court, still a more or less uninterrupted sequence of tranquil 18th-century lanes and squares, were Elizabethan London's postgraduate centre, and a forcing-house of youthful ambition – political, ecclesiastical and literary, as well as legal. The route passes two 16th-century halls which saw very early outings for Shakespeare's comedies, *The Comedy of Errors* and *Twelfth Night*, and the lovely *Temple Gardens*, the plucking of whose roses anticipated such devastating events in *Henry VI*.

Start:	Temple Underground Station.
Finish:	Chancery Lane Underground Station.
Length:	2.5 km (1½ miles).
Time:	1½ hours.
Refreshments:	The Edgar Wallace and the Devereux, both Devereux Court; numerous places on Fleet Street and Chancery Lane; the Castle, corner of Furnival and Norwich Streets; the Seven Stars, Carey Street.

Turn left outside Temple Station and then immediately right through Victoria Embankment Gardens, Temple section. Turn right out of the gardens; head for the gate that takes you into the Middle Temple. Oxford and Cambridge have for so long assumed an historical sovereignty over higher education in England that it is easy to forget that London too had a university of a kind in its Inns of Court and Chancery. For many, the Inns were the natural next step after taking a degree, and there is hardly a famous name in Elizabethan and Jacobean political, ecclesiastical, military and literary life who did not pass through one of the Inns: Hawkins, Drake, Cotton, Hakluyt, Carew, Davies, Ford, Gascoigne, Marston, Raleigh, Bacon, Hatton, Wotton, Young, Beaumont and Fletcher.

The Temple

The Temple was originally the property of the Knights' Templar. When they were discredited it passed to the Knights' Hospitaller, who until the Reformation leased it to the lawyers. Edmund Spenser gives the history a characteristically Protestant emphasis in his *Prothalamion*:

> Those bricky towers
> The which on Thames broad, ancient back do ride
> Where now the studious lawyers have their bowers
> There whilom wont the Templer Knights to bide,
> Till they decayed through pride.

On the other side of the car park you can see Temple Gardens. It is here in *1 Henry VI* that the white and red roses, badges of the rival Houses of York and Lancaster, are plucked:

RICHARD PLANTAGENET:	Let him that is a true-born gentleman And stands upon the honour of his birth, If he suppose that I have pleaded truth, From off this briar pluck a white rose with me. *He plucks a white rose.*
SOMERSET:	Let him that is no coward nor no flatterer, But dare maintain the party of the truth, Pluck a red rose from off this thorn with me. *He plucks a red rose.*

There follows some sinister repartee, as the other nobles present declare their allegiances. The significance is not lost on Warwick, who, later alone with Richard Plantagenet, prophesies:

> This brawl today,
> Grown to this faction in the Temple garden,
> Shall send, between the red rose and the white,
> A thousand souls to death and deadly night.

And so, *Exeunt*. The rose brier is removed.

Turn left up the steps to Garden Court. Did Shakespeare ever study law? His plays and poems (the sonnets in particular) are filled with legal terms – *bond, plea, recovery, action, statute, fine, indenture, conveyance, session, mortgage, suit, fee, proof* – and many of the plays turn on crucial trial and trial-like scenes: Portia v Shylock in *The Merchant of Venice*; Angelo v Isabella in *Measure for Measure*; the debate over the Law Salic at the beginning of *Henry V*; Desdemona before the Venetian Senate in *Othello*; the mock trial of Goneril in *King Lear*; the trial

Opposite: Middle Temple Hall, where the first recorded performance of Twelfth Night *took place on 2 February, 1602. It has the finest Elizabethan interior in London.*

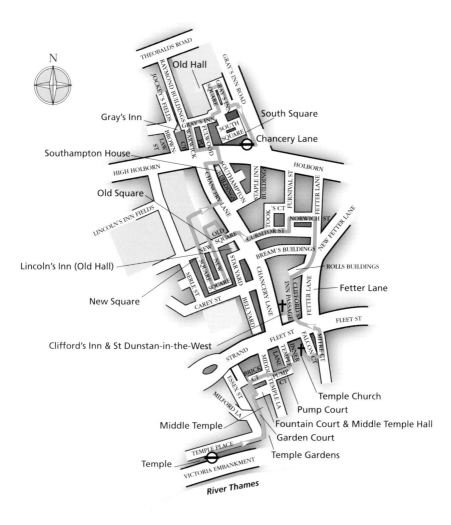

N

of Hermione in *The Winter's Tale*. Some people (lawyers of course) have claimed that his 'lost' years were spent as a legal clerk, but there is no evidence and it hardly seems necessary. Shakespeare's was a litigious age, and some of the plays by his contemporaries are equally legalistic. A stock of legal jargon picked up from a few Inns of Court men, some experience of forensic procedure (which Shakespeare had) would be enough to furnish him with what he needed for the stage. And then his plays, while not necessarily representative of Shakespeare's views, are often hardly respectful towards the profession. Dogberry the constable is incompetent, Angelo the magistrate is corrupt. 'The first thing we do, let's kill all the lawyers' says the butcher who follows Jack Cade, and hardly more complimentary is Hamlet's speculation on the second skull thrown up during the graveyard scene: 'Why might not that be the skull of a lawyer? Where be his quiddities now, his quillets, his cases, his tenures, and his tricks?'

Middle Temple Hall

Walk up the steps to Fountain Court. To your right is Middle Temple Hall. Built in 1572, it has the finest Elizabethan interior in London. It is the social heart of the Inn, and was the venue, at certain times of the year, of 'revels' that sometimes included masques and plays presented before the sovereign and the Court. On 2 February 1602, the first recorded performance of *Twelfth Night* took place here. The event was recorded by the student John Manningham: 'At our feast we had a play called Twelfth Night, or What You Will.' It was, Manningham observes learnedly, very like the *Maenechmi* of Plautus, and even more like the Italian play *Inganni*. He finds the comedy of Malvolio more memorable than the tale of Viola – or at least that is what he chose to record. It was 'good practice' he says to introduce a counterfeit letter which made the steward (ie Malvolio) understand that 'his lady widdowe' (ie Olivia) was in love with him; Malvolio's smiling and cross-gartering clearly appealed to him 'and then when he came to practise making him believe they took him to be mad'. The play was probably not more than a few months old at the time, though some have argued that this was the first performance and that the script was written or adapted for a legal audience. An all-male production to celebrate the quatercentenary of this performance was staged by the Globe Theatre Company in 2002, with Oliver Cotton as Malvolio and Mark Rylance as Olivia.

Nobody is quite sure how the play would have been presented. This hall, like those in Oxford and Cambridge colleges, has at one end a large screen with serving doors, similar in many respects to the permanent backdrop (or *frons scenae*) at the rear of a stage such as the Globe: a natural place, you might think, before which to perform a play. But the few plans which exist for the adaptation of halls for performance suggest that they took place at the 'top table' end of the hall, on the raised platform which stands there. Who can say?

Some two months after the Chamberlain's Men appeared here, Manningham's room-mate Edward Curle told him an anecdote about Shakespeare and Burbage. Burbage, who was playing Richard III, had arranged a tryst with a woman, but Shakespeare got there first. When Burbage arrived, he found Shakespeare already 'entertained, and at his game'. Shakespeare sent word that 'William the Conqueror was before Richard III'. It seems a bit too good to be true, and has the flavour of something invented outside the theatrical world, but who knows? It shows Shakespeare and his company were common currency for jokes in London student life.

Go through the passage opposite into Essex Court and Brick Court. Turn right into Pump Court, one of the oldest parts of the Temple. The playwright John Marston studied here. His is the bitterest consciousness of the age and he paid for his satirical attacks on the establishment with two spells in jail. *The Malcontent* probably appeared at about the same time as *Othello* (1603). *Measure for Measure*, with its disguised duke and the sense of sexual corruption, was clearly an influence.

Temple Church and the Inns of Chancery

Look left towards the old houses at the top as you cross Temple Lane. Beyond the colonnade (called the Cloister), you will find Temple Church. It was built by the Knights Templar in 1185 in imitation of the Dome of the Rock in Jerusalem (or perhaps the Church of the Holy Sepulchre) and still contains, as it would have in Shakespeare's day, effigies of some of the old knights, referred to by playwrights of the time. In 1585, the first of Shakespeare's 'lost years', the church suffered the doctrinal indignity of offering Richard Hooker's Anglican sermons in the morning and Walter Travers' Calvinist sermons in the afternoon.

Turn right out of the church, go through the arch and onto King's Bench Walk. Turn left through the arch under Mitre Court Buildings. Cross Fleet Street, looking left, towards the site of Temple Bar. Turn left into the yard in front of St Dunstan's in the West. The statue of Elizabeth I was removed from Ludgate. Turn right out of the churchyard and next right up Clifford's Inn Passage. By the Elizabethan period Clifford's Inn was attached to the Inner Temple, and served, like the other Inns of Chancery as a kind of residential college to prepare students before they were called to the bar by one of the Inns of Court – in this case, the Inner Temple. Sir Edward Coke, Lord Chief Justice to James I and Bacon's great rival, studied here.

Keep going around the back of the church, through the passage and left on Fetter Lane. Ben Jonson lived here for a while, when it supported a number of pawnbrokers, and a character in his *Every Man Out of His Humour* refers to the '40 shillings more' he can borrow on his gown in Fetter Lane. The London residence of the Bishops of Norwich was once here; it was possessed at the Reformation, but is remembered in the next street.

Turn left at Norwich Street and left again at the end on Furnival Street. Furnival's Inn was another of the Inns of Chancery, attached in this case to Lincoln's Inn. Thomas More was a student here. Turn right to the end of Cursitor Street. Opposite you, on the other side of Chancery Lane, stands Lincoln's Inn, and according to the biographer Thomas Fuller, Ben Jonson, who started life (to his everlasting chagrin) as a bricklayer, helped his stepfather build 'the new structure of Lincoln's Inn', 'when, having a trowel in one hand, he had a book in his pocket'. He may have put a few bricks into that

Right: '*Inky blots and rotten parchment bonds.*'
Shakespeare's signatures to three legal documents.
Top: *Shakespeare's deposition of 11 May 1612 in the Belott-Mountjoy suit.* Middle: *The Conveyance for the Blackfriars gatehouse, 10 March 1613.*
Bottom: *The mortgage for the same dated the following day.*

wall. Further up the street was the discreet *Domus Conversorum* for London's Jews (see page 63).

Lincoln's Inn

Cross Chancery Lane and pass through the arch to the right of the gatehouse that leads to Lincoln's Inn. The Old Hall has a handsome 15th-century interior, with 17th-century furnishings, including a fine carved screen. Unlike the halls at the Inner Temple, Middle Temple and Gray's Inn, it escaped damage in World War II. To the right of the hall is the chapel. Three years after Shakespeare's death, the great experimental poet John Donne, then Reader of Lincoln's Inn, laid the foundation stone of the new chapel, an early exercise in 17th-century gothic, probably by Inigo Jones. It replaced an earlier building. Four years later, on Ascension Day 1623, the same year as the publication of the First Folio, Donne, now Dean of St Paul's, preached the consecration sermon here. The open undercroft, perhaps designed as an alternative to the Temple Church, was intended to allow students to reflect and lawyers to meet their clients. The building escaped enemy action, but not heavy-handed restoration.

Pass through the arch into the Old Square, familiar to Thomas Lodge who studied here in the late 1570s. Lodge was one of the clever generation of wits – Greene, Lyly, Kyd and, to an extent Marlowe, are others – who made a stir in London's literary and theatrical life just before Shakespeare came on the scene, and who were in various ways important to his success. Lodge started out with a brief spell in the thick of London's theatrical world, writing a defence of the theatre against the puritan Stephen Gosson (see page 60) and turning out a few plays for the Lord Admiral's company, of which two survive. But his career really took off with prose and verse romances: *Scillaes Metamorphosis*, 'dedicated to the gentlemen of the Inns of Court and Chancery' was the first such handling of a classical subject in English (Shakespeare adapted it in *Venus and Adonis*). *Phillis*, which offered more of the same, followed his great hit *Rosalynde*, a bestseller which went through ten editions but is now remembered (if at all) as the basis for *As You Like It*. Lodge was a friend of the wretched Robert Greene (see page 56), with whom he collaborated on at least one play. Lodge was perhaps the kind of fellow-victim Greene had in mind when he intimated Shakespeare's plagiarism in Greene's *Groatsworth of Wit*. Some years after Greene's death, Lodge became dissatisfied with literature and did what Greene perhaps should (and could) have done himself: gave up scribbling and became a doctor.

Turn left and walk around the lawn of New Square. This was called Fickett's Field in Shakespeare's time, and before the dissolution of the monasteries belonged to the Priory of St John of Jerusalem in Clerkenwell. Keep straight ahead at the top towards the austerely handsome Stone Buildings. Contemporary maps show this part of the Inn laid out with trees, possibly a place for 'the walks of Lincoln's Inn / Under the elms' Jonson refers to in *The Devil is an Ass*. Turn right at the bottom of Stone Buildings and leave the Inn here, turning left on Chancery Lane.

Towards the top to your right is Southampton Buildings, the site of Southampton House. In 1605, *Love's Labour's Lost* was revived here for Anne of Denmark, Queen to James I. She was keen on the theatre, becoming patron of Worcester's, later the Queen's, Men in 1603. *Love's Labour's Lost* was some 10 or 11 years old by 1605, and rather antique by the standards of the time, but it seems there was 'no new play that the queen has not seen'. Southampton House was the London residence of Henry Wriothesley, Shakespeare's patron.

Gray's Inn

Cross Holborn, a residential district favoured by lawyers in the 16th and 17th centuries (see page 42). At the traffic lights, walk straight up Warwick Court and in to Gray's Inn. Shakespeare's patron, the Earl of Southampton was a member of Gray's Inn. So was Elizabeth's great minister, William Cecil, Lord

Burleigh (see page 93). The playwrights George Chapman, Thomas Middleton and James Shirley (see page 159) were all Gray's men, as was Sir Philip Sidney, the supreme courtier and *beau ideal* of the age. It is Sir Francis Bacon, though, whose presence is most strongly felt here.

Turn right through Field Court and through the passage to Gray's Inn Square. Verulam buildings honour Bacon, who was created 1st Lord Verulam (the Latin name for St Albans). The building at the end is the Old Hall, which dates from 1556. According to the Gestae Greyorum – the account of activities at Gray's Inn – events got out of hand on the night of 28 December 1594. A performance intended for the evening had to be abandoned and instead

> it was thought good not to offer anything of account saving dancing and revelling with gentlewomen; and after such sports a comedy of errors (like to Plautus his Menaechmus) was played by the players. So that night was begun, and continued to the end, in nothing but confusion and errors; whereupon it was for ever afterwards called 'The Night of Errors'.

This was *The Comedy of Errors*, newly written, short enough to be played towards the end of an evening, and unquestionably based on Plautus' play. The lawyers knew their Roman comedy, evidently. It was not for nothing that Shakespeare took Plautus as a model, knowing he could at least equal if not excel his dramatic technique. The same questions as to how *Twelfth Night* was staged at Middle Temple Hall also apply to *The Comedy of Errors* at Gray's Inn.

The statue here in South Square is of Sir Francis Bacon, Lord Chancellor, lawyer, philosopher, essayist and debtor. He was a prominent member of the Inn, and as well as his more serious contributions, laid out the walks and wrote speeches for the entertainments in the Inn. His great essays return often to the struggle for wealth and power, and Bacon himself used all he had to get senior government office. This included not allying himself with the faction led by the Earl of Essex (the downfall of many less vigilant in the Elizabethan corridors of power). In his prosecution of Essex and later report of the Earl's treachery he mentions the seditious production of *Richard II* at the Globe on 7 February 1601 (see page 96). Some confused occultists, taking their lead from Delia Bacon, have asserted that Bacon wrote Shakespeare's plays – or, less confidently, that the world does not know that he did not. To which there is only one sane response: *Exeunt omnes*.

Leave the Inn under the arch. Chancery Lane Underground Station is to your left.

ST JAMES'S AND WHITEHALL

Summary: You see some of London's most splendid views on this walk through and around St James's Park, once a royal hunting ground and still surrounded by royal estates. The Tudor range of St James's Palace evokes the Chapel Royal and some of Shakespeare's surprising theatrical rivals, as well as the appearance of the much larger Palace of Whitehall on the other side of the park. The walk ends with a visit to the only surviving part of the palace, Inigo Jones's exquisite Banqueting House, once home of the Court masque, and the building symbolically associated with the end of theatrical life in 17th-century London. The walk from Westminster to Lambeth on page 97 is a convenient continuation of this route.

Start:	St James's Park Underground Station.
Finish:	Embankment or Charing Cross Underground Stations.
Length:	2 km (1¼ miles).
Time:	1 hour. Allow an additional ½ hour for a visit to the Banqueting House or the royal chapels.
Refreshments:	Stalls in St James' Park; the Two Chairmen, Dartmouth Street; the Red Lion, Crown Passage (off Pall Mall); the Golden Lion, King Street; the Red Lion, Duke of York Street.

Cross the road outside the Broadway/Tothill Street exit and walk down Queen Anne's Gate, turning right with the street and left at the end down Cockpit Steps. Cross Birdcage Walk, turning left and then second right down the lane into St James's Park (past the water fountain). This, the oldest royal park in central London, was formed by Henry VIII for St James's Palace. It had been a boggy field where the lepers at St James's Hospital kept their pigs. In Henry's time much of it was wooded and given over to deer, but there were also a tiltyard and a bowling alley. Elizabeth I hunted in the park and there was an attempt to assassinate her here by one William Parry. The park was transformed by Charles II.

Opposite: The gatehouse to St James's Palace with, to its right, the Chapel Royal – survivors of Henry VIII's large palace. The great musicians of the Tudor and Stuart periods were employed here.

The birds you can see from the bridge over the lake are not a modern adornment. An aviary – the birdcage of Birdcage Walk – formed part of the peculiar zoo that James I established in the park, together with a long-vanished physic and formal garden. The polymath Henry Peacham wondered at the beavers in the ornamental pond, which were reputed to bite off their testes when frightened to create a decoy to predators. Shakespeare makes no mention of them, unfortunately. He makes no mention of the two crocodiles apparently kept here either; their ancestry in *Antony and Cleopatra* is strictly literary.

To the left is Buckingham Palace. Continue through the park, cross The Mall and go down Marlborough Road to Inigo Jones's Queen's Chapel on the right, the first classical church in this country, begun for the proposed marriage of Charles I to the *Infanta* of Spain, which fell through, and finished for his marriage to Henrietta Maria.

St James's Palace and the Chapel Royal

To your left is St James's Palace, built in 1531 by Henry VIII on the site of St James's Hospital, which towards the end of the medieval period had an almost comically chequered career as the repository of brewing, embezzling, drunkenness and general unseemliness, and ended up as a leper hospital for young women. The gatehouse on Pall Mall and, to its right, the Chapel Royal are all that remain of a substantial Tudor building of four courts (a fire destroyed the rest in 1809). It was a principal residence of the English monarchy for 300 years, especially after Whitehall Palace (of which St James's gives a flavour) burned down once and for all in 1698. Both Elizabeth and James held court here. It does not seem to have been a venue for plays, but some masques by Ben Jonson were performed here – of which more later.

To the right of the large gatehouse on Cleveland Row is the Chapel Royal, which was famous for its church music and for employing some of the greatest names in 16th- and 17th-century English music: Thomas Tallis, William Byrd and Henry Purcell were all organists here. The chapel maintained a choir to match, some of whom were recruited into the companies of children who performed plays at the indoor theatres at St Paul's, Blackfriars and elsewhere (see page 25). These companies were competition for the adult players like Shakespeare's Chamberlain's Men, and Hamlet refers to them slightly as 'an eyrie of children, little eyases [baby hawks]' who are 'most tyrannically clapped'. Management of the children's companies usually had an air of exploitation about it, run as they were by opportunistic characters who only managed to keep performances going by pretending they were strictly educational. This was not so difficult to achieve since drama was seen as a way of instilling presentation skills and formed a central part of school curricula. The boys must have been accomplished

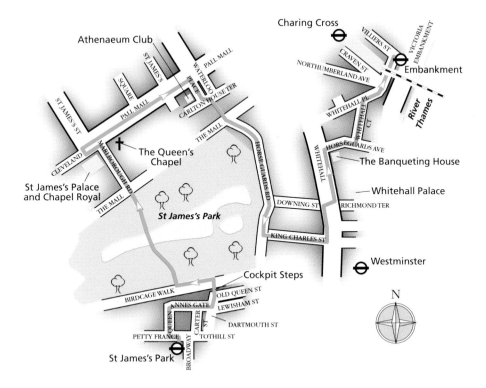

players to cope with the emotionally sophisticated plays of Jonson and Marston which they tackled in the early years of the 17th century.

Whitehall Palace

Cross the double-zebra and turn right onto Pall Mall. Turn right at Waterloo Place, past the Athenaeum Club (see page 186). Walk down Duke of York Steps at the end, turn left and right down Horse Guards Road. At the end of Horse Guards Parade, turn left up Clive Steps, and walk down King Charles Street to Whitehall. You pass the gates of Downing Street to your left. Whitehall Palace stood here, the principal residence of the monarch from Henry VIII until William III. It was an enormous, rambling place that stretched from a point near Westminster Bridge up to Scotland Yard halfway up the corner to your left, and from the Thames (which was wider and closer in the Elizabethan period) to St James's Park. Before Henry appropriated it, the palace was a vast ecclesiastical property owned by the Archbishop of York and known as York Place. Its last resident was Cardinal Wolsey. After a disastrous fire at the Palace of Westminster, and the fall of Wolsey, Henry VIII took it and renamed it:

You must no more call it York Place, that's past;
For since the Cardinal fell, that title's lost;
Tis now the King's and called Whitehall.

Henry developed the palace, adding splendid gatehouses over this street, one of stone and flint flushwork, allegedly designed by Hans Holbein and known as the Holbein Gate near the Banqueting Hall. Elizabeth also improved it, in 1581 adding a new banqueting hall made, like its predecessor out of wood and canvas, but richly painted and decorated with nearly 300 glass windows. It sounds a rather strange building. James I certainly didn't think much of it, describing it contemptuously as an 'old, rotten slight-builded shed'. In 1606 he replaced it with something more substantial and stately, some of its building materials being supplied by Peter Street, who had built the Globe Theatre about seven years before. This hall survived until the comprehensive destruction wrought by the palace fire of 1619. Both these halls, probably converted for the occasion, were venues for plays by Shakespeare and his contemporaries. Sometimes the performances were routine, sometimes for a special occasion.

Performance at Court was lucrative and prestigious, and lent respectability to what was often perceived to be a disreputable profession. This was especially so under James I. Only ten days after his accession, letters patent were drawn up to advertise the royal protection Shakespeare's company, renamed the King's Men, would receive:

freely to use and exercise the art of playing comedies, tragedies,
histories, interludes, morals, pastorals, stage plays as well for the
recreation of our loving subjects as for our solace and pleasure

Moreover, it was the King's pleasure that these courtesies and favours be observed by provincial justices, mayors and other officials, so often opposed to dramatic activity. The King's Men played 187 times before James between the issuing of this patent and 1616, the year of Shakespeare's death – that is approximately 13 a year (ten more annually than they had played before Queen Elizabeth). The year between November 1604 and October 1605 is fairly representative. The Court was presented with a mixture of recent material – *Othello, Measure for Measure* – and old stuff – *The Comedy of Errors, Love's Labour's Lost, The Merry Wives of Windsor, The Merchant of Venice* (played twice) and *Henry V*. The company also performed two plays by Ben Jonson: *Every Man In* and *Every Man Out of His Humour*. Most of these were performed at Whitehall.

The Banqueting House

Cross the road and turn left, towards Trafalgar Square. On your right, you will reach the Banqueting House. When the old Palace of Whitehall burned down, James planned to have the whole place rebuilt by Inigo Jones and John Webb. Their plans show that it would have been one of the greatest palaces in Europe, but only this corner, the Banqueting House, was completed. It is the first pure Renaissance building in London and when it was finished in 1622, clearly showed up the rest of the palace for what it then was: a vast, formless, piecemeal jumble of 2,000 rooms. In 1698 another fire destroyed everything but the Banqueting House.

As well as plays, the old banqueting halls had been used for court masques – one of them, Jonson's *Masque of Beauty*, had christened the hall James had built in 1606. For 13 years, before the installation of the ceiling by Rubens (which was considered too precious to spoil with candle smoke), masques were performed here.

Of all the artistic achievements of the Elizabethan and Jacobean age – and in spite of the often really good literary contributions by Jonson, Chapman, Beaumont and others – masques are perhaps the most difficult to grasp. These half-dramas, with their dance, music and, later, elaborate scenery and spectacle seem very remote. They were less naturalistic than the theatre, bringing on classical deities and personifications of abstract qualities, although Jonson livened them up when he started introducing anti-masques – rustics and grotesques which provided an antidote. In the hands of Inigo Jones, Jonson's collaborator (they came to hate each other), the sets followed rational Italianate principles, with a vanishing point best seen from where the monarch sat (which reinforced their royal commission), and complex machinery was employed to work scenes of transformation: deities appearing from the skies, landscapes split asunder to reveal palaces and so on. They mixed professional and amateur (that is, courtly) performers – which must have made for some backstage tension – and the whole affair wound up with a dance. It all sounds rather well-behaved, but contemporary accounts suggest otherwise, with courtiers sometimes performing an unseemly scramble for seats and sending the glasses flying when it was time for refreshment.

Shakespeare did not write masques, but some of his plays have masque-like episodes: the confrontation between Oberon and Titania in *A Midsummer Night's Dream* for instance, or the dance of Ceres and the appearance of Ariel as a harpy in *The Tempest*. Indeed, *The Tempest* was performed at the old banqueting house along with Beaumont's *The Masque of the Inner Temple and Gray's Inn* as part of the celebrations of the wedding between Princess Elizabeth (the daughter of James I) and the Elector Palatine.

Royal patronage of drama reached its highest point during the reign of

Charles I, long after Shakespeare's death, but when his plays were still performed. If there is a symbolic moment at which that theatrical tradition came to an end it happened here in 1649, when Charles stepped out of a first-floor window onto the scaffold erected to stage his execution. In his great 'Horation Ode', Andrew Marvell made the association between theatre and monarchy explicit at the very moment at which it seemed to have come to an end.

> ...thence the royal actor borne
> The tragic scaffold might adorn:
> While round the armed bands
> Did clap their bloody hands.
> *He* nothing common did or mean
> Upon that memorable scene...

For Embankment and Charing Cross Underground Stations, turn right down Horseguards Avenue, left up Whitehall Court and right at the end. Cross Northumberland Avenue and walk down Embankment Place opposite. Embankment is at one end and Charing Cross at the other end of Villiers Street.

HAMPTON AND HAMPTON COURT

Summary: Hampton Court was the largest house in Tudor England and this royal palace advertises itself as the greatest in Britain. Elizabeth entertained lavishly here and the palace is the greatest material legacy of the Tudor and early Stuart courts. Shakespeare's company appeared here and Shakespeare himself probably acted in the Great Hall. This walk combines a stroll around the edges of the palace with a visit to one of London's more eccentric monuments and an eloquent architectural expression of the elevated place Shakespeare had come to occupy in the 18th century: Garrick's Temple to Shakespeare. In between lies Bushy Park, once the palace's hunting reserve, now a landscape divided by magnificent tree-lined avenues.

Start:	Hampton Station.
Finish:	Hampton Court Station or Hampton Station.
Length:	3.5 km (2 miles) or 5 km (3½ miles).
Time:	2–3 hours. Allow at least 3 hours extra if you want to tour the palace.
Refreshments:	Several cafés and pubs at Hampton; restaurant and café in Hampton Court Palace Gardens.

Turn left out of the station, down Station Road. Turn right onto Plevna Road and left at the end down Thames Street. At the Bull Inn, you can cross the road and walk for a little way along the foreshore. Turn up to Thames Street. A few yards on your right a little lane leads off to the lawn on which stands David Garrick's Temple to Shakespeare. There is a well-situated bench with views along the river on the other side. The temple is a little Palladian shrine, designed by the then-unknown Robert Adam, and occupying a (now much reduced) pleasure garden landscaped by Capability Brown. Inside stood Roubiliac's much-imitated life-sized statue of Shakespeare, for which, with endearing vanity, Garrick himself posed and which cost him £500. He bequeathed the statue to the British Museum and it now stands in the foyer of the British Library. (See page 8).

Garrick and Shakespeare
More than anyone else, Garrick ensured Shakespeare's survival and reputation in the 18th century. As well as keeping his plays in the repertory as a manager

and actor, he adapted his work, and extolled it in prologues and epilogues. The temple anticipates by 14 years Garrick's 1769 Shakespeare Jubilee in Stratford and is a concrete expression of the 18th-century cult of Shakespeare. Garrick frankly described the playwright in his Jubilee 'Ode upon dedicating a building, and erecting a statue, to Shakespeare, at Stratford-upon-Avon' as 'the god of our Idolatry'. Five years late, high prices, heavy rain and a dose of heavier satire did what they could to spoil the fireworks, horse-racing, masquerade ball and grand parade of Shakespearean characters, but the Jubilee somehow came off. Garrick's rendition of his ode (to an accompaniment written by Thomas Arne) took place inside a temporary Rotunda. His introductory preamble was tellingly interrupted by a Frenchified 'plant' in the audience who complained of the untutored and overrated Bard, charges robustly met by Garrick and further confounded by his ode to the 'Genius of our Isle'. The Jubilee did much to put both the Bard and Stratford on the cultural map of Europe.

Above the road, which cut through Garrick's property even then, stands his handsome neo-classical villa. Enlarged and improved by its owner with advice from Robert Adam, it was paid for by Garrick's income as a player and manager of Drury Lane. He entertained a distinguished company here in a style hitherto unknown to anybody in his profession. 'Ah David,' said Dr Johnson, much taken with the house, 'it is the leaving of such a place that makes a death-bed terrible.'

Bushy Park

At the end of the lawn, return to the road. Pass St Alban's Lodge, cross the road and pass through the gates into Bushy Park. Henry VIII acquired the park from Wolsey when he got the palace from him in 1526, and enclosed it for hunting in 1538. After his death the fences were removed and Shakespeare must have known it as a public park, and perhaps used it for exercise with his fellow players when his troupe came to perform at Hampton Court. The great tree-lined avenues of Bushy and Hampton Court Parks were introduced by William III, and in the 16th century it was probably, as its name suggests, a shrubbier, bushier place than it is now. It is likely that *As You Like It* was performed at Hampton Court in the late 1590s or early 1600s, and the courts of Elizabeth and James recreated themselves in Bushy as do those of the Duke in Shakespeare's Arden. It perhaps suggested to its audience the 'wood near Athens' of *A Midsummer Night's Dream*, the 'marvelous convenient place for our rehearsal'

Opposite: The west entrance to Hampton Court. Visitors who arrived by boat – including, perhaps, Shakespeare's troupe – entered the palace by this gatehouse.

praised by Peter Quince: 'This green plot shall be our stage, this hawthorn brake our tiring house, and we will do it in action as we will do it before the Duke.'

Hampton Court Gardens

Bear right down the long Lime Avenue; bear right at the roundabout at the end; cross Hampton Court Road and walk through the Lion Gate. You are entering the palace gardens from the north, not the obvious point of entry in Shakespeare's time, which would have been from the river. To your right is the maze, not Elizabethan but planted in 1702 and almost certainly very different from anything Shakespeare would have known. Hedge mazes like this are mentioned by one Elizabethan gardening writer as a place 'to make your friend wander in gathering of berries till he cannot recover himself without your help', but if there was a maze at Hampton Court it would probably have been a dwarf version of hyssop, thyme or lavender, perhaps with an arbour decked with roses in the middle. Shakespeare's mazes are chiefly low-lying affairs, like the one Gonzalo refers to in *The Tempest* amongst the 'forth-rights and meanders', or the fast-vanishing network of sheep-tracks lamented by Titania:

> …the quaint mazes in the wanton green
> For want of tread are undistinguishable.

Turn left through the arboretum and past the old lawns. In Tudor times this was Henry VIII's Great Orchard, and the fruit trees that were grown here supplied the palace kitchens. Courtiers listening to the Ghost of old Hamlet in the evening need only have cast their minds back to their afternoon walk to imagine a plausible setting for the king's murder:

> Sleeping within my orchard,
> My custom always of the afternoon,
> Upon my secure hour thy uncle stole
> With juice of cursèd hebenon in a vial,
> And in the porches of mine ears did pour
> The leperous distilment…

Turn left at the end towards Wren's palace, and past the Real (or Royal) Tennis Court to your right. Henry VIII built a tennis court at Hampton Court, but this one dates from the 1620s. A royal game, it was also, in *Henry V* the inspiration for the famous royal insult, when the Dauphin sends Henry, instead of the dukedoms he demands, a tun of tennis balls, as more befitting his 'spirit'. The King resolves to repay the pleasantry:

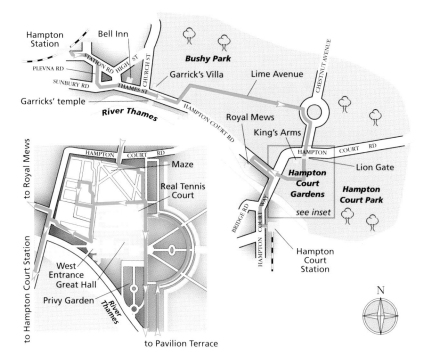

When we have matched our rackets to these balls,
We will in France, by God's grace, play a set
Shall strike his father's crown into the hazard.

Keep going along the Broad Walk – what Gonzalo would describe as a 'forthright' – past Wren's building. The Tudor apartments of Wolsey's and Henry's palace were demolished to make place for William III's developments. Likewise, the formal gardens to your left were parkland in Tudor times. Where the wall drops, you have a good view of the Tudor range of the palace and of the Privy Garden, once Tudor, now largely a reconstruction of William III's. The 16th-century Privy Garden would have included a formal knot garden, one of many kinds of garden suggested by the enraptured account of the Duke of Württemberg, which praises 'the many beautiful gardens both for pleasure and ornament – some planted with nothing but rosemary; others laid out with various other plants, which are trained, intertwined, and trimmed in extraordinary shapes'. One Elizabethan gardening writer exhorts the gardener to cut the 'lesser wood'

Above: 'Our bodies are gardens, to the which our wills are gardeners.' A small formal garden from Thomas Hill's The Gardener's Labyrinth.

(commonly yew and privet) in the shape of 'men armed in the field ready to give battle, of swift running greyhounds, or of well-scented and true-running hounds to chase the deer or hunt the hare'. Francis Bacon, who wrote an essay on gardens, did not approve: 'I, for my part, do not like images cut out in juniper or other garden stuff; they be for children.' As well as topiary, there were vases of lead or stone, statues, fountains and sundials.

Elizabeth maintained and improved her father's gardens, sometimes working in them herself in the morning, 'briskly when alone'. Rare plants brought back from the New World by such as Hawkins, Drake and Raleigh – including the tobacco and potato, for which Sir Walter takes credit – were put in the hothouses and flowerbeds. Many plants perhaps planted here and now common in English gardens – daffodils, fritillaries, tulips, hyacinths, anemones – would have been classified as 'outlandish', that is foreign, by the gardening professionals.

There is a small modern knot garden to the west, between the Privy Garden and the Pond Gardens. In Shakespeare's time these were occupied by towers, turrets, an elaborate summerhouse and ornamental sunken ponds surrounded by striped poles surmounted by a Tudor bestiary of unicorns, dragons, lions and greyhounds, similar to those the Queen kept on pedestals at Whitehall and recalling, perhaps, the beasts which crouch on top of the Great Hall. The ponds supplied fish for the palace kitchens. There was also a complex of buildings that led to the water-gate, used by the king, and later monarchs, when they came to Hampton Court by barge.

Hampton Court Palace

At the end of the Broad Walk, bear left, turn left over the top of William III's garden and leave this part by the way you came in, but continuing along the east range of the palace. You can see the top of the Great Hall above the lower Tudor buildings. It was chiefly used for banqueting and as a reception room, as many as 600 courtiers dining there at two sittings twice a day, but it also lays claim to being the oldest surviving playhouse in England. In Elizabeth's time the tone of festivities at Christmas was lavish but not unseemly: banquets, balls, masques and masquerades, music and dancing. James, too, was lavish in his entertainment, but sometimes allowed matters to reach bacchanalian extremes.

Elizabethan players were experienced in presenting plays at all kinds of venues, not just purpose-built theatres. Shakespeare's company performed at Hampton Court on numerous occasions and Shakespeare himself would have acted in the Great Hall. A room adjacent to the hall, perhaps the nearby Horn Room, where the Queen's collection of antlers was hung, was perhaps made available as a tiring house in which the players might dress. Unlike performances in the public theatres, productions in the hall would have taken place in the evening, the walls and ceilings hung with the candles that illuminated not only the stage but also the hangings that covered the walls and the vast and richly carved hammerbeam roof. Peter Quince and his fellow mechanicals expect to perform at night and in a place such as the hall at Hampton Court when they rehearse 'Pyramus and Thisbe' for Theseus' wedding in *A Midsummer Night's Dream*:

QUINCE:	...there is two hard things: that is, to bring the moonlight into a chamber – for you know Pyramus and Thisbe meet by moonlight.
SNOUT:	Doth the moon shine that night we play our play?...
BOTTOM:	...you may leave a casement of the great chamber window where we play open, and the moon may shine in at the casement.
QUINCE:	Ay, or else one must come in with a bush of thorns and lantern and say he comes to disfigure, or to present, the person of Moonshine...

Although the screen at the end of the hall may sound like a promising area for staging a play, the drama actually took place at the other end, where the high table stood. It was this end of the hall which was associated with display, and where at other times the sovereign's meals were served with elaborate ceremony. A small army of carpenters, painters and other technical staff would be mustered to create a temporary stage and auditorium. At its centre, enthroned on a raised dais, sat the monarch, occupying the best place in which to see the action and be seen. With the development of masques, such as those created by Ben Jonson and Inigo Jones, the king sat at the only perfect viewing point for the newly invented perspective scenery, reinforcing the sense that the production was for the royal pleasure. In other respects, however, court performances such as those at Hampton Court were far from dignified or comfortable occasions. In fact, they could be a scrum.

In the Christmas festivities of 1603–4, soon after the accession of James I, Hampton Court was the venue for 30 plays, many of which would have been presented by Shakespeare's company, the recently named King's Men.

The Tiltyard and the apartments of the palace

At the crossroads, follow the sign for the Tiltyard; turn right and then left at the tearooms and through the gate into the rose garden. These gardens cover the site of the Tiltyard, where tournaments took place and which added to Henry's recreational collection of bowling alleys, tennis court and hunting park. Turn left at the end, through the gate to your right; there is an excellent view of the Tudor range of the palace here. From right to left, you see the buildings enclosing the courts of the Lord Chamberlain (in Elizabeth's day, Lord Hunsdon, the patron of Shakespeare's company) and the Master Carpenter; next, at ground level, come the first rooms of the kitchen complex – the boiling house, flesh larder, fish court, and great kitchens; behind them, below the Great Hall, lies the vast beer cellar; beyond these, on top of the wine cellar, and beyond are the surviving Tudor apartments – the Horn Room, converted for a display of antlers and horns, the Great Watching Chamber, the Garderobe with its 28 lavatories, the Pages' Chamber and the exuberant Chapel Royal. The royal apartments were decorated with rich tapestries of pure gold and fine silk, paintings, tables inlaid with mother-of-pearl, organs and other musical instruments. In Elizabeth's time, the Queen's own apartments, *inner sanctum* of the cult of the Virgin Queen, were the most sumptuous of all. The Duke of Württemberg was bowled over by one apartment.

> Costly beyond everything; the tapestries are garnished with gold, pearls and precious stones not to mention the royal throne, which is studded with very large diamonds, rubies, sapphires, and the like, that glitter among other precious stones and pearls as the sun among the stars.

Notwithstanding the inspiration provided by Plutarch, Shakespeare's Roman source, it is easy to imagine how Cleopatra must have appealed to the Elizabethan feeling for excess:

> For her own person,
> It beggared all description: she did lie
> In her pavilion, cloth-of-gold of tissue,
> O'erpicturing that Venus where we see
> The fancy outwork nature.

As royal servants under James, members of Shakespeare's company were probably quartered in some corner of the palace, finding their way, with other staff and with courtiers, through the vast complex of courts, passages and saloons. It is difficult to know how much exposure 'base' players would have had to everyday Court life, that hotbed of scandal-mongering and intrigue, with its unrelieved jockeying for position and preferment – especially under the comparatively lax management of James. Perhaps some model for the facile and pretentious Osric, that 'waterfly' of a 'drossy age' and creature of Claudius, was glimpsed here.

Clock Court and the Royal Mews

Turn left and then right at the long brick wall, towards the West Entrance of the palace. Behind the gatehouse is the Base Court, in which, according to the Duke of Württemberg, was set 'a splendid high and massy fountain with an ingenious waterwork, by which you can, if you like, make the water to play upon the ladies and others who are standing by and give them a thorough wetting'. Most visitors would have arrived by river, mooring at one of the jetties built by Wolsey. Behind the first court lies Clock Court, on whose west wall is set an astronomical clock which gives not only the time and the phases of the moon, but also – invaluable to those who had arrived and would return by boat – the time of high water at London Bridge.

Leave the palace grounds by the main Hanoverian Gate. Cross the road and turn right, and then left (signposted for Hampton). You reach on your right the Royal Mews. The mews buildings on the left were built by Henry VIII in 1536, those on the right by Elizabeth I in 1570. The King's New Stable, as Henry's was called, had stables and coach-houses below and accommodation for grooms above; the Queen's were chiefly two barns and a coach-house with garrets above for storage. Horses for conveying Elizabeth to town, should she desire it, or for hunting in the park, were quartered here.

Retrace your steps and turn right at the crossroads for Hampton Court Station. Alternatively, follow Hampton Court Road or the park to your right to return to Hampton Station.

DEPTFORD
AND GREENWICH

Summary: There is still a salty, piratical quality to Deptford, a handful of elegant streets and a couple of interesting churches relieving the sight of scrap-metal merchants and seedy-looking shops and pubs – an appropriate *milieu*, perhaps, in which to revisit an old crime: the murder of Christopher Marlowe. But beyond the other side of Deptford's sluggish creek lies one of the great architectural ensembles of Europe, once the site of Queen Elizabeth's favourite palace and a splendid venue for Shakespeare's company.

Start:	Deptford Station.
Finish:	Maze Hill Station.
Length:	3.5 km (2 miles).
Time:	2 hours.
Refreshments:	SE10 Restaurant and Bar, 62 Thames Street; The Bird's Nest, 32 Deptford Church Street; Ashburnham Arms, 25 Ashburnham Grove; Cutty Sark, Ballast Quay, off Lassell Street; Trafalgar Tavern, Park Row, SE10.

Turn left out of the station down Deptford High Street. The Deptford Marlowe knew was not really part of London but Kent, and lay within the Diocese of Rochester – sufficiently remote for some Londoners to consider themselves safe from the plague of 1593, the year of Marlowe's murder. This High Street, once Butt Lane, ran through fields and orchards; there were market gardens here which supplied London, and which were in their turn fertilized by the manure collected in the city. Royal dogs were kennelled in Deptford, in readiness for courtly hunting at nearby Blackheath and Lewisham, and the town retained some of the characteristics of a village, with its local parish church, manor at Sayes Court and village green. Yet, like its distant neighbour Woolwich, it had also been in a sense promoted above ordinary provincial status. The nearness of the court at Greenwich brought to the town minor courtiers, officials and servants, some artistic and cosmopolitan, such as royal musicians. More important was the local industry, for Deptford was a hub of Tudor shipbuilding.

Opposite: A skull and crossbones on top of the gatehouse at St Nicholas' Church, Deptford. Christopher Marlowe is buried here.

On your right is St Paul's churchyard, leading to St Paul's Deptford. It has no Shakespearean connections, but since it has one of the finest 18th-century exteriors in London, you might like to take a look. It was built by Thomas Archer, who also designed the equally baroque St John's Smith Square. Further on, to the right, lies Albury Street, a street of handsome early Georgian houses, which gives a flavour of Deptford's prosperous past.

St Nicholas' Church

Turn right at the end on Creek Road; cross at the lights and follow the (rather ambiguous) sign for St Nicholas' Church down McMillan Street. The church is at the end on your left. It retains most of its medieval tower, but the body of the church – which is late 17th-century – was ruined by wartime bombing. Marlowe was buried here, according to tradition near the north tower, the only surviving bit of the church from Elizabethan times. There is a plaque on the east wall of the churchyard. Charles Nicholl, in his exciting book on Marlowe's death, *The Reckoning*, suggests that his funeral may have been attended by his old patron Sir Francis Walsingham, the administrator of Elizabeth's secret service, and also Marlowe's publisher, Edward Blount. Blount suggests as much in a dedication to Walsingham in his edition of Marlowe's great erotic poem, 'Hero and Leander':

> We think not ourselves discharged of the duty we owe to our friend when we have brought the breathless body to the earth. For albeit the eye there taketh his ever-farewell of that beloved object, yet the impression of the man that hath been dear unto us, living an afterlife in our memory, there putteth us in mind of further obsequies due unto the deceased.

Was Shakespeare there, too? It is possible. He was probably in London in the early summer of 1593, when Marlowe was murdered, and he had good reason to pay his last respects. He was indebted to Marlowe artistically and professionally, and they must have known each other at least quite well, having probably worked together in Lord Strange's company in the early 1590s, and possibly also having collaborated on *Henry VI*. Shakespeare also makes what has been taken to be a direct allusion to the circumstances of Marlowe's death and subsequent reputation in the riddling words of Touchstone in *As You Like It*:

> When a man's verses cannot be understood, nor a man's good wit seconded with the forward child understanding, it strikes a man more dead than a great reckoning in a little room.

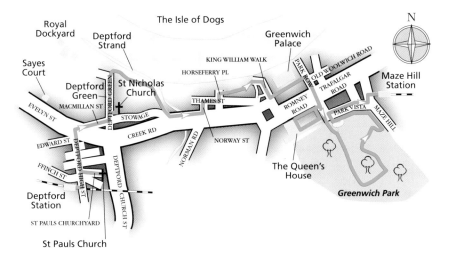

That is, when the work and reputation of a dead poet is misinterpreted and misrepresented it is even more fatal than actual death – met in this case in a room in Deptford over a 'reckoning'. Of this reckoning, more later.

Deptford Green and the Royal Dockyard

Leave the churchyard by the way you came in and turn right down Deptford Green, now far from verdant. The green, too, has Marlovian associations. Lord Howard of Effingham, famous as the admiral who led the English navy against the Spanish Armada, lived on its edge. He it was whose name lent distinction to the Lord Admiral's Men, one of the most famous playing companies in London. Most of Marlowe's plays were presented by them at their resident playhouse, the Rose, with the titanic Edward Alleyn taking the great roles. On another side of the green lived the old sea-dog and slave-trader Sir John Hawkyns, a comrade of Effingham's against the Armada.

At the end bear right to the river; to your left was the place at which Hawkyns worked as Treasurer: Henry VIII's Royal Dockyard. He developed it to serve the nation's growing maritime needs of war, trade, exploration and piracy. There were two docks, the Private for merchant ships and the Royal for the navy. Between them lay a complex of sheds, ropeyards and warehouses. It was a large, efficient factory where timber came in and ships came out. It also had a certain symbolic and ceremonial function. Frobisher set off from here in search of the North West Passage in 1576. Twelve years later, Sir Walter Raleigh left here for Virginia to establish the first English colony in North America.

On 4 April 1581, the Queen visited Drake's *Golden Hind* at Deptford after his circumnavigation of the world and conferred a knighthood upon the captain.

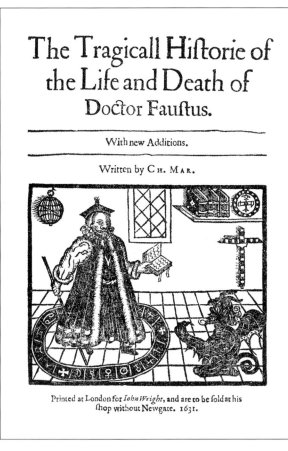

The Tragicall Hiſtorie of the Life and Death of Doctor Fauſtus.

With new Additions.

Written by C H. M A R.

Printed at London for *Iohn Wright*, and are to be ſold at his ſhop without Newgate. 1631.

Left: 'Why this is hell, nor am I out of it.' Title page from the 1631 Quarto edition of Marlowe's Doctor Faustus.

The ship was preserved here for many years, rather in the manner that the *Cutty Sark* is today, and its cabin was used as a kind of floating hospitality suite for visitors. It was, on at least one occasion, searched by the authorities on suspicion of being one of the 'secret and unsuspected places' where meat was illegally butchered during Lent. The celebrated galleon was moored at Deptford until it literally fell to bits. There is a reconstructed *Golden Hind* at St Mary Overy dock in Southwark.

South of the dockyard was the site of Sayes Court, later lived in by the diarist John Evelyn. In Shakespeare's time it was the chief house in Deptford, with three gables and a walled garden which sheltered fruit orchards and a summerhouse. The Lord of the Manor was Christopher Browne, a senior member of the royal household, responsible for its finances and, rather incongruously, for overseeing the provision of meat when the court was in residence at Greenwich. There were slaughterhouses near the house and shambles on the river, which must conveniently have borne off the detritus.

Before and behind you lay Deptford Strand which covered an area running from Sayes Court to Deptford Creek, and inland to what is now Evelyn Street. Fishing boats were moored along the river's gravelly beach, and here lived many of those connected in some way with the ship business of Deptford: craftsmen like joiners, caulkers and hemp-dressers, cadets from the naval college at Trinity House on Deptford Strand and sailors passing through.

Somewhere on the Strand stood the house of Eleanor Bull, according to Charles Nicholl not the tavern usually spoken of but a kind of private boarding house, offering accommodation and food. It was in a room there that Christopher Marlowe was murdered on 30 May 1593. There are two versions of his death. The official version was that, in the company of three others – Ingram Frizer, Nicholas Skeres and Robert Poley – and after a 'quiet' day spent eating, drinking and walking in the garden, he was stabbed through the eye on impulse by Frizer, in a sordid disagreement over their 'reckoning' – that is, the bill for refreshment received at Eleanor Bull's house. Some later attributed it to an old grudge or romantic jealousy, but nevertheless a domestic incident. The unofficial version was that his death was the result of intrigue. Skeres and Poley were agents of, respectively, the Earl of Essex and Sir Robert Cecil. Marlowe had become an obstruction to the ambitions of the Earl of Essex. Attempts had been made to frame him, based on his homosexuality and alleged atheism, and force him to declare evidence against Raleigh, Essex's rival. These had been unsuccessful; a further attempt was made to coerce him in Deptford, which failed, and so Marlowe had to be silenced once and for all. But it is difficult to know how far his murder was premeditated and to what extent he incited it. In Nicholl's words: 'The killing happens in the hermetic confines of the secret world: a dirty trick, a rogue event, a tragic blunder.'

The Isle of Dogs and Greenwich

Turn right, along the river. On the other side is the low-lying Isle of Dogs, in Shakespeare's day a sewage-fringed marshy place, difficult to drain, hardly populated and a bleak refuge for fugitives and criminals. It might have got its name from kennels there, or it might originally have been the Isle of Ducks. It might simply have been a term of derogation. Ben Jonson collaborated with the satirist Thomas Nashe on a play entitled *The Isle of Dogs* in 1597, which was considered sufficiently offensive to send Jonson and the actors for a short stay in the Marshalsea Prison. Nashe gave the authorities the slip by fleeing to Great Yarmouth.

Pass the statue of Peter the Great, Tsar of Russia, who picked up ideas about shipbuilding at the dockyard. Follow the river, and at the end turn left on Creek Street; cross Deptford Creek and turn left on Norway Street; right at the end on Thames Street and right on Horseferry Place, where a ferry carried horses to the other side of the river.

Turn right on the Thames Path. Turn right past the *Cutty Sark* up King William Walk and go left through the gates to the Royal Naval College. Keep going until you reach the middle of the college, with the river to the north and a distant view of the Queen's House to the south, one of London's great prospects. This was the site of Greenwich Palace, which was first built by Humphrey, Duke of Gloucester in the mid-15th century. It was one of the finest houses in England and the duke called it 'Bella Cort'. He lent it to Henry VI and Margaret of Anjou for their honeymoon and they took it over after the Duke's arrest and precipitate death. In 1501, Henry VIII's older brother, Arthur, Prince of Wales, was married to Catherine of Aragon here. Henry himself was born at Greenwich and later made it his chief residence, renaming it Placentia, the 'Manor of Pleasaunce'. The palace was a rambling complex of buildings with a long river front, a great tower (built by Henry VII) and a core of three courtyards; the main entrance was from the river, from where a massive gatehouse led into the central court. There was a large tiltyard and an armoury staffed by German craftsmen. Here the king might hunt or watch with complacency the wealth of the nation swell before his eyes, as the ships brought in silk and spices and sent out wool and metal.

Elizabeth and Mary were born at Greenwich. Elizabeth made her principal summer residence here and it was allegedly a Placentia puddle over which the gallant Raleigh was permitted to throw his cloak before her. Distinguished foreign visitors were greeted at the palace, disembarking on the quay before the gate. The German traveller Paul Hentzner was received here and caught sight of the Queen in the Presence Room in 1598, bare-breasted and with narrow lips and black teeth. She spoke graciously 'first to one, then to another, whether foreign ministers or those who attended for different reasons, in English, French and Italian'. She was followed by the ladies of the Court and a guard of fifty pensioners with gilt halberds. Three years later, the antiquarian William Lambarde recorded a less amiable conversation with the old Queen. This was when, irked by Essex's illicit revival of Shakespeare's *Richard II*, she had made her famous complaint: 'I am Richard II, know ye not that?' Like Richard, Elizabeth had no heir, and was therefore, as the ambitious Essex and his supporters claimed, a candidate for deposition. 'This tragedy,' she went on bitterly, 'was played 40 times in open streets and houses' (see page 96).

Plays were often presented before the Court at Greenwich, where performance brought the troupe not only prestige but also one of its most important sources of income. On 15 March 1595 the accounts of the Treasurer of the Queen's Chamber record payments made to William Kempe, Richard Burbage and William Shakespeare, servants of the Lord Chamberlain, for plays performed before the Queen here on the previous St Stephen's Day – that is, 26 December 1594. It is the first record that connects Shakespeare's name with an acting company and the only time he is officially cited in connection with a theatrical performance. What was the play? An early outing for *A Midsummer*

Night's Dream perhaps, which might also have been performed at the marriage of the Earl of Derby a month later. Shakespeare's company returned many times to Greenwich, particularly at Christmas, New Year and Shrovetide, when their services were most in demand. They would have performed here, as in the other royal palaces such as Hampton Court and Whitehall, not in a purpose-built theatre but on a temporary stage in the great banqueting hall. The palace staff oversaw the installation of the necessary tiered seating, partitions and doors. The players may have arrived by boat, embarking at Bankside or Blackfriars and unloading their costumes and other gear here at the great river gate.

The Queen's House and Greenwich Park

Walk straight on in the same direction to Park Row; cross Romney Road and up the continuation of Park Row, turning right for the Queen's House. In 1605 James settled Greenwich Palace upon his queen, Anne of Denmark. She commissioned Inigo Jones to build her a house in 1616, the year of Shakespeare's death. It is built on arches that once spanned the old road that ran from Deptford to Woolwich. It was the first neo-classical house built in England. In 1652 the Parliamentarians stripped the place of its paintings, tried to sell it and, failing, turned it into a biscuit factory.

Beyond the house lies Greenwich Park. Henry VI gave Duke Humphrey of Gloucester a licence to enclose 80 hectares (200 acres) of pasture, heath, woods and gorses, the same area as the present park. He built a watchtower at the top of the park to enjoy the view, described as one of the best in Europe. When the king took it over the park became a place of resort: archery, fighting with spears and swords and wrestling all took place here. Elizabeth's accession in 1558 was celebrated with a great entertainment in the park paid for by the City of London. Fourteen years later she reviewed the militia that had been raised to confound the Duke of Norfolk's plot and watched it conduct a mock battle. James I, never fond of such spectacles but very keen on hunting, spent £2,000, a vast sum, enclosing the park with a brick wall.

The walk ends here. There is easy access to the park, otherwise return to Park Row and turn right down Park Vista for Maze Hill Station.

ST PANCRAS TO MARYLEBONE

Summary: Some of London's least-visited Georgian streets, squares and gardens are the settings for latter-day interpreters of Shakespeare: the hero-worship of Thomas Carlyle and the iconoclasm of George Bernard Shaw; the pioneering scholarship of Edmund Malone; the paintings of Henry Fuseli and the music of Hector Berlioz. Between the Berlioz and Carlyle sites stands a building housing one of the great popular disseminators of Shakespeare; beside it the site of a long-forgotten hall where some of the earliest and most radical modern experiments in 'authentic' Shakespeare were performed.

Start:	King's Cross Station.
Finish:	Great Portland Street Underground Station.
Length:	4 km (2½ miles).
Time:	2 hours.
Refreshments:	Cafe and restaurant at the British Library; McLynn's, Argyll Street; Marlborough Arms, Torrington Place; The Hope, Tottenham Street; The King and Queen, The Crown and Sceptre both Foley Street; The Yorkshire Grey, corner of Middleton Place and Langham Street.

Turn right out of King's Cross Station on Euston Road; you pass on the right St Pancras Station. Parts of Roman Polanski's *Macbeth* were filmed in St Pancras Chambers. Keep going and turn right into the forecourt of the British Library, in the foyer of which stands a statue of Shakespeare by Roubiliac, originally in the grounds of Garrick's villa at Hampton (see page 123).

Walk upstairs past the information desk and follow signs to the John Ritblatt Gallery. At the time of writing the following collection of Shakespearean documents and first editions are on display:

The autograph copy of *The Book of Sir Thomas More* (see page 38)
The 'good' and 'bad' quartos of *Hamlet* (see page 28)

Opposite: Shakespeare in Fitzrovia. George Bernard Shaw, self-proclaimed rival to Shakespeare and one of his most robust critics, and Virginia Woolf, inventor of Shakespeare's sister, both lived here at different times.

GEORGE BERNARD SHAW
LIVED IN THIS HOUSE
FROM 1917 TO 1898
FROM THE COFFERS OF HIS GENIUS
HE ENRICHED THE WORLD

GREATER LONDON COUNCIL
Virginia
Stephen
(VIRGINIA WOOLF)
1882 - 1941
Novelist and Critic
lived here
1907-1911

29

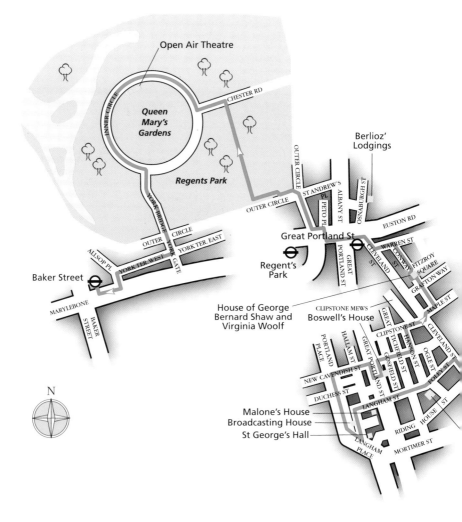

William Smith's 'View of Westminster, London and Bankside' (1588)
Ben Jonson's *Masque of Queens* (1609) copied for presentation to Henry, Prince of Wales (see page 121)
Sir Walter Raleigh's notes for his *History of the World* (see page 71)
Sketch and plan for New Place, Shakespeare's home in Stratford-upon-Avon
The Sonnets (1609)
The mortgage deed for Shakespeare's gatehouse property in Blackfriars (11 March 1613) (see page 54)

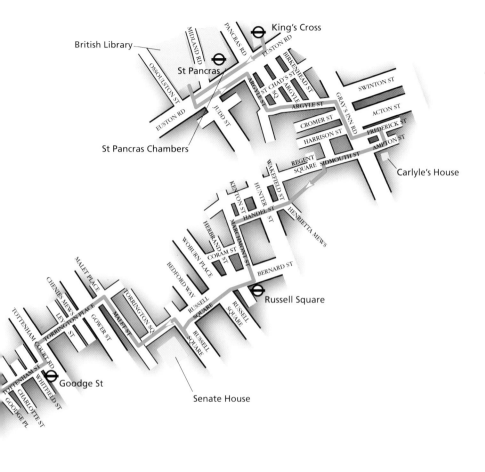

British Library

St Pancras

King's Cross

St Pancras Chambers

Carlyle's House

Russell Square

Goodge St

Senate House

Fuseli's House

The First Folio (1623) (see page 35)

Elsewhere in the gallery is an audio recording of Laurence Olivier and Stanley Holloway in the graveyard scene from *Hamlet*.

British Library to RADA
Leave the British Library by the main gates, cross Euston Road at the lights and turn left and then right down Argyle Street; left at the end and along the

bottom of Argyle Square; turn right on Gray's Inn Road crossing at the lights; turn left down Frederick Street and right down Sage Way. Turn right up Ampton Street. On your left, at No 33, a brown plaque identifies the house of Thomas Carlyle. For Carlyle, Shakespeare was a prime subject for his book *Heroes and Hero Worship*, an incarnation of transcendent will and artistic power, whose soul struggled to gain mastery over the loathsome business of writing to order for the theatre. But there are more engaging associations:

> I recollect when I first heard of Shakespeare my Father never, I believe, read a word of him in his life. But one day in the street of Annan I found a wandering Italian resting a board with very bad imagery – 'images' (*C. imitated the cry*), and among them a figure leaning on a pedestal with 'The Cloudcapt towers', etc. Various passers-by looked on, and a women read aloud the verses, very badly, and then the name below, 'Shankespeare', that was the way she gave it, 'Shankespeare' (laughing).

Cross Gray's Inn Road and down Sidmouth Street; turn left down the path at the beginning of the Georgian terrace on your left through St George's Gardens. At the end, go straight ahead down Handel Street. Don't stop. Handel is an English (or half-English) composer unusual in having added nothing to the Shakespearean musical literature. Cross Hunter Street and walk up the steps past the Brunswick Shopping Centre. Turn left on Marchmont Street, right on Bernard Street and across the top of Russell Square – on the corner of the square and Thornhaugh Street, to your left is the University of London Senate House, which features in Richard Loncraine's film of *Richard III* with Ian McKellen,who played 'that bottled spider, that foul bunch-backed toad' in Oswald Mosley fashion.

Turn right on Market Street. On your left is the recently revamped RADA, illustrious forcing house of young actors and where Shakespeare has been part of the staple diet since its foundation, in 1904, by the grand old fruit of Edwardian Shakespeare, Sir Herbert Beerbohm Tree.

Turn left on Torrington Place and Gower Street; at the end of Torrington Place cross Tottenham Court Road, which was once a market road leading to the village of Tottenham about seven miles north-east of central London, and in Shakespeare's time a pleasant-sounding place of numerous greens, taverns and almshouses.

Henry Fuseli and Edmund Malone
Turn left and right at Tottenham Street; cross Charlotte Street and turn right at the end of Cleveland Street; turn left at Foley Street, opposite the top of

Hanson Street you will see the house of the painter Henry Fuseli.

Strange, intense, intellectual, Fuseli loved Shakespeare from his Swiss childhood. He also loved the theatre and after settling in London in the 1780s was an habitué of Drury Lane and Covent Garden. Shakespeare offered Fuseli subjects appropriate to the calling of a great 'history' painter (that is, of lofty historical, allegorical or heroic themes). But although he executed drawings of *King Lear* and *Macbeth* in his early days in Berlin, it was less the heroic and more the supernatural aspects of Shakespeare's work that caught his imagination and stimulated the latent fantasies of the age. The three witches in profile, Titania and Oberon, both commissioned for Boydell's famous – later infamous –. Shakespeare Gallery on Pall Mall (see page 119) are his most memorable Shakespearean images. Like Blake, whom he resembles, Fuseli had an idiosyncratic, rather abstract and not very attractive, way of rendering the human anatomy. 'Nature puts me out' he once said, and looking at the musculature of his Bottom one can see why. He was more at home with supernature. Like Blake, also, he was sometimes considered insane.

Cross Great Titchfield Street and down Langham Street. On the left is the house of Edmund Malone who has some claim to be the greatest of all Shakespeare scholars, a brilliant pioneer who swept away the editorial and documentary rubble of centuries to reveal the life and work of a Shakespeare more or less as we know him today. His work everywhere betrays an heroic zeal to separate the authentic from the spurious, to start from first principles with respect to both biography and textual scholarship. Malone made the first serious attempt to establish a chronology for the plays; he was the first to consistently seek out the quartos and Folio as the only reliable evidence for what Shakespeare actually wrote. He threw a *cordon sanitaire* around Shakespeare's certain achievements and so banished plays we now know to have been written by some contemporary into the appropriate obscurity of the Apocrypha. He shed light on the mediations of often interfering or bungling editors and printers and he was a scourge of the notorious 18th-century literary fakers. Chatterton was exposed by Malone, and so was the Shakespeare forger William Henry Ireland. The titular restraint of Malone's *Inquiry into the Authenticity of Certain Miscellaneous Papers* betrays little of the forensic zeal with which its author went about belaying his subject.

It would be nice to know whether the sarcastic, extreme Fuseli, his German accent thick enough to have been affectionately imitated by Blake, was on conversational terms with the Anglo-Irish Edmund Malone, the model of scholarly detachment and impartiality. At first glance they could hardly be more different. But their preoccupations with an 'authentic' Shakespeare – Fuseli's atavistic and archetypal, Malone's historical and documentary – do mark them out as figures characteristic of their age.

The BBC

Cross Great Portland Street; at the end of Langham Street you find on your right Broadcasting House. Richard Imison, the BBC Script Editor for Radio Drama for over 20 years, once said that Shakespeare, although writing 300 years before its invention, was a great writer for radio, Chekhov an awful one. It's easy to see why. When audiences went to the Globe Theatre in 1600 it was not chiefly to see but to *hear* a play. Shakespeare's language is full of pictures, internal directions and accounts of what's happening on stage. Consider how little needs to be seen, and how much can be imagined in this passage from *Macbeth*, for instance:

Enter lady macbeth with a taper.

GENTLEWOMAN:	Lo you, here she comes. This is her very guise, and, upon my life, fast asleep. Observe her. Stand close.
DOCTOR:	How came she by that light?
GENTLEWOMAN:	Why, it stood by her. She has light by her continually. 'Tis her command.
DOCTOR:	You see her eyes are open.
GENTLEWOMAN:	Ay, but their sense are shut.
DOCTOR:	What is it she does now? Look how she rubs her hands…

Shakespeare has done the work already. This has not been lost on the BBC, which has been broadcasting Shakespeare since the corporation was founded. In this, they were in sympathy with the prevailing movement in the theatre, which was moving away from a Victorian pictorial style and towards visual simplicity and an emphasis on language. The first Shakespeare programmes were broadcasts of live extracts. Later in the 1920s came broadcasts of full-scale (if cut) productions. In the 1930s music, sound effects and inter-cut dialogue were added. Then the development of recording brought editing, and repeat broadcasts. The BBC made Shakespeare accessible to millions and the attitude towards listening to and recording Shakespeare for the radio was more or less stable until 1946, when the Third Programme was added to the Light and Home services.

Producers were then allowed to experiment with the repertory, recording some of the less-performed plays. Unfortunately, this almost certainly cost the BBC a major part of its Shakespeare audience, since people who might have tuned in to the Home Service and listened to a play, did not necessarily do the same for the Third Programme where Shakespeare came increasingly to be placed. It is one of the casualties of Shakespeare's elevation to 'serious' entertainment. None of this is to take away from the BBC the fact that the relatively short contracts required for radio has meant that the medium has been able to employ many well-known Shakespeareans, from Thorndike, Gielgud and Richardson in the early days to Harriet Walter and Michael Maloney for the recent Millennium recordings.

William Poel and St George's Hall

To the left, beyond All Souls' Langham Place is the dismal St George's Hotel, where a green plaque commemorates the Queen's Hall, but not its lost neighbour, the St George's Hall. It was here in 1881 that the actor, director, antiquarian and inspired crank William Poel played the prince in the 'bad' quarto version of *Hamlet* – a perverse choice, one might think, in view of that version's botched speeches, misremembered lines and stark omissions. But for Poel, the 'bad' quarto could tell us much about revisions made for performances of the play by Shakespeare's company. It seemed to offer direct access to the early performance of *Hamlet*. It was the first of Poel's experiments into an 'Elizabethan' staging of Shakespeare. Poel believed that Shakespeare's texts held the key to his stage practice, and that in order to understand his plays in performance we must first rediscover that practice.

Poel's ardent pursuit of Elizabethan authenticity was matched only by his abiding detestation of the ways of the established Victorian theatre, with its extravagant pictorial effects and generally redundant opulence. His results were often rather idiosyncratic, particularly in the vocal delivery. Poor Poel was commercially unsuccessful in nearly all his theatrical enterprises, but he exerted a great influence on the movement to adopt open staging and to attain directness and transparency in performance – which won him the admiration of Shaw. Harley Granville-Barker played his Richard II (for one performance) and took much from Poel's example if not his practice. Poel also tried to get a project going to rebuild the Globe Theatre, something not achieved until 1997 (see page 86). In 1929 the uncompromising antiquarian was offered a knighthood for his achievements, but the thought of being lumped together with Beerbohm Tree, Henry Irving and the rest was too much for his uncompromising nature and he rejected the honour with contumely.

Turn right up Portland Place and right on New Cavendish Street. Turn left down Great Portland Street where at No 122 you will find the house of James Boswell. James Boswell senior was egged on by Edmund Malone to finish his great biography of Samuel Johnson. The family repaid him, for Boswell's son, James the younger, himself a considerable Shakespeare scholar, completed Malone's 21-volume edition of Shakespeare after Edmund died.

George Bernard Shaw

Retrace your steps to New Cavendish Street; turn left up Hanson Street; turn right at the end (Clipstone Street), and over Cleveland Street, down Maple Street and left on Conway Street – there's a suspiciously bard-like countenance staring from the keystone over the door to No 7, Conway Street – and into Fitzroy Square. At No 29, but not at the same time, lived Virginia Woolf and George Bernard Shaw.

'With the single exception of Homer, there is no eminent writer, not even Sir Walter Scott, who I can despise so entirely as I despise Shakespeare when I measure my mind against his.' Shaw's deliberately outrageous, often funny, remarks about Shakespeare were directed as much at the actor-managers and worshippers of the 'poor foolish old Swan' as they were at the man himself.

Shaw, with some justice perhaps, resented the perpetual revivals of Shakespeare on the Edwardian stage. How was he to make his mark as Ibsen had in Norway, and as Strindberg had in Sweden, with an oppressive Bard hogging the boards? Moreover, Shakespeare was to blame for keeping his beloved Ellen Terry at the Lyceum, stuck in a rut with Henry Irving instead of spreading modernist (Shavian) wings. 'It would positively be a relief to me', Shaw goes on in the same article, 'to dig him up and throw stones at him.' His iconoclasm was only partly sincere. His work is in fact filled with Shakespearean allusion, sometimes introduced with affection, sometimes in a spirit of rivalry or a desire to get even. Shaw re-wrote and 'improved' the last act of *Cymbeline*, cast Shakespeare as a plagiarist in *The Dark Lady of the Sonnets*, who shamelessly rips off everyone's best lines, and, most revealingly, right at the end of his long life sets himself up against Shakespeare in the puppet show *Shakes v Shav*. His theatre criticism, though, shows a profound desire to understand Shakespeare and to see him performed with understanding rather than reverence (see page 182). The Edwardian actor-managers diminished and deformed Shakespeare at their reverential altars. 'He does not superstitiously worship William,' Shaw said of Forbes-Robertson's Hamlet, but 'plays him as Shakespeare should be played, on the line and to the line, with the utterance and acting simultaneous, inseparable and in fact identical.'

Virginia Woolf

Virginia Woolf enlisted Shakespeare in two explorations of sexual politics. The shape-changing, sex-changing protagonist of the peculiar historical caprice *Orlando* sports with *As You Like It*. More seriously, she explores the dismal outlook for the woman of genius in Shakespeare's time in the fantasy of Shakespeare's sister in *A Room of One's Own*. What, she asks, if Shakespeare had had a sister as gifted as he? What opportunities would have come her way in 16th-century Stratford? Not many: 'she was not sent to school. She had no chance of learning grammar and logic, let alone of reading Horace and Virgil. She picked up a book now and then, one of her brother's perhaps, and read a few pages. But then her parents came in and told her to mend the stockings or mind the stew and not moon about with books and papers.'

She escapes the misery of an enforced marriage by running away to London to try and follow in her brother's footsteps, is laughed at, fails, takes up with an actor-manager who gets her pregnant. The tale ends badly. She kills herself 'one winter's night and lies buried at some cross-roads where the omnibuses now stop outside the Elephant and Castle.' The story is the inspiration for the title of a gloomy song by Morrisey and for the band, 'Shakespeare's Sister'.

Hector Berlioz

Leave the square by the other end of Conway Street; turn left up Warren Street and right at the end; ahead of you at the top of Cleveland Street is Osnaburgh Street. Hector Berlioz, greatest of the French Romantic composers and France's most passionate advocate of Shakespeare, stayed at No 26 on a visit to London in 1848. Shakespeare, Berlioz always maintained, fell on him like a thunderbolt in Paris in 1827. The artistic experience was at first virtually indistinguishable from the romantic, because it was at this performance that he fell in love with the Irish actress Harriet Smithson. He later married her, but his relationship with Shakespeare proved to be the more enduring, inspiring operas (*Beatrice et Benedict* and the great love duet from *Les Troyens*), and some of his most beautiful orchestral works – the dramatic symphony *Romeo et Juliette*, a passionate essay on Romantic yearning, the fantasy on *The Tempest* and the glowering *Roi Lear* overture. Berlioz revered the intensity, variety and formal freedom of Shakespeare's plays; after centuries of Gallic reservation or opprobrium, he stands out as a frank idolator: 'The English are quite right when they call him the supreme creator, after the Good Lord.' A couple of years before his stay in Osnaburgh Street, he had a few pungent remarks to make about the London productions he saw. 'They had condescended,' he writes in a letter, 'to give us *Hamlet* as written, practically complete, a rare thing in this country, where there are so many people superior to Shakespeare that most of his plays are corrected and augmented by the Cibbers and the Drydens and other rogues who should have their bottoms publicly spanked.'

Turn left for Great Portland Street Underground Station or if you want to walk on, cross Euston Road and bear left for Regent's Park. Follow the signs for the Open Air Theatre and then Baker Street Underground.

SHAKESPEARE IN THE RESTORATION

Summary: Quiet streets and back-lanes in the unfrequented streets south of Fleet Street and one of London's finest squares set the tone for an intriguing walk which visits sites associated with the years leading up to the closure of London's playhouses in the Commonwealth period and the revival of Shakespearean activity in the Restoration. Some of the greatest buildings of Charles II's London were theatres, and the settings for the first really spectacular productions of Shakespeare's plays. They were presented by one of the two licensed companies, often in drastically re-written versions – which is not so different from contemporary filmed versions of the plays. One of these adaptors was John Dryden, Shakespeare's first major critic. The walk can easily continue that on page 30 or be followed by that on page 88.

Start:	Blackfriars Underground Station.
Finish:	Charing Cross or Embankment Underground Stations.
Length:	2.5 km (1½ miles).
Time:	1½ hours.
Refreshments:	Ye Olde Cheshire Cheese, Fleet Street; Seven Stars, Carey Street; Ye Olde White horse, St Clement's Lane; Red Lion, Whitehall; numerous cafes and pubs in Covent Garden; Kastner and Ovens, Floral Street.

Leave Blackfriars Underground at Exit 8; turn left down Watergate and right at Kingscote Street. The Bridewell Palace stood here. Originally built for Henry VIII, by Shakespeare's time it had been donated to the City and put to use as a prison, workhouse, hospital and refuge for destitute children and orphans. It was well known for its public floggings. The Bridewell may have been intended in some of the vaguely specified scenes that call for a 'council chamber' and 'antechamber in the palace' in *Henry VIII* (who often held Court here), but its later history of hemp-beating and flogging 'rogues, bawds and whores' is more vividly conjured up in Thomas Dekker's play *The Honest Whore*, where one character asks: 'Do you know the brick-house of castigation by the river-side...the school where they pronounce no letter well but "O"?'. Dekker's is a rare voice of social conscience in Shakespeare's London. In the period in which this walk begins, the Bridewell's facilities were augmented by the introduction of stocks and a ducking stool on the river.

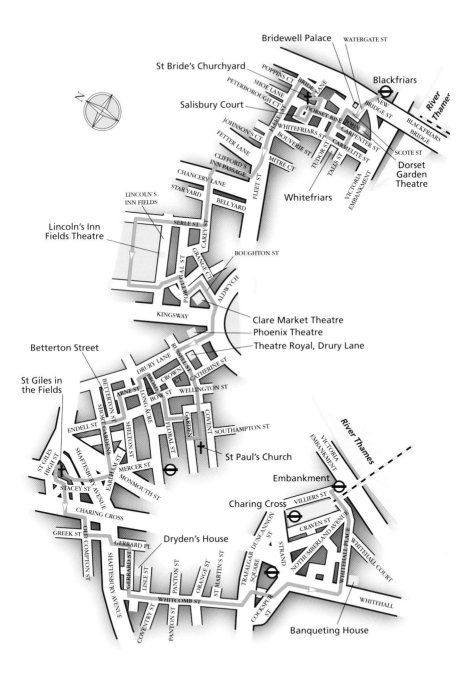

N

Bridewell Palace   WATERGATE ST

St Bride's Churchyard

POPPINS CT

SHOE LANE

BRIDE LANE

Blackfriars

PETERBOROUGH CT ST

Salisbury Court

DORSET RISE   JOHN

NEW BRIDGE ST

River Thames

JOHNSON'S CT

WHITEFRIARS ST   CARPENTER ST

BLACKFRIARS BRIDGE

FETTER LANE

BOUVERIE ST

CARMELITE ST

SCOTE ST

CLIFFORD'S INN PASSAGE

TUDOR ST

TALES ST

Dorset Garden Theatre

CHANCERY LANE

MITRE CT

Whitefriars

VICTORIA EMBANKMENT

STAR YARD

FLEET ST

BELL YARD

LINCOLN'S INN FIELDS

SERLE ST

Lincoln's Inn Fields Theatre

CAREY ST

PORTUGAL ST

GRANGE CT

BOUGHTON ST

ALDWYCH

KINGSWAY

Clare Market Theatre

Phoenix Theatre

Theatre Royal, Drury Lane

DRURY LANE

RUSSELL ST

CATHERINE ST

Betterton Street

CROWN CT

BOW ST

WELLINGTON ST

BETTERTON ST

ARNE ST

LONG ACRE

St Giles in the Fields

SHORT GARDENS

ENDELL ST

SHELTON ST

FLORAL ST

COVENT GARDEN

SOUTHAMPTON ST

ST GILES HIGH ST

SHAFTESBURY AVENUE

EARLHAM ST

MERCER ST

MONMOUTH ST

St Paul's Church

River Thames

VICTORIA EMBANKMENT

STACEY ST

CHARING CROSS

Embankment

VILLIERS ST

Charing Cross

CRAVEN ST

GREEK ST

OLD COMPTON ST

GERRARD PL

Dryden's House

DUNCANNON ST

STRAND

NORTHUMBERLAND AVENUE

WHITEHALL PLACE

WHITEHALL COURT

SHAFTESBURY AVENUE

GERRARD ST

LISLE ST

PANTON ST

ORANGE ST

ST MARTIN'S ST

TRAFALGAR SQUARE

COVENTRY ST

PANTON ST

WHITCOMB ST

COCKSPUR ST

WHITEHALL

Banqueting House

The Dorset Garden Theatre

Turn left on Tudor Street and left on John Carpenter Street where Christopher Wren's magnificent Dorset Garden (or Duke's) Theatre once stood. The theatre was the home of the Duke of York's Company after 1671, one of only two licensed companies allowed to perform in the city after the Restoration. Before the construction of the theatre on Drury Lane (a predecessor of the one that still stands) it was unquestionably the finest theatre in London and the venue for the most ambitious and innovative staging of Shakespeare. The theatre was run by Sir William Davenant, one of the two courtier-managers appointed to oversee productions by Charles II (the other was Thomas Killigrew, of whom more later). The performing rights to the plays written before the advent of Cromwell were divided between the two, Killigrew getting what was considered the choice Shakespeare while Davenant got the rest. Davenant, by getting what was thought of as the dreary old-fashioned Shakespeare was deemed to have drawn the short straw. What was to be done with Shakespeare's language, 'as affected as it is obscure', and all those embarrassing rustics and low characters? The solution was radical and highly successful: they must be adapted to the taste of the age. Davenant grasped this principle whole-heartedly and so created the most vigorous Shakespearean productions of the Restoration. At the Dorset Garden, all the scenic and musical resources of the theatre were ambitiously deployed in Davenant and Dryden's adaptation of *The Tempest; or The Enchanted Island*. From the 'tempestuous noise of thunder and lightning heard' required for the Globe, Davenant wrought grand phantasmagoria:

> While the Overture is playing, the Curtain rises the Scene represents a thick and Cloudy Sky, a very Rocky Coast, and a Tempestuous Sea in perpetual Agitation. This Tempest has many dreadful objects in it, as several Spirits in horrid shapes flying down amongst the Sailors, then rising and crossing in the Air. And when the Ship is sinking, the whole House is darkened...

It is difficult to conceive of anything much further from the bare platforms of the Globe and the Blackfriars on which the play had first been performed some 60 years before. And, with the introduction of two additional female roles, the production made the most of the English theatre's latest innovation: actresses.

Opposite: Lincoln's Inn Fields, home of the theatre of that name and the first in London to incorporate a proscenium and changing scenery. It was, for a while, a home for Davenant's company, the most innovative and successful of the late 17th century.

Whitefriars and the Salisbury Court Playhouse

Turn right onto Tallis Street and right again up Carmelite Street, which marks the place of the great Carmelite Priory, or Whitefriars, which once stood here. The place has a walk-on part in *Richard III*, when Gloucester orders the body of Henry VI to be sent 'to Whitefriars'. The large site was transformed in the Reformation, its fine church was pulled down and large houses built over the ancillary buildings of the old monastery. The privilege of sanctuary survived here, as it did in other 'liberties' (old ecclesiastical estates): in Shakespeare's day and right up to the end of the 17th century the place became an assorted refuge for fraudulent debtors, refugees from justice, and prostitutes. It was a no-man's-land nicknamed 'Alsatia', after the doubtful territory between Germany and France. Characteristic, again, was the survival of the priory's old refectory, which, like that in the Blackfriars (see page 52), was converted into a theatre. Two children's acting companies appeared here, one of which performed Ben Jonson's comedy *Epicoene* in 1610, Jonson himself taking the part of the noise-hating Morose. The company owned a highly distinguished repertoire of non-Shakespearean plays, including Chapman (*Bussy d'Ambois*), Marston (*The Insatiate Countess*) and Beaumont and Fletcher (*The Knight of the Burning Pestle*). And who could forget Tailor's *Hog hath lost his Pearl*?

James Shirley, the last playwright for the King's Men and the Globe and final representative of the pre-Commonwealth theatrical tradition, spent his declining years here before the Great Fire drove him up to St Giles, where he died. Turn right at the top and left at Dorset Rise, which passes through what were once the gardens of Dorset House, the property of the Sackville family and, before the Reformation, of the Bishops of Salisbury.

Turn left onto Salisbury Square, where a plaque marks the site of the Salisbury Court Playhouse, one of only a very few places to keep up theatrical activity (which was illegal), during the Commonwealth. Although in 1649 a militia pulled the place down. The theatre was revived in the Restoration by Christopher Beeston, an old manager of children's companies. Davenant's company started here, but stayed only six months. Pepys, that inveterate playgoer, was pleased to have sat next to a 'pretty and ingenious lady' when he saw a revival of John Ford's great tragedy of incest *'Tis Pity She's a Whore*, which made up for the tedium of sitting through 'a simple play and ill acted'.

Milton and Pepys

Turn right down St Bride's passage, turn left at the bottom of the steps and left down St Bride's Avenue for St Bride's Church. In the old church was buried the notorious transvestite and thief Moll Cutpurse, the original of Middleton's play *The Roaring Girl*. The poet and statesman Lord Sackville, who lived nearby, was also buried here. He co-authored *Gorboduc*, the first English tragedy in blank verse. He was a vast landowner, one of Shakespeare's most powerful contemporaries, and entertained a poor opinion of democracy: 'O let no prynce put trust in commontie / Nor hope in fayth of giddy peoples mynde.'

John Milton lodged in the churchyard at the house of a tailor called Russell in 1639. Milton was greatly indebted to Shakespeare. His first published poem was a sonnet 'To Shakespeare', which appears without acknowledgement in the Second Folio of Shakespeare's plays, and in which he speaks in terms of affectionate possession: 'What needs my Shakespeare for his honoured bones / The labour of an age in piled stones...'. Milton liked to think of Shakespeare as an untutored home-grown genius who could freely 'warble his native wood-notes wild'. *Comus* recalls *The Tempest*, *Othello* and *A Midsummer Night's Dream*; *Macbeth* is discernible in the Satan of *Paradise Lost*; *King Lear* and *Coriolanus* are there in the arrogant, suffering prophet of *Samson Agonistes*. In his youth, Milton loved the theatre, and as a Londoner probably went to see plays at the Globe, which survived into Milton's mid-thirties.

While Milton lived here, Pepys, who was born in a house in Salisbury Court, very near this churchyard, was six years old. His *Diary* provides a great record of theatre-going in 17th-century London. All those innovations introduced into Shakespearean production during the Restoration – scenic effects, actresses, radical adaptations of the plays – are vividly recorded there. He did not mince his words, as enthusiastic about Dryden's adaptations of *Macbeth* ('one of the best plays for a stage') and *The Tempest* as he was withering about the unadapted *A Midsummer Night's Dream*: 'the most insipid ridiculous play that ever I saw in my life'. He preferred his Shakespeare rewritten.

Lincoln's Inn Fields Theatre

Turn left out of the churchyard and right at the end where a plaque on your right marks the site of Pepys's birth. Turn left on Fleet Street; cross the road and then turn right into Clifford's Inn Passage. Cross Chancery Lane and turn left on Carey Street; turn right up Serle Street into Lincoln's Inn Fields and turn left. The Lincoln's Inn Fields Theatre once stood to your left, behind the Royal College of Surgeons. It was converted from a tennis court by Davenant in 1660 and was the second home of the Duke's Company. It was one of the most important playhouses in London's theatrical history, the first to have incorporated a proscenium arch and movable and changeable scenery (previously reserved for masques). It was a theatre for the age of Newton, in which the actor was placed in a rational, receding space, a long way from the vertical cosmology of theatres such as the Globe, with their Heavens above and Hells below. Thomas Betterton's legendary Hamlet played here. The company also revived *Romeo and Juliet* without revisions to accommodate itself to contemporary taste in 1662 – and so earned Pepys's disgust, who declared it 'the worst that ever I heard'. He was more complimentary about the *Macbeth* which appeared here, with music by Matthew Locke, 'new Clothes, new Scenes, Machines, as flying for the Witches...Singing and Dancing'. Illustrations probably based on this production show the witches in semi-classical dress, Macbeth himself dressed in rich contemporary garb. Davenant's production drew an explicit parallel between Macbeth and Cromwell (the usurper), and Malcolm and Charles II (the Restorer). It was one of the theatrical triumphs of the Restoration.

Clare Market Theatre

Turn left; cross Sardinia Street, bear left for Portsmouth Street; at the end turn right on Portugal Street and immediately left down Clare Market. Like the playhouse at Lincoln's Inn Fields, Clare Market Theatre was an adapted tennis court – 'the finest playhouse, I believe, that ever was in England', Pepys thought when it opened in 1660. It was the first home of the King's Company, whose manager was the 'trusty and well beloved' Thomas Killigrew, dramatist, actor and courtier. Beside Davenant, Killigrew seems the more conservative of the two. He hired older actors who had been active before the Civil War, and, although he inherited exclusive rights to perform 20 of Shakespeare's plays, the King's Company produced only four of them in the course of its career (it eventually merged with the Duke's in 1682). Moreover, Killigrew was less bold in his Shakespeare productions. They did not enjoy (or endure) the radical alterations Davenant undertook, and that the age seemed to require. But in one sense Killigrew was experimental. At the first performance of *Othello* at Clare Market on 8 December 1660 the audience heard this prologue:

> I come, unknown to any of the rest,
> To tell you news; I saw the lady dress'd!
> The woman plays today, mistake me not,
> No man in gown, or page in petticoat

This Desdemona (perhaps played by Anne Marshall) is probably the first woman on the English stage. Charles II approved. He'd acquired a taste for the good-looking actresses he'd seen in theatres in France (where they had long been the norm) and the sight of women on the stage must have reinforced the sense of victory over the Commonwealth and all its odious Puritanical associations. The Elizabethan tradition of using boys in the theatre, with the exception of a few comic parts (Juliet's Nurse, for instance) became more or less a thing of the past in the professional theatre.

The Cockpit Theatre and Drury Lane

Turn right down Houghton Street and right at the end on Aldwych. Turn right up Drury Lane. Before the Theatre Royal, Drury Lane was home to the Cockpit Theatre, founded by the actor-manager Christopher Beeston (of the Salisbury Court) in 1617, and probably designed by Inigo Jones. It was an exclusive indoor playhouse – too exclusive for some of the locals, maybe, for the theatre was smashed up by rioting apprentices. Beeston renamed it the Phoenix after its repair. It was a rare survivor of the old theatrical tradition in the Restoration period. The remnants of the King's Men risked a performance of a play by Fletcher and Massinger here in 1648, when a government militia broke in and arrested the players, some of them in their 60s and 70s, and marched them to prison in costume, where they were flogged and their costumes confiscated. It was the last performance by Shakespeare's old company.

Old John Lowin, one of Shakespeare's players, was almost certainly of that party. Lowin, like the Phoenix itself, represented a bridge between the King's Men and the Restoration. Thomas Betterton's great performance of Henry VIII was attributed to what he had learned from Davenant, who had himself 'had it from old Mr Lowin, that had his instructions from Shakespeare himself'. The Phoenix was one of two theatres where Shakespeare's plays were revived after the Restoration. It was also the first home to Davenant's Company after Charles II granted him a royal licence, and so represents the end and beginning of two distinct theatrical traditions.

Turn left on Russell Street for the Theatre Royal, Drury Lane. The current Theatre Royal is (more or less, in view of the amount of alterations it's had since 1812), the third theatre on this site. The second theatre was built for Killigrew by Christopher Wren in 1673 on a scale intended to rival Davenant's Dorset Garden. Wren's plans survive, and show a theatre designed on neo-classical proportions, with elaborate perspective scenery and a proscenium arch, setting the action within a picture frame – very different to what Killigrew's company was used to, the still more-or-less bare open stage of the Phoenix. Edward Kynaston, the great and last player of female parts, played here. He was an enormously attractive and versatile performer. Pepys saw him play several parts in Jonson's *Epicoene*, in which he 'was clearly the prettiest woman in the whole house; and lastly as a man; and then likewise did appear the handsomest man in the house.' Colley Cibber saw his Henry IV here:

> This true majesty Kynaston had so entire a command of, that when he whispered the following plain line to Hotspur, 'Send us your prisoners, or you'll hear of it!' he conveyed a more terrible menace in it than the loudest intemperance of voice could swell to.

Finally, unable to compete with the Duke's Company, the King's took to parody and burlesque. Davenant's most successful Shakespearean adaptations, *Macbeth* and *The Enchanted Isle*, were both sent up by Thomas Duffet in his 'Epilogue' to *Macbeth* and his *Mock Tempest*, where Prospero, usurped from his office as keeper of the king's dog kennels, is appointed over the prostitutes at the Bridewell. Its *mise en scene* apparently render it too obscene for revival.

Betterton and St Giles-in-the-Fields

Continue on Russell Street – on your left is the Theatre Museum, with items relating to the Restoration stage in the Main Gallery (case 10) – into Covent Garden Market; on the north (or right hand side as you face the portico of St Paul's Church) side of the Piazza turn up James Street and right up Floral Street for Covent Garden Theatre, (see page 166). Turn left up Bow Street; cross at the zebra and down Broad Court, turning left at the passage leading past the Sun Tavern; cross Long Acre and turn left up Arne Street, passing Dryden Street on your right. Turn left at the end then right at the end of Shelton Street; Betterton Street is on the right.

By general consent, Thomas Betterton was the greatest Shakespearean actor between Burbage and Garrick. Highly literate, Betterton's genius resided in vocal delivery rather than actions, which were 'few, but just'. His style probably resembled John Gielgud's – 'serious, venerable and majestic' – an impression that is reinforced by Betterton's own remarks on the power of speech, in which he recognized 'a sort of music, with respect to its Measure, Time and Tune...'. He played many major Shakespeare roles, inluding Henry VIII, Mercutio, Sir Toby Belch and Macbeth, but his greatest was Hamlet. Pepys saw him play the Prince when he (Betterton) was 26 'beyond imagination', and he was still playing it at 74 with apparently undiminished power. The actor-manager Colley Cibber has left us a fine description of his performance of Hamlet's first encounter with the Ghost:

> he opened with a pause of mute amazement, then rising slowly to a solemn, trembling voice, he made the Ghost equally terrible to the spectator as to himself, and in the descriptive part of the natural emotions which the ghastly vision gave him, the boldness of his expostulation was still covered by decency, manly, but not braving, his voice never rising into that seeming outrage or wild defiance of what he naturally revered.

Turn left down Short's Gardens (Neal's Yard). At Seven Dials turn right down Mercer Street (two streets to your right at the end of Short's Gardens); cross Shaftesbury Avenue and go down St Giles Passage ahead of you; cross the road (there are seats in the Phoenix garden to your left) into the churchyard of St Giles-in-the-Fields. The great Bohemian engraver, Wenceslaus Hollar, to whom we owe the lovely 1647 panorama of London – which includes the only reliable image of the (second) Globe – was married here. James Shirley, driven out of his house in the Bridewell by the Great Fire, ended his chequered life at St Giles with his wife (the parish records include the registrations of their deaths on the same day). Shirley was the last resident playwright at the Globe. And Shakespeare's great contemporary, George Chapman, playwright, poet and translator of Homer, is buried here too: see his severe memorial inside. Their careers dogged each other's: Chapman sent up the tradition Shakespeare launched with *Venus and Adonis* in his *Ovid's Banquet of Senses*; Shakespeare was indebted to Chapman's Homer for *Troilus and Cressida*. One notion, now lapsed, proposed Chapman as the 'rival poet' in Shakespeare's sonnets.

Dryden and Soho

Turn left out of the church down Flitcroft Street; cross Charing Cross Road and turn left; turn right down Old Compton Street; left down Greek Street; cross Shaftesbury Avenue and turn left on Gerrard Place; turn right on Gerrard Street, where a plaque above the Loon Fung Supermarket honours John Dryden. 'I admire him,' wrote Dryden of Jonson, 'but I love Shakespeare.' Dryden was a Shakespeare nut, writing adaptations, imitations and critical defences of his work. He collaborated with Davenant on *The Tempest* and he wrote an adaptation of *Troilus and Cressida* which he called *Truth Found too Late*. Unlike the two damaged survivors at the end of Shakespeare's original, Dryden's Cressida is proved virtuous and Troilus is killed on the battlefield.

His *All for Love; or The World Well Lost*, in which he professes to have imitated 'the Divine Shakespeare' is not really an adaptation of *Antony and Cleopatra*, but it does tell its story. Shakespeare's is a kind of tutelary presence throughout. It is the only play Dryden wrote in blank verse (he favoured rhyme, usually in couplets). Dryden was a robust defender of Shakespeare against the notorious criticism of the pedant Thomas Rymer (for whom *Othello* was a 'bloody farce'), and his eloquence promoted Shakespeare 'far beyond anything of the Ancients'. 'He was the man,' he wrote, 'who of all Modern, and perhaps Ancient poets, had the largest and most comprehensive soul. All the images of Nature were still present to him, and he drew them not laboriously, but luckily: when he describes any thing, you more than see it, you feel it too.' Dryden is Shakespeare's first great critic and the familiar reverence for his genius receives an early and powerful amplification in his essays and prefaces.

Turn left down Whitcomb Street and left on Pall Mall East; cross at the lights straight ahead, bearing left for Whitehall. Bear right across Trafalgar Square for Charing Cross Underground Station.

THE AGE
OF GARRICK

Summary: The 18th century is the age of David Garrick, the actor-manager who elevated Shakespeare to semi-divine status and placed him at the centre of London's cultural life. Sites associated with the great actors and actor-managers, poets, scholars, critics and painters who fashioned him in their own image and claimed him as their own are scattered throughout the lively streets of Covent Garden, Soho and St James's. This walk traces a vital thread in the artistic fabric of life in the 18th-century city.

Start:	Holborn Underground Station.
Finish:	Piccadilly Circus Underground Station.
Length:	2.5 km (1½ miles).
Time:	1 hour.
Refreshments:	The Sun, corner of Betterton Street and Drury Lane; The Chequers, Duke Street St James's; Lamb and Flag, Rose Street.

Turn left out of the High Holborn side of Holborn Underground; cross the top of Kingsway; turn left on Newton Street; turn right on Macklin Street.

Charles Macklin

Charles Macklin excelled in the portrayal of Shakespeare's outsiders – Malvolio, Iago and, most famously, Shylock. This violent Irishman raised Shakespeare's Jew from its long-held position of low comedy to one of tragic dignity. 'The first words he utters,' wrote Charles Lichtenburg, 'when he comes on to the stage, are slowly and impressively spoken':

> 'Three thousand ducats,' which Macklin lisps as lickerishly as if he were savouring the ducats and all that they would buy, make so deep an impression in the man's favour that nothing can destroy it. Three such words uttered thus at the outset give the keynote of his whole character. In the scene where he first misses his daughter, he comes on hatless, with disordered hair a finger standing on end, as if raised by a breath of

Opposite: Enlightening Shakespeare. A copy of William Kent's design stands in the centre of Leicester Square. The quotation is from Twelfth Night.

THERE IS
NO DARKNESS
BUT
IGNORANCE

THIS ENCLOSURE
WAS PURCHASED, LAID OUT
AND DECORATED AS A GARDEN
BY ALBERT GRANT ESQᴿᴱ M.P.
AND
CONVEYED BY HIM ON THE 2ᴺᴰ JULY 1874.
TO THE
METROPOLITAN BOARD OF WORKS
TO BE PRESERVED FOR EVER
FOR THE FREE USE AND ENJOYMENT
OF THE PUBLIC.

wind from the gallows, so distracted was his demeanour. Both his hands are clenched, and his movements abrupt and convulsive. To see a deceiver, who is usually calm and resolute, in such a state of agitation, is terrible.

It was one of the great performances of the 18th century, and Macklin played the part for 48 years. It was too long, for a sad account survives of his appearance in the green room before his own benefit performance asking: '"Who is to play Shylock?" – The imbecile tone of voice, and the inanity of look with which this last question was asked, caused a melancholy sensation in all who heard it.' Things did not improve on the stage, and he had to take his leave after two or three speeches. He was nearly 90 years old.

Drury Lane and David Garrick

At the end turn left on Drury Lane; turn right on Russell Street, along the north side of the Theatre Royal, Drury Lane. Drury Lane in this period is associated with the name of David Garrick, who first appeared as Hamlet here in 1742 and shared the management of the theatre from 1747. He was the greatest Shakespearean actor of his time: 'the Master,' as his teacher and fellow Lichfield man, Samuel Johnson said, 'both in tragedy and comedy'. A detailed record of Garrick's revival of *Hamlet* at Drury Lane in the 1770s survives:

Hamlet has folded his arms under his cloak and pulled his hat down over his eyes; it is a cold night and just twelve o'clock; the theatre is darkened, and the whole audience of some thousands are as quiet, and their faces as motionless, as though they were painted on the walls of the theatre; even from the farthest end of the playhouse one could hear a pin drop. When the ghost appears, Garrick: turns sharply and at the same moment staggers back two or three paces with his knees giving way under him; his hat falls to the ground and both his arms, especially left, are stretched out nearly to their full length, with the hands as high as his head, the right arm more bent and the hand lower, and the fingers apart; his mouth is open. The almost terror-struck silence of the audience, which preceded this appearance and filled one with a sense of insecurity, probably did much to enhance this effect. At last he speaks, not at the beginning, but at the end of a breath, with a trembling voice: 'Angels and ministers of grace defend us!' What an amazing triumph it is.

Alexander Pope and Russell Street

Cross Bow Street for the second stretch of Russell Street, passing the Theatre Museum. Alexander Pope spent his time in Will's Coffee House on this

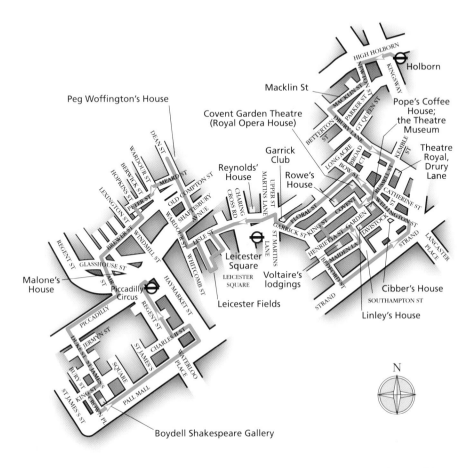

street. In an age when things medieval were just beginning to affect public taste, Pope described Shakespeare's work as 'an ancient majestick piece of *Gothick* Architecture'. He followed his predecessor Dryden in praising Shakespeare as the poet of nature, and like nature sometimes in need of cultivation. His not-very-scholarly 1723 edition of Shakespeare, with its most particular literary beauties advertised by asterisks and quotations, and its defects and obscurities relegated to the footnotes, gives a wonderful idea of 18th-century literary taste. His edition was put in the shade by that of the brilliant and scholarly Lewis Theobald, who brought to bear on his own edition (and his attack on Pope's) all the historical discipline of contemporary classical and biblical studies. Pope, though, was not a man to cross, and 'Tibbald' was promoted to the king of the Duncad in the first version of *The Dunciad* (an honour which later befell the actor-manager

Colley Cibber). In Pope's *Epistle to Dr Arbuthnot,* Theobald appears as the very type of mediocrity and pedantry, one whose fame can only be sustained by the subject in which he worked:

> Each wight who reads not, and but scans and spells,
> Each word-catcher that lives on syllables,
> Ev'n such small critics some regard may claim,
> Preserved in Milton's or in Shakespeare's name.
> Pretty! in amber to observe the forms
> Of hairs, or straws, or dirt, or grubs, or worms

Not a very generous appraisal of the work of the greatest Shakespeare scholar of the first half of the 18th century. One of Pope's *Imitations of Horace* betrays a refreshingly unsentimental idea of Shakespeare's artistic imperatives:

> Shakespeare (whom you and every playhouse bill
> Style the divine, the matchless, what you will)
> For gain, not glory, wing'd his roving flight,
> And grew immortal in his own despite.

Rowe, Linley, Voltaire and Cibber

In Covent Garden piazza turn right, walk along the east side and then left along the top of the market and down King Street. Nicholas Rowe, Shakespeare's first scholarly editor, died in lodgings here in 1718. Rowe was the first to modernize Shakespeare's spelling and to supply lists of *dramatis personae.* He was also the first to attempt a biography of Shakespeare, which constituted part of the introduction to his six-volume edition of the plays published in 1709. A dramatist himself, Rowe was more interested in performance than text. His Shakespeare was illustrated, and the engravings show the style of many productions of the late 17th and early 18th centuries.

Turn right down the narrow passage leading to St Paul's Church; through the churchyard, turn left on Henrietta Street and right down Southampton Street. Thomas Linley, the composer to Drury Lane, lived at No 11. Linley was friendly with Mozart when he studied in Italy as a child, and is now chiefly remembered for his lively and imaginative Shakespeare music, *A Lyric Ode on the Fairies, Aerial Beings and Witches of Shakespeare* and his incidental music for *The Tempest.* He was killed in a boating accident at the age of 22.

Turn right on Maiden Lane. 'A coarse and barbarous piece, which would not be tolerated by the lowest rabble of France and Italy... You would suppose it to be a product of the imagination of a drunken savage.' Voltaire's notorious view of *Hamlet* has served to obscure his more judicious appraisal of Shakespeare during his exile in England. When he lived at No 10, Voltaire was able to overcome his neo-classical principles and confess an admiration for Shakespeare, even paying him the compliment of importing chunks of *Macbeth* into his own tragedy *Mohamet*. But it was not to last. He became unable to overcome his antipathy towards Shakespeare's awful taste and irregularities, his indifference to the rules of drama. Samuel Johnson, himself alert to Shakespeare's artistic 'defects', was impatient with these cavils: 'Such violations of rules merely positive, become the comprehensive genius of *Shakespeare*, and such censures are suitable to the minute and slender criticism of *Voltaire*.'

Turn left on Bedford Street and left at the bottom on the Strand. Turn right up Wellington Street. On the left-hand side, a few doors up from Tavistock Street, lived the actor-manager Colley Cibber, a man in the thick of the feuds of literary and theatrical London. He undertook an adaptation of *Richard III* (in which he played the lead), and he became poet laureate in 1730, which did not endear him to Pope, who elevated him to the king of the Dunces in *The Dunciad*, pushing even the detested Theobald off his throne.

Cibber played a number of arrogant and villainous parts – Wolsey, Iago and Edmund as well as Richard – but his greatest role was probably Shallow. 'His manner,' wrote Thomas Davies:

> ...was so perfectly simple, his look so vacant, when he questioned his cousin Silence about the price of ewes, and lamented, in the same breath, with silly surprise, the death of Old Double, that it will be impossible for any surviving spectator not to smile at the remembrance of it. The want of ideas occasions Shallow to repeat almost everything he says. Cibber's transition from asking the price of bullocks, to trite, but grave, reflections on mortality, was so natural, and attended with such an unmeaning roll of his small pig's-eyes that I question if any actor was ever superior in the conception or expression of such solemn insignificancy.

Cibber wrote his *Apology for his Own Life*, an important and entertaining source for the theatrical history of the period, here. His contemporary, the tragedian Barton Booth, lived and died in the same house.

James Quin at Covent Garden Theatre

On your left on Bow Street you see the Royal Opera House, once the Covent Garden Theatre, where James Quin asserted his grandiloquent self-important style in the theatre's earliest years. The pompous declamatory Quin –

'Bellower' Quin – was the quintessence of Shakespearean importance, an unprepossessing creature. The critic Francis Gentleman, while 'sorry to mention him so often disadvantageously', did not spare him. Quin's Othello 'was – though Othello is in the vale of years – not a very probable external appearance to engage Desdemona, his declamation was as heavy as his person; his tones monotonous; his passions bellowing, his emphasis affected, and his understrokes growling'; his 'magpye' appearance 'tended greatly to laughter', an unintended parody of an earlier generation.

Only his Falstaff, where Quin could subvert his own heroic declamations, seems to have really come off, achieving an 'impudent dignity', apparently exquisite. All the same, Garrick had put the writing on the wall for Quin and others of his type by 1740. 'If that young fellow is right,' Quin said of Garrick, 'I and the rest of the players have all been wrong.'

Garrick Street

Turn left on Floral Street; turn right at the end on Garrick Street until you reach the Garrick Club. This solemn black palazzo is the most concrete memorial to Garrick, and testifies to the status he enjoyed by the end of his life: a man who seemed to have single-handedly reformed the stage in England. It was Garrick who threw the spectators off the stage and the backstage areas; who reformed theatrical costume, dance, lighting and stage effects. For better and for worse, he was also the greatest promoter of Shakespeare in the national consciousness. He co-ordinated the Jubilee celebrations in Stratford, hoarded editions, collected and promoted Shakespearean tat, adapted the plays, wrote odes to them and their author and threw up a temple to the playwright in his garden at Hampton (see page 123). He was Shakespeare's high priest, mediating between him and the public, the playtexts themselves the Good Book to ward off the incursions of weaker talents: 'Never let your *Shakespear* be out of your hands, or your Pocket – Keep him about you as a Charm.'

The Garrick Club has a great collection of theatrical portraits, many Shakespearean – including Zoffany's lovely Thomas King as Touchstone in *As You Like It*, with King in sumptuous silken garb, and the same artist's famous depiction of Garrick and Mrs Pritchard in *Macbeth* – that 'wonderful expression' described by Thomas Davies, 'of heartfelt horror, which Garrick felt when he shewed his bloody hands, can only be conceived and described by those who saw him!'

Sir Joshua Reynolds and William Hogarth

Cross Long Acre, turn down Great Newport Street. The handsome black house was once lived in by Sir Joshua Reynolds, painter and President of the Royal

Academy. Reynolds' artistic ambitions lay in History painting. The gallery founded by John Boydell (of whom more later) enshrined artistic values very much to his taste. His painting of the bedchamber of Cardinal Beaufort, with the cardinal writhing in remorse over his part in the murder of Humphrey, Duke of Gloucester in *2 Henry VI*, was considered one of his best efforts at narrative painting. The peculiar contortions of Beaufort's face seem partly disturbing, partly ridiculous now as Reynolds sought to render in paint Warwick's observation, 'See how the pangs of death do make him grin'. Reynolds intensified the cardinal's anguish after painting over a little fiend beside his head who had bodied forth the cardinal's guilty conscience. The painting is now at Petworth House, in West Sussex.

Cross Charing Cross Road, turn right on Little Newport Street; turn down Lisle Street and left on Leicester Place; walk through Leicester Fields, past the bust of William Hogarth. Hogarth's painting of Garrick as Richard III startled by the apparitions outside his tent was one of the most celebrated Shakespearean images of the 18th century. It records one of those moments of extravagant artifice that broke through the more usual naturalism of Garrick's performances. It is now at the Walker Gallery in Liverpool. In another picture of Garrick, the actor is depicted (this time not in character) but proprietarily seated upon a chair fashioned from the mulberry tree supposed to have been planted by Shakespeare in Stratford. The statue of Shakespeare in the fountain is a copy of a statue designed by the architect William Kent in Westminster Abbey (see page 104) and executed in the 1870s by George Fontana. 'There is no darkness but ignorance', though an admirable Enlightenment sentiment, seems a strange quotation to have chosen, when you consider its context in *Twelfth Night*: Feste tormenting the imprisoned Malvolio.

Peg Woffington

Pass the bust of Reynolds, walk up Leicester Street (there's no sign at the bottom); turn left on Lisle Street; turn right up Wardour Street, right down Dansey Place and over Shaftesbury Avenue at the lights and up Dean Street. The beautiful Peg Woffington lived at No 33, one of the most accomplished and versatile actresses of the mid-18th century. She was a great Cordelia, playing opposite Garrick (with whom she had an affair), and a great Lady Anne to his Richard III. There were few Shakespearean parts she didn't attempt: Rosalind, Viola, Desdemona, Lady Macbeth, Gertrude. One of her greatest was clearly Portia, which, 'while in petticoats, she shewed the woman of solid sense, and real fashion; when in breeches, the man of education, judgement and gentility.' Her career was cut cruelly short by a stroke during a performance of *As You Like It* at Covent Garden. The actor Tate Wilkinson witnessed it:

when [she] arrived at – 'If I were among you I would kiss as many of you as had beards that pleased me.' – her voice broke, she faltered, endeavoured to go on, but could not proceed – then in a voice of tremor screamed, 'O God! O God!' [and] Tottered to the stage door speechless, where she was caught. The audience of course applauded till she was out of sight, and then sunk into awful looks of astonishment, both young and old, before and behind the curtain, to see one of the most handsome women of the age, a favourite principal actress, and who had for several seasons given high entertainment, struck so suddenly by the hand of death in such a situation of time and place, and in her prime of life, being then about forty-four.

She survived another three years, however, as Wilkinson recalled with a grim consciousness of mortality, 'a mere skeleton; sans teeth, sans eyes, sans taste, sans every thing. – Vain is Beauty's gaudy flower!'

Retrace your steps a few yards and turn right on Meard Street, a well-preserved 18th-century lane; cross Wardour Street and down Peter Street; turn left on Green Street and right at the end on to Brewer Street; turn left at the end of Brewer Street down Glasshouse Street. The great scholar Edmund Malone lived at No 22 when he first came to London in 1777 (see page 145).

The Shakespeare Gallery to Pall Mall

Turn right down Air Street, crossing Regent Street at the lights and continuing down Air Street cross Piccadilly, and turn right on Jermyn Street and left down Duke Street St James's; cross King Street, turn right and left down Crown Passage to Pall Mall at the end.

At No 52 was situated the Shakespeare Gallery, the venture of John Boydell, engraver, publisher and Lord Mayor. The idea was to 'form an English School of Historical Paintings [depicting] scenes of the immortal Shakespeare', and to make a great deal of money from both gallery receipts and the sale of prints. Boydell commissioned 35 artists to do the work, notably the chief historical painters of the day – including Reynolds, Romney, Fuseli and Benjamin West. The gallery opened its doors in 1789, by the next year displaying in its saloons 67 pictures depicting scenes from the plays. Shakespeare, flanked by the Genius of Painting and the Dramatic Muse, adorned the façade. James Gillray executed one of his most brilliant and elaborate caricatures satirizing Boydell's alleged greed: *Shakespeare Sacrificed – or the Offering to Avarice*. The gallery cost £100,000 to build, fit-out and decorate, a huge sum, but it was not a commercial success. During the Napoleonic Wars Boydell could find no continental market for the prints (supposed to have been the biggest money-spinner), the gallery was lampooned in the press, public taste wearied of the historical style, and Boydell was forced to sell up – which he did by lottery. The engravings are still occasionally seen in print shops.

At the end of Pall Mall, turn left up Haymarket for Her Majesty's and the Theatre Royal. Neither theatre had a distinguished Shakespearean pedigree in the 18th century.

Turn left down Charles II Street and right up Regent Street for Piccadilly Circus Underground Station.

ROMANTIC
SHAKESPEARE

Summary: In the Romantic period, Shakespeare, whether on the stage or the page, was enlisted in the political and literary debates of the age. Were you for Kemble's Tory *Coriolanus* or Kean's radical *Richard III*? Did you agree with Byron that *Hamlet* was impenetrable to a fault, or with Coleridge, who found there 'admirable indefiniteness'? While Hazlitt was in one street writing the greatest theatre criticism of the age, Lamb was in another declaring that Shakespeare should never be staged. This walk follows in the paths of the great actors, poets, novelists and critics for whom Shakespeare was at the centre of lives never more intensely lived nor deeply felt.

Start:	Covent Garden Underground Station.
Finish:	Piccadilly Circus Underground Station.
Length:	2 km (1¹⁄₄ miles).
Time:	1 hour.
Refreshments:	Kemble's Head, corner of Long Acre and Bow Street; The Sun; Long Acre; The Opera Tavern, Catherine Street.

Turn right on the James Street exit; turn left on Floral Street. Beside you stretches the north side of the Royal Opera House, once known as the Theatre Royal Covent Garden. Covent Garden and Drury Lane dominated Shakespearean performance in London up to the Victorian period. From 1802, the theatre was run by John Philip Kemble who, with his sister Sarah Siddons and his brother Charles, bridges the gap between the 18th-century Garrick and the high Romantic Edmund Kean.

John Kemble and Eliza O'Neill

According to the critic Leigh Hunt, 'Were it not for Mr Kemble's exertions the tragedies of our glorious bard would almost be in danger of dismissal from the stage.' Kemble was a great manager – what we would now call a director – as well as actor, chasing authenticity in his costumes and design – not Elizabethan authenticity, but an accuracy proper to the period in which the plays were set. As a manager Kemble was studious, as an actor declamatory and formal. He had a patrician style, so perhaps it's not surprising that his greatest role was Coriolanus, often revived at Covent Garden to an

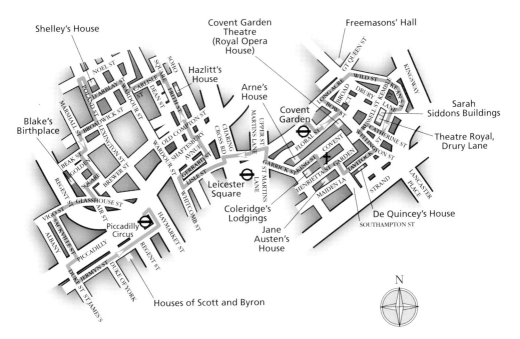

Shelley's House

Covent Garden
Theatre
(Royal Opera
House)

Freemasons' Hall

Hazlitt's
House

Arne's
House

Covent
Garden

NOEL ST

SOHO
SQUARE

IRISH ST

DEAN ST

CARLISLE
ST

D'ARBLAY ST

TOLAND ST

WARDOUR ST

OLD COMPTON ST

SHAFTESBURY
AVENUE

CHARING
CROSS RD

MARTIN'S LANE

UPPER ST

FLORAL ST

LONG ACRE

BROAD
ST

BOW ST

DRURY
LANE

WILD ST

GT QUEEN ST

KINGSWAY

RUSSELL ST

KEMBLE ST

CATHERINE ST

Sarah
Siddons Buildings

Blake's
Birthplace

Theatre Royal,
Drury Lane

MARSHALL ST

LEXINGTON ST

BROADWICK ST

WARDOUR ST

BEAK ST

GOLDEN
SQUARE

BREWER ST

GERRARD ST

LISLE ST

GARRICK ST

KING ST

COVENT
GARDEN

HENRIETTA ST

TAVISTOCK ST

WHITINGTON ST

STRAND

LANCASTER
PLACE

Leicester
Square

MAIDEN LA

REGENT ST

GLASSHOUSE ST

AIR ST

WHITCOMB ST

ST MARTIN'S
LANE

De Quincey's House

SOUTHAMPTON ST

VIGO ST

SACKVILLE ST

PICCADILLY

HAYMARKET ST

Coleridge's
Lodgings

Jane
Austen's
House

Piccadilly
Circus

ALBANY

JERMYN ST

DUKE ST
ST JAMES'S

DUKE OF YORK

REGENT ST

Houses of Scott and Byron

N

overwhelming reception up to Kemble's retirement in 1817. His death scene in *Coriolanus* suggested to Walter Scott the 'most striking resemblance to instant and actual death we ever witnessed, and saved all that rolling, gasping and groaning which generally takes place in our theatres, to the scandal of all foreigners.'

Kemble's greatest successes were during Britain's 20-year war with France, when he made explicit the association between the national poet and traditional (that is, Tory) values. Under Kemble's management, especially after the theatre was rebuilt following a disastrous fire in 1808, Covent Garden became associated with the establishment, and Shakespeare at the heart of a semi-official national theatre. Riots greeted Kemble's revival of *Macbeth* (first performed at Drury Lane) when the theatre was reopened with higher ticket prices – riots that were kept up for an amazing 67 performances until Kemble caved in and put the prices down.

Eliza O'Neill's great debut as Juliet was at Covent Garden in 1814. Sometimes seen as the heir to Sarah Siddons, she was her temperamental opposite: beautiful rather than sublime, reflective rather than active. She satisfied the Romantic appetite for sensibility.

Turn left up Bow Street; at the top on your left is the Kemble's Head; turn right on Long Acre; cross Drury Lane; ahead of you is the Freemasons' Hall.

Berlioz was guest of honour at a dinner in a previous building on this site. Charles Kemble, John Philip's brother, played Romeo to Harriet Smithson's Juliet in Paris in 1827, the production that turned Berlioz's Shakespearean (and romantic) head (see page 149).

Sarah Siddons

Turn right down Wild Street, cross the top of Kemble Street and down Kean Street, at the end of which turn right up Drury Lane and then immediately down Tavistock Street, where the buildings on your right acknowledge the great Sarah Siddons. She and her brother John Philip Kemble were the great double-act of the Romantic stage; she was Desdemona to his Othello, Cordelia to his Lear, Ophelia to his Hamlet and Cleopatra to his Antony. But she was far from skulking in his shadow. She was, for one thing, quite a different kind of actor to her brother. Where he was formal and classical, she was intensely sympathetic, striving always to get inside her characters, and drawing upon powers of concentration which she did not forsake in the Green Room: no gossip and jokes in the easy Garrick way for her.

She was an early 'Method' actress, too, using her observations of real sleepwalkers in her depiction of Lady Macbeth, one of the greatest performances of the period and memorably painted by Fuseli. She revised the popular conception of Lady Macbeth as a monster of unnatural cruelty and cunning, portraying her rather as wicked (like her husband) in spite of herself. Sarah Siddons clearly excelled in the moments of great internal stress or terror rather than those of reflection or tenderness – the special qualities of her looked-for successor at Covent Garden, Eliza O'Neill.

Edmund Kean

Turn right up Catherine Street; on your left is the Theatre Royal Drury Lane, best known in this period for the performances of Edmund Kean. Hazlitt recognised Kemble's merits, but his declamatory style was in the end not what the period required. Edmund Kean offered something more vivid, direct and spontaneous. He was the Romantic actor par excellence, the favourite of London's young political radicals and to be weighed against the respectability of Kemble. Hazlitt's review of Kean's Richard III at Drury Lane, in which his genius was first described, is a classic of theatre criticism. He brought an 'animation, vigour, and relief' to the part 'which we have never seen surpassed'. Kean conveyed a sense of indomitable will, an adamantine, Byronic quality.

Opposite: The Royal Opera House. Before its dedication to opera, several versions of the Theatre Royal Covent Garden stood here.

Left: A portrait of Jane Austen whose novels were influenced by Shakespeare's stories and characters.

Yet, there was a partial quality too. Coleridge famously described Kean's acting as like 'reading Shakespeare in flashes of lightning' – exciting, bringing brilliant flashes of inspiration to the part, often marvellous in his effects, but also leaving us in the dark or half-light for much of the time. Kean's Hamlet was presented here in 1814. It did not disappoint Hazlitt either. His description of the closet scene between Hamlet and Gertrude in which Kean returned gives a good idea of what the Romantics looked for in their Shakespeare: 'It had an electrical effect on the house. It was the finest commentary that was ever made on Shakespeare. It explained the character at once (as he meant it), as one of disappointed hope, of bitter regret, of affection suspended, not obliterated, by the distractions of the scene around him!' Kean achieved this in spite of a harsh voice and unimpressive physique.

Charles and Mary Lamb

Turn left down Russell Street, where at No 21 Charles Lamb lived with his sister Mary from 1817–23. Their *Tales from Shakespeare* are still in print, and for generations were the medium by which many children first encountered Shakespeare. Charles Lamb was also an important champion of Shakespeare's playwriting contemporaries; he records his visit to No 19 on this street to buy a copy of Beaumont and Fletcher, about whom he chats in his essay, 'Old China'. Lamb was also responsible for a significant and highly characteristic essay, 'On the Tragedies of Shakespeare Considered with Reference to their Fitness for Stage-Representation', in which he argued that *King Lear* should not be staged and that we are better off reading it.

On the stage we only *see* Lear and 'nothing but corporal infirmities'; but when we read it we *are* Lear. With a few exceptions (such as Hazlitt) the Romantics couldn't conceal from themselves a discontent about the performance of Shakespeare's plays. They suspected that they were better appreciated in the study, where they could be effectively worked upon by the imagination, than in the playhouse. This said nothing about the quality of performance. Indeed, the more charismatic it was, the more it distracted attention from the *idea* of the character (or play) as a whole. In the end the performance eclipsed the idea and, as Lamb complained, 'we speak of Lady Macbeth, while we are in reality thinking of Mrs S[iddons]'. This reservation is not limited to the Romantic era.

Thomas de Quincy
Cross Bow Street (on your left is the Theatre Museum); turn left on Wellington Street and right on Tavistock Street. At No 36 lived Thomas de Quincey, author of an essay 'On the Knocking at the Gate in *Macbeth*' – a famous piece of what the author called 'psychological criticism'. Its aim was to reveal Shakespeare's talent for creating intense dramatic sympathy (and anxiety) through sound. The real analysis of the essay is devoted to the silence which precedes the knocking at the gate of Macbeth's castle, when 'life is suddenly arrested – laid asleep – tranced – racked into a dread armistice; time must be annihilated; relation to things without abolished; and all must pass self-withdrawn into a deep syncope and suspension of earthly passion.' The knocking itself brings this to a close, making us aware of the 'awful parenthesis' that had suspended the 'pulses of life'.

Austen and Coleridge
At the end of Tavistock Street, turn right up Southampton Street and at the end left on Henrietta Street, where a blue plaque on the left-hand side advertises the house of Jane Austen. Henry Crawford, the plausible suitor to Fanny Price in *Mansfield Park*, is usually taken to be speaking for his creator when he considers the natural and artless stealth with which Shakespeare seems to take hold of the English mind: 'But Shakespeare one gets acquainted with without knowing how. It is a part of an Englishman's constitution. His thoughts and beauties are so spread abroad that one touches them every where, one is intimate with him by instinct.' The three daughters in *King Lear* and the love story in *All's Well That Ends Well* clearly influenced the writing of *Mansfield Park*, just as Elizabeth Bennett and Mr Darcy constitute a latter-day Beatrice and Benedick.

Turn up the passage opposite Jane Austen's house, pass through the garden of St Paul's church, through the passage on the other side, and onto King

Street. Samuel Taylor Coleridge lived at No 10 King Street in 1801–2. The greatest Shakespeare critic of his day, and one of the greatest of all, Coleridge never troubled to put his writings on Shakespeare in any systematic order. They are scattered throughout his works, in letters, conversation and lectures (some transcribed by John Payne Collier, later notorious for his forgeries of Shakespearean documents), but what is constant is his conviction that Shakespeare's work grows organically out of the power of his language. Shakespeare also plays a role in Coleridge's attitudes to politics and society. Like his friend William Wordsworth, Coleridge was a political radical in his youth, his hopes bound up with the ideals and ambitions of the French Revolution. With the rise of Napoleon and Britain's war with France, the radical youth became a middle-aged conservative, and his writings on Shakespeare offer a kind of index of his changed views.

Step out of the Romantic period for a moment and glance up at Thomas Arne's house on the opposite side. Arne (composer of 'Rule Britannia') was the most important English theatrical composer of the mid-18th century, and composed incidental music for seven of Shakespeare's plays. Many of his song-settings have stood the test of time and include: 'Blow, blow, thou winter wind' from *As You Like It*, 'Where the bee sucks' from *The Tempest*, 'When daisies pied' from *Love's Labour's Lost*. His version of 'Under the Greenwood Tree' in the famous production of *As You Like It* with Hannah Pritchard as Rosalind, became one of the most popular songs of the 18th century.

Turn left on King Street and right up Garrick Street; cross Long Acre at the end, over Upper St Martin's Lane at the lights and down Great Newport Street; cross Charing Cross Road and turn left; turn right on Little Newport street, onto Lisle Street, where Edmund Kean was born in 1787.

William Hazlitt

Turn right at the end and right again onto Gerrard Street; turn left up Gerrard Place and over Shaftesbury Avenue; turn right up Frith Street, where at No 6, near the top, you'll find William Hazlitt's house. 'The striking peculiarity of Shakespeare's mind,' wrote Hazlitt, 'was its generic quality, its power of communication with all other minds – so that it contained a universe of thought and feeling within itself, and had no one particular bias....His genius shone equally on the evil and on the good, on the wise and the foolish, the monarch and the beggar.' Hazlitt, who shares with Coleridge the highest place amongst Romantic critics of Shakespeare, always kept before him the notion of the playwright's sympathetic genius – an ability to transcend egotism in order to offer an education in humanity 'in all is shapes, degrees, elevations, and depressions'.

In his *Characters of Shakespeare's Plays*, the first generally available comprehensive survey of every play, Hazlitt sought to define the distinct qualities or characteristics of each play, its peculiar tonality. As a theatre critic he favoured performers who conveyed Shakespeare's sympathetic powers: the Juliet of Eliza O'Neill, the Lady Macbeth of Sarah Siddons, the Othello and Iago of Edmund Kean (whose champion he was). All three could achieve an identification with their roles that took the audience out of itself and the petty egotism of everyday life.

Shelley

Keep going up to Soho Square, bear left and turn left on Carlisle Street, cross Dean Street and Wardour Street at the end; turn right and left down D'Arblay Street; turn right up Poland Street at whose corner with Noel Street you will find the house of Percy Bysshe Shelley.

Shelley's grim verse play *The Cenci*, a Shakespearean–Jacobean pastiche which he hoped he could get staged with Kean and O'Neill in the main roles, is not a very likeable work. The Shakespearean influence is better felt when it sought an echo in Shelley's own temperament. *Ariel* was the title of Andre Maurois' biography of Shelley, it was the name of his boat and of all Shakespeare's plays, it is probably *The Tempest* that worked most magically upon him. It is often felt in 'Prometheus Unbound', and more explicitly in 'With a Guitar, to Jane', a monologue by an aggrieved Ariel (Shelley) to Miranda (his friend Jane Williams):

> Many changes have been run
> Since Ferdinand and you begun
> Your course of love, and Ariel still
> Has tracked your steps, and served your will.

William Blake

Turn back down Poland Street and right on Broadwick Street at the end; turn left on Marshall Street; cross Beak Street and down Upper James Street into Golden Square where William Blake was born. Shakespeare was grist to Blake's literary and painterly mill. Bits of Shakespeare lie behind passages in his (to some) impenetrable prophetic books, and Blake painted a portrait of Shakespeare and engraved some of Fuseli's famous Shakespearean subjects. But Shakespeare was probably as important as an example and model. He found in his work that 'firm and decided hand' he also recognized in Milton and Michelangelo.

Turn right on Brewer Street over Glasshouse Street, where the great Irish Shakespeare scholar Edmund Malone lived at No 22 when he first came to London in 1777 (see page 145). Cross Regent Street; turn left on Sackville

Street; cross Piccadilly and turn right, then right again down Duke Street St James's; turn left on to Jermyn Street, where both Byron and Scott lived.

Byron and Scott

Lord Byron, who lived at No 55, liked to depreciate Shakespeare in favour of Alexander Pope and Sir Walter Scott, attributing his popularity to 'want of education and having written above 200 years before our time'. He was not altogether sincere. Leigh Hunt heard him 'quote passages from [Shakespeare] repeatedly; and in a tone that marked how well he appreciated their beauty'. In a conversation with Shelley, Byron describes *Hamlet* as 'wonderful', but charges it with many faults detected by earlier generations. The Ghost, he complains,

> seems to come and go without any reason at all. Why should it make all that bustle in the cellarage when it cries out 'Swear!' in echo to Hamlet? Why should it appear so unexpectedly and uselessly in that scene with his mother?

Shelley, after a few melancholy moments, comes to Shakespeare's defence. Byron is induced to listen to Shelley read a longish essay on the subject of the artistic wholeness of the play, which sends him to sleep. Nevertheless, Byron was influenced by Shakespeare. His *Manfred* is a kind of reworking of *Macbeth*, as *Don Juan* is of *Hamlet*.

Sir Walter Scott – once described by the critic and short-story writer V.S. Pritchett as 'the single Shakespearean talent of the English novel' – lived at Nos 85–6. It seems a bold claim to make for perhaps the greatest of the world's Unread. In fact it was nothing new. 'The Shakespeare of novelists', was a comparison often made in Scott's lifetime, and one he did nothing to discourage. The historical range of his work, the variety of characters, his authorial detachment, his very profuseness all begged comparison. There is a good deal of Shakespearean allusion throughout his work, too. Shakespeare himself even enjoys an anachronistic walk-on part in Scott's 'Elizabethan' novel *Kenilworth*, where he is facetiously upbraided by the Earl of Leicester for having 'given my nephew, Philip Sidney, love-powder – he cannot sleep without thy *Venus and Adonis* under his pillow!'

Turn right down St Alban's Street and right on Charles II Street. In front of you is the Haymarket Theatre, which was not distinguished for its Shakespeare revivals in the Romantic period, but saw some great triumphs from Samuel Phelps and William Macready in the late 1830s and 1840s (see page 187).

Turn left up Haymarket for Piccadilly Circus Underground Station.

VICTORIAN SHAKESPEARE

Summary: Like it or not, when it comes to Shakespeare in our cinemas and theatres we are still often living with the legacy of a pictorial tradition, in which the action and diction seem remote. The Victorians, who more than anyone else put Shakespeare behind a frame, must take some of the blame for this. Some of them – like Macready and Irving – pulled it off with genius; others didn't. The busy shopping streets of Victorian London – Soho, Oxford Street, Covent Garden and St James's – yield up a few unsuspected Shakespearean secrets, like the ghosts who haunted Dickens on his night walks. But they also lead you to other, more concrete reminders of a fascinating period of opulent sets, interfering music, drastically cut scripts and extraordinary acting.

Start:	Oxford Circus Underground Station.
Finish:	Piccadilly Circus Underground Station.
Length:	2.5 km (1½ miles).
Time:	1 hour, allowing 30 minutes each for visits to the Theatre Museum or the National Portrait Gallery.
Refreshments:	Bar des Amis, 11–14 Hanover Place; Coach and Horses, 42 Wellington Street; Lamb and Flag, 32 Rose Street (near Long Acre); Opera Tavern, 23 Catherine Street; The French House, Dean Street.

Leave Oxford Circus Underground by the Oxford Street North/Regent Street East exit; walk straight ahead at the top of the steps; on your left, under the bronze ballerina, you will see the Plaza Shopping Centre, site of the Princess's Theatre. Throughout the 1850s, under Charles Kean's management, the Princess's occupied a central place in Shakespearean production in London. Tubby, nasal and with an inexpressive face, Charles seemed an unpromising heir to his father Edmund, the disreputable genius of the Romantic stage.

The Prince's Theatre and Charles Kean

But in spite of what must have been an oppressive paternal example, Charles had his hour. When the versatile William Macready threw in the towel at Drury Lane (we'll pass him in a minute) Kean bore off his promptbooks to help him recreate and develop the kind of Shakespearean productions Macready had created at Drury Lane. The result was an elaborate, remote sequence of plausible and romantic oil paintings. The actors had to hold their own against the lights, scenery, music, 'effects' and crowds which jostled and shook around them. Kean was a master of the theatrical tableau, and lost few opportunities to mine the plays for grand, sometimes ponderous spectacles.

When Shakespeare describes Richard II miserably following Bolingbroke through London and '...rude misgoverned hands from windows' tops / Threw dust and rubbish on King Richard's head' Kean was not content with a mere recital of Bolingbroke's triumph; he had to have it enacted, with crowds, medieval scenery and all.

His efforts divided the critics. *King Lear* was well received by one: 'All the scenes were exquisitely painted; each had also some special merit of its own, but so judiciously introduced that the action was in no wise interfered with by its illustrative accessory.' The person sitting next to the German writer Theodor Fontane at *The Winter's Tale* though thought differently of the Kean style: '"It is too heavy." That hit the nail on the head. Everything in this production is overloaded, and perhaps no play has more claim than this to travel light. The poetry collapses under the burden of stage effect imposed on it.'

The Princess's was also notable for presenting in 1880 the Hamlet of Edwin Booth, the greatest American tragedian of his day, a 'beautifully musical and distinct' performance, with a 'quiet, unconscious, method of American humour. Hamlet bantered Polonius and the courtiers without a smile, as Bret Harte in a lecture makes jokes with a grave face.' The Princess's, perhaps the most comfortable and respectable theatre of its time, folded up in 1902 and was demolished to make room for Woolworth's in 1931.

Dean Street

Cross the road at the lights and turn down Dean Street; on the left-hand side a blue plaque above Quo Vadis honours Karl Marx, who lived here in miserable circumstances. Marx knew his Shakespeare and was particularly taken with Timon's rant on gold, which he quotes approvingly in his *Economic and Philiosophic Manuscripts of 1844*:

> This yellow slave
> Will knit and break religions, bless th' accursed,
> Make the hoar leprosy adored, place thieves,
> And give them title, knee, and approbation
> With senators on the bench. This is it
> That makes the wappered widow wed again.

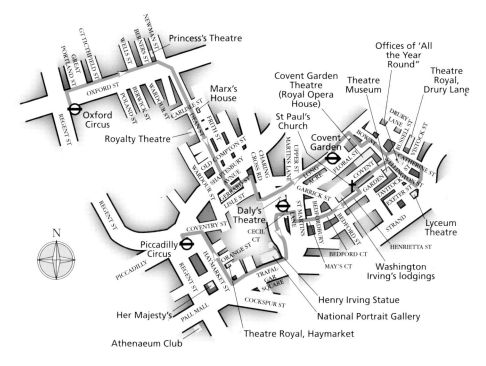

Marx cites Shakespeare many times throughout his work. The compliment has been returned by Shakespeare, or rather by his critics, for Marxist criticism of Shakespeare constitutes a large, not altogether united, province in the ceaselessly expanding territory of Shakespeare studies.

On the other side, at No 72 Dean Street, Royalty House occupies the site of the Royalty Theatre. It was here in 1845 that Charles Dickens (of whom more later) played Captain Brobadil in a very 'fierce, bright, colour' in his amateur production of Jonson's *Every Man in His Humour*.

Some 48 years later, the uncompromising, severely anti-establishment William Poel introduced his portable replica of the stage of the Elizabethan Fortune playhouse (see page 19) and acted *Measure for Measure* on it. The play was not then often revived, and Poel's choice, in combination with some of his eccentric ideas of vocal delivery, grated on critical ears. William Archer was representative: '...there is no other play of Shakespeare's in which so much of the dialogue is absolutely unspeakable before a modern audience.' None of Poel's Shakespearean productions enjoyed commercial success, but he was a central figure in the movement to recover some of the essential principles of the Elizabethan and Jacobean theatre (see page 147).

At the end of Dean Street, cross Shaftesbury Avenue and walk down

Macclesfield Street; turn left on Gerrard street and right on Newport Place, over Charing Cross Road, turning left onto Cranbourn Street, site of Daly's Theatre.

'Grandfather' Daly, as George Bernard Shaw deridingly called him, was an Irish-American critic, playwright and owner-manager of theatres in London and New York. He followed the fashions set by Macready and Kean and offered heavy pictorial productions, adapting the texts to accommodate the tableaux and dioramas that had become *de riguer* by the late Victorian period. These he effected with more matter and rather less art than some of his predecessors. Shaw, for one, was far from impressed with the effects he saw in Daly's production of *A Midsummer Night's Dream*: 'His "panoramic illusion of the passage of Theseus's barge to Athens" is more absurd than anything that occurs in the tragedy of Pyramus and Thisbe in the last act.' Shaw's funniest observations, though, were spent on Daly's *Two Gentlemen of Verona*: the textual havoc wrought by Daly's inartistic cuts, the ludicrous scenery, the 'indescribably atrocious' effect of the music, the dim lighting, and the stumbling performances all come in for a pasting.

Macready at Covent Garden

At the end of Cranbourn Street cross Upper St Martin's Lane and walk down Long Acre; take the second right after the tube – Hanover Place; at the end you'll see the north side of the Royal Opera House. William Macready, the Victorian model of dignity and good stage management (that is, direction), launched his London career at the Covent Garden Theatre here in 1816. More than anyone else, Macready was responsible for establishing the principles of Shakespearean production that set the standards for the rest of the century. He was the ideal Victorian actor-manager, co-ordinating all the forces available in the service of his artistic vision: diligent, learned, respectable.

Macready was also an intellectual and a scholar, dedicated to revealing the psychological qualities of the parts he played, which were usually tragic and grand. 'The actor's art,' he wrote, 'is to fathom the depth of character, to trace its latent motive, to feel its finest quiverings of emotion, to comprehend the thoughts that are hidden under words, and thus possess one's soul of the actual mind of the individual man.' When playing Shylock he warmed himself up by standing in the wings cursing to himself, working up his anger on backstage furniture as if it had given offence. His verse-speaking, though, wasn't to everyone's taste.

Macready's *King Lear* was famous not merely for the excellence of his performance but also for restoring the Fool to the play absent since the intervention of Dryden and Cibber in the later 17th century, and thereby '[banishing] that disgrace from the stage forever'. Macready's Fool was, in Victorian style, rather more delicate and pathetic than astringent. He was, as Macready himself said, 'the sort of fragile, hectic, beautiful-faced, half-idiot-looking boy that it should be.' Like a creature conceived by the young Dickens, in other words. This innovation was characteristic of Macready, who was dedicated to reclaiming Shakespeare's original texts for the theatre.

Turn left; then right down Bow Street and left on Russell Street. In front, you will see the Theatre Royal, Drury Lane. Macready was the manager here from 1841–3. His *Julius Caesar* was performed at Drury Lane in 1843, a production heavy on 'supers': 24 senators, 12 lictors, 16 guards and 24 citizens supplemented the speaking roles. Only revivals of large-scale Shakespearean opera can give us something of the size of those Victorian theatrical crowds.

The Lyceum Theatre
Turn right down Catherine Street and at the end right up Exeter Street. At the end, you will see the Lyceum Theatre, the temple of late Victorian Shakespeare. Henry Irving's Lyceum was a national theatre in all but name, and its prestige chiefly Shakespearean. An ungainly body and an unmusical voice presented no obstacle to his dominance of the late 19th-century theatre. He was a kind of hypnotist on the stage, his performances occasionally coming across to his contemporaries as somehow superior to the words he spoke: not great qualities for a performer of Shakespeare, perhaps. Shaw, at least, found the style insufferable, claiming he spoke 'in flat contradiction of the lines, and positively acted Shakespeare off the stage'. But in the 1870s Irving's Hamlet, Macbeth, Othello and Richard III were all enthusiastically received.

Accounts of Shakespearean productions at the Lyceum suggest symbolism rather than the antiquarianism of an earlier generation. The critic and adaptor William Winter (responsible in part for many of the excisions in Daly's productions) has left a wonderfully detailed account of Irving's Shylock. After Jessica has eloped the

...clamorous rabble streamed away; there was a lull in the music, and the grim figure of Shylock, his staff in one hand, his lantern in the other, appeared on the bridge, where for an instant he paused, his seamed, cruel face, visible in a gleam of ruddy light, contorted by a sneer, as he listened to the sound of revelry dying away in the distance. Then he descended the steps, crossed to his dwelling, raised his right hand, struck twice upon the door with the iron knocker, and stood, like a statue, waiting – while a slow-descending curtain closed in one of the most expressive pictures that any stage has ever presented.

It was, said the symbolist critic Arthur Symons, 'noble and sordid, pathetic and terrifying... one of his great parts, made up of pride, stealth, anger, minute and varied picturesqueness, and a diabolical subtlety.' A disturbing combination, and it's no surprise to learn that Irving excelled in impersonating the haunted: Iago, Macbeth and Iachimo among them.

Dickens and Tennyson

Turn right up Wellington Street; you will pass on your right the offices of *All the Year Round* and the apartment of Charles Dickens from 1859–70. Dickens's great essay 'Night Walks' appeared in this magazine in 1860. The insomnia Dickens suffered after the death of his father forced him out of bed and sent him wandering through the night all over the city. His thoughts were haunted by Shakespeare. The great theatres (probably Covent Garden and Drury Lane) suggest the graveyard scene in *Hamlet*: 'the rows of faces faded out, the lights extinguished, and the seats all empty. One would think that nothing in them knew itself at such a time but Yorick's skull'. Again, Macready may have contributed to this association, as we shall see.

Turn left on Russell Street, passing the entrance to the Theatre Museum, which has displays dedicated to the Victorian theatre in the Main Gallery. On the corner of Russell Street and the Piazza stood Hummums Hotel, where Alfred Tennyson stayed in 1844. Then in his early thirties, Tennyson had made his mark with 'Poems of 1842' and had his greatest poems ahead of him, including *In Memoriam* (inspired in part by Shakespeare's Sonnets) and the great mad monologue *Maud*, which he described as 'my little Hamlet'. Like most of his contemporaries, Tennyson soaked up Shakespeare from his childhood and took his love of him to the grave – literally. He was especially fond of *Cymbeline* (he was buried with a copy in his hand), and on his deathbed clasped the play open on the beautiful passage of reconciliation between Posthumous and Imogen:

> Hang there like fruit, my soul,
> Till the tree die.

St Paul's Church

Walk through the Piazza and down King Street, on the right-hand side of the church as you face the portico. A signed covered passage to your left will take you into the gardens of St Paul's Church. The great Lady Macbeth, Ellen Terry, is one of many 19th- and 20th-century players commemorated in the church.

Turn down the passage on the opposite side of the churchyard, and right on Henrietta Street. Washington Irving stayed at No 22, now Global House, in 1824, some four years after the publication of his *Sketch Book*. On his 'poetical pilgrimage' to Stratford, he declares himself willing to be deceived by the relics

Opposite: The Lyceum, a temple to the magnetic style of Henry Irving which, according to Shaw, 'positively acted Shakespeare off the stage'.

shuffled forth for his approval by the curator of Shakespeare's 'small and mean looking' birthplace, 'a garrulous old lady, in a frosty red face, lighted up by a cold blue anxious eye, and garnished with artificial locks of flaxen hair, curling from under an exceedingly dirty cap'.

Cross Bedford Street, walk down Bedford Court, over Bedfordbury, and down Mays Court to your left. Ahead, you will see the Duke of York's Theatre; cross St Martin's Lane, turn right and left down Cecil Court; cross and turn left on Charing Cross Road, passing the statue of Henry Irving on your right. Next to him is the National Portrait Gallery, where in Rooms 24 and 28 there are portraits of many of the people encountered on this walk. Turn right on Trafalgar Square and down Pall Mall East; to your left is the Athenaeum Club where member Matthew Arnold imagined Shakespeare as a literary alien:

> And thou, who didst the stars and sunbeams know,
> Self-school'd, self-scann'd, self-honour'd, self-secure,
> Didst tread on earth unguess'd at. – Better so!

Tree at Her Majesty's

Turn right up Haymarket. To your left stands Her Majesty's Theatre, forever associated with the management of Sir Herbert Beerbohm Tree, the last and most opulent of the Victorian actor-managers. Accounts of Tree's productions suggest the search for a kind of Shakespearean *Gesamtkunstwerk*. All the ancillary arts of the theatre – the pageant-masters, crowd-controllers, scenic artists, antiquarians and academicians – were drilled in the service of his stupendous theatrical ambitions. Plays less tolerant of the picturesque, where some high-class casts could be discerned amongst the scenic embellishment, sometimes came off well. His *Julius Caesar*, for instance, was admired by William Archer 'whatever its defects in detail'. But where Tree's fancy was unchecked: the four mini-Malvolios who aped Olivia's steward; and Shylock's room-after-room search for his daughter; the results could be artistically disastrous. Still, they were popular. The huge auditorium of Her Majesty's was not too big for the audiences which came in their hundreds of thousands to enjoy Shakespeare manipulated by the decadent genius of Tree.

Sir Herbert was also a founder of RADA and enjoys the distinction of appearing in the earliest surviving Shakespearean film, in which he performs the death scene from *King John*.

Theatre Royal, Haymarket

On your right you see the Theatre Royal, Haymarket. Samuel Phelps, contemporary of Charles Kean and Macready, gave his first London performance, as Shylock, at the Haymarket in 1837. Most reviews suggest a well-balanced and correct performance, though he clearly made the most of his trial scene, bringing out the 'utter prostration' of Shylock's 'corporal and mental faculties' and clinging to the walls of the court room as he groped his way out. Phelps became one of the most conscientious Shakespearean actor-managers of the mid-19th century, presenting 32 Shakespeare revivals at Sadler's Wells over a period of 18 years.

That Haymarket revival of *The Merchant of Venice* had been produced by Ben Webster, another major Shakespearean of the Victorian period. Webster anticipated the experiments of William Poel by some 40 years, attempting an Elizabethan staging of *The Taming of the Shrew*, itself almost never performed in its entirety. Placards were brought on stage to describe location – 'a public place in Padua', 'a room in Baptista's house' – and Christopher Sly's 'induction', when the tinker falls asleep and 'dreams' the action, was restored for the first time since before the Restoration. 'The revival,' recollected the playwright James Planche, 'was eminently successful, incontestably proving that a good play, well acted, will carry the audience along with it, unassisted by scenery...'

Unfortunately, these principles had to wait some 70 years to catch on. Macready, too, appeared at the Haymarket. His 1849 Lear was reviewed by his friend, Charles Dickens, who was deeply moved: 'Only of such tenderness, could come such rage; of both combined, such madness; of such strife of passions and affections, the pathetic cry:

> Do not laugh at me;
> For, as I am a man, I think this lady
> To be my child Cordelia.

Only of such recognition and its sequel, such a broken heart.' Dickens probably saw Macready play Lear some eleven years before, at about the time he was writing *The Old Curiosity Shop*, a novel in which the presence of Lear and Cordelia are felt throughout.

At the top of Haymarket turn left for Piccadilly Circus Underground Station.

LAMBETH AND SOUTHWARK

Summary: The modern bumps up roughly against the antique in this route through the unlovely back streets of Lambeth, Southwark and Newington. The walk passes a clutch of great theatres which have been at the heart of the 20th-century staging of Shakespeare, and a couple which have long vanished into oblivion, but which played distinct walk-on parts in the theatrical history of Shakespeare's time. It is not commonly known that Shakespeare almost certainly acted in a street off South London's most notorious traffic island.

> *Start:* Southwark Underground Station.
> *Finish:* Elephant & Castle Underground Station.
> *Length:* 4 km (2½ miles).
> *Time:* 1½ hours.
> *Refreshments:* Rose & Crown, Paris Garden; Konditor and Cook café, The Cut (Young Vic) and Rouppell Street; White Hart, Broad Street.

Turn right out of Southwark Underground, down The Cut; cross the top of Greet Street, named in honour of Sir Ben Greet, one of the lesser-known heroes of British Shakespearean production.

Sir Ben Greet

Greet was largely responsible for bringing Shakespeare to the Old Vic, since Lilian Baylis, who re-established the theatre in the 1910s and knew her opera, had little knowledge or experience of Shakespeare. He was 50 when he first ran into Baylis, with about 30 years' experience in touring Shakespeare to school halls, parks and gardens, a genius of the fit-up performance.

'He had done the plays so often,' said the actress Margaret Webster, 'in so many extraordinary ways and places, that I don't think he took any of it seriously any more. In the face of some particularly fearful or ludicrous happening, his eyes would twinkle with enjoyment. Anything short of

Opposite: The Old Vic, home to London's most important productions of Shakespeare from the 1920s to the 1970s.

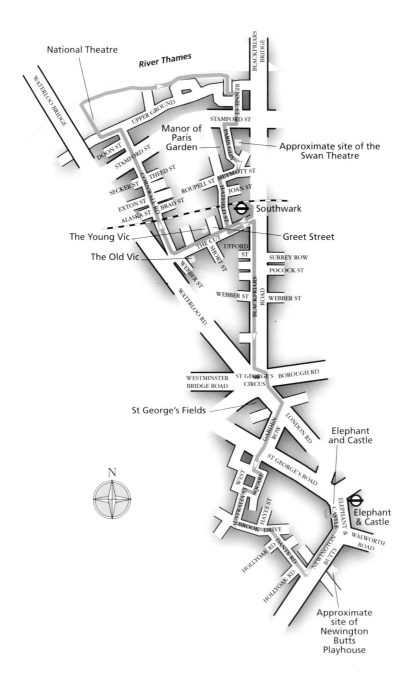

190

total disaster simply passed him by. He had become so accustomed to making the actors fend for themselves that he knew he would, between us, get the shows on somehow.'

Greet resembles William Poel in his disinterested devotion to the idea and practice of making Shakespeare accessible to people, and it's easy to imagine that a kind of inspired pragmatism characterised his work. He was very well aware of the ideal way of presenting the plays – on a plain stage with the whole of the text – but he felt that this would nearly always be beyond the capacity of audiences and players. His solution was his 'acting versions', done with 'changes of scenery to make them entertaining and interesting to ordinary audiences. The intellectual ones and the youngsters who study the plays can supply with their knowledge the omitted scenes. The regular playgoer can understand the plot as it stands and imagination will help him fill in the gaps.' As you might guess, Greet was also an important promoter of Shakespeare in education. In 1933, he founded the Open Air Theatre in Regent's Park.

The Young Vic

On your right you pass the Young Vic, an offshoot of the National Theatre, founded by its then-director Sir Frank Dunlop. It was built on an old bomb-site in 1971, and incorporates an old butcher's shop. The place still has a hasty, makeshift look, not surprising, because it was built as a temporary measure, a place to offer good theatre and cheap seats especially to young people. Michael Bogdanov's 'Action Man Trilogy' caused a stir here in 1979, introducing shock tactics and contemporary politics into *Richard III*, *Hamlet* and, rather awkwardly, *The Tempest*. It was a rigorous, anti-romantic vision of, according to the actor Bill Wallis, 'modern dress, telephones, bicycles, combat dress, and general scorn of spectacle and magic'. The results may not always have been artistically successful, but Bogdanov's Young Vic productions set a precedent for performing politicized Shakespeare in studio-type theatres and in a non-naturalistic style. The Young Vic remains a regular venue for Shakespeare.

The Old Vic

At the end on your left is the Old Vic. The foundation stone of the theatre and other bits used in its construction came from the Savoy Palace – once John of Gaunt's great house on the Strand (see page 93). It seems appropriate for the theatre with such a long and distinguished 20th-century Shakespearean history. It was not always so. Although opened in 1818, the Old Vic (previously the Royal Coburg) started its career as a home of melodrama and (with the exception of a short run by Edmund

Kean in 1831) only gained a reputation for Shakespeare from World War I when Lilian Baylis became sole manager. Knowing little about production, in 1914 she hired Rosina Filippi to direct the first two productions, *The Merchant of Venice* and *Romeo and Juliet*. Resources were limited, relying on 'art muslin, two changes of scenery and two hired orange trees'. Shakespeare continued precariously until she met and hired the resourceful and seaman-like Ben Greet (see above).

Greet was succeeded by Robert Atkins, who, between 1918 and 1923, produced every play in Shakespeare's First Folio. He also raised the technical standards of production, introducing better lighting, moving the action closer to the audience by bringing the acting area beyond the proscenium. Atkins was a ubiquitous actor-manager. As well as pushing the crowd around in *Coriolanus*, and cueing in the music, he found time to play Wolsey, Belch and Caliban in his last season.

In 1929, Harcourt Williams was appointed director and some of the greatest names in 20th-century Shakespearean performance came to light under his management. In that year Edith Evans appeared here with John Gielgud and the theatre was the venue for Gielgud's famous Richard II, Oberon and Antonio (from *The Merchant of Venice*) – all characteristic parts, allowing him to exercise his melodious voice. His legendary Hamlet, a matchless romantic interpretation of the role, was first seen here: 'noble,' the critic James Agate said, 'in conception…thought out in the study and…lived upon the stage, with the result that these things are happening to Hamlet for the first time and that he is here and now creating words to express new-felt emotion.'

In the early 1930s Gielgud partnered Ralph Richardson at the Old Vic, playing Richard to his Bolingbroke, Prospero to his Caliban, Antony to his Enobarbus, Malvolio to his Belch, and (a very young) Lear to his Kent. Richardson also partnered Edith Evans, playing Iago to her Emilia. Peggy Ashcroft, too, first came to Shakespearean prominence under Williams, playing a range of young romantic leads that included Imogen, Rosalind, Portia, Juliet and Miranda.

Tyrone Guthrie succeeded Williams in 1933 and brought with him Charles Laughton and his wife Elsa Lanchester, and Flora Robson. In his *Measure for Measure* of 1933, Laughton's Angelo played to Robson's Isabella. In 1937, Guthrie directed a balletic production of *A Midsummer Night's Dream* with the dancer Robert Helpmann as Oberon, Vivien Leigh as Titania and Ralph Richardson as Bottom, a role in which he excelled: 'never pushful and eager, thrusting his mates out of the way. He is impelled in front of them by his own quiet certainty, which they [share] as often as not, that he is right.' Guthrie also brought Laurence Olivier to the Old Vic. The critic W.A. Darlington saw his Richard III here in 1944:

As he made his way downstage very slowly and with odd interruptions in his progress, he seemed malignity incarnate. All the complications of Richard's character – its cruelty, its ambition, its sardonic humour seemed implicit in his expression and his walk, so that when at last he reached the front of the stage and began his speech, all that he had to say of his evil purpose seemed to us in the audience less like a revelation than a confirmation of something we had already been told.

From 1963 to 1976, Olivier led the National Theatre Company at the Old Vic (about which more later). Turn right down Cornwall Road; cross Stamford Street that was built across the Lambeth Marsh Shakespeare knew. Turn left on Upper Ground, past the south side of the National Theatre. Take a seat in the garden on the south side.

The idea of a state-supported national theatre on continental models was first proposed in the mid-19th century, and then again in the 1900s by the director and writer Harley Granville-Barker and the critic (and Ibsen champion) William Archer. But little happened until the 1960s, when the Old Vic Company and the Shakespeare Memorial Theatre in Stratford jockeyed for position. Parliamentary approval and a grant of £1 million came after London County Council made the present site available.

The National Theatre

Olivier assembled a national theatre company in 1963 at the Old Vic. In this period appeared Olivier's Othello, who entered 'smelling a rose, laughing softly with a private delight; barefooted, ankleted, black.' Thirteen years passed before Sir Denys Lasdun's complex was finished – not one theatre but three, by which time Peter Hall had succeeded Olivier as director of the company. Since Peter Hall's retirement in 1988, the National's directors have been Richard Eyre, Trevor Nunn (who succeeded Eyre in 1997) and Nicholas Hytner. Approximately one in ten National productions is of a Shakespeare play.

Turn right down the lane along the west side of the theatre. Vertical signs advertise the three theatres. The foyer is usually open and you will find there a plaque inscribed 'to the living memory of William Shakespeare', and an excellent bookshop. You will also come across signs to the Olivier, Cottesloe and Lyttelton theatres.

The critic Michael Billington summed up Peter Hall's 1987 National Theatre production of *Antony and Cleopatra* as a tale of 'two middle-aged people – carnal, deceitful, often sad – seeking in love a greater reality than themselves.' In Judy Dench's Cleopatra he detected a queen, 'capricious, volatile, the mistress of all moods who in the course of a single scene can switch easily from breathy langour...to cutting humour...to a pensive melancholy...at the frank acknowledgement of the passing years.' He found Anthony Hopkins 'a real old campaigner', able to express 'false gaiety – and overpowering inward grief – in the short scene where he bids farewell to his servants. From that point on, the knowledge of death sits on Antony; and when Mr Hopkins says he will contend even with his pestilent scythe, it is with a swashbuckling bravura that moves one to tears.'

Leave the National Theatre foyer by the doors nearest the bookshop into Theatre Square and turn right (east) along the river. For a description of the river view to the north, see page 94. On this side of the river, to the west lay Lambeth Palace (see page 106). In Shakespeare's day the herbalist John Gerard botanised his way along the river front, coming across the 'narrow-leafed' rocket, found, in his words, 'as ye go from Lambeth bridge to the village of Lambeth, under a small bridge that you must pass over hard by the Thames side'. Alheale he found in the Lambeth meadows and spiked willow-herb or loose-strife 'under the Bishop's house-wall at Lambeth' near the river.

Paris Garden

Turn right up Marigold Alley, running beside Sea Containers House; turn left on Upper Ground and right down Rennie Court; cross Stamford Street at the lights, turn right and left down Paris Garden. The Manor of Paris Garden was a 40-hectare (100-acre) estate of marsh and riverbank, once the property of Jane Seymour, Henry VIII's third wife. It later passed to the Bailiff of Southwark, one William Baseley, who, in a spirit of uncommon public-spiritedness, opened the grounds to the public for bowling and gambling.

Paris Garden was a landing stage for visitors to Bankside's theatres and animal-baiting arenas. A bear garden stood here in the 1580s, which, on 13 January 1583 collapsed. It was a notorious disaster, seized upon by Puritans such as the Preacher John Field as a judgement of God against the 'cruel and loathsome exercise of baiting bears' on a Sunday: 'the yard, standings, and galleries being full fraught, being now amidst their jollity, when the dogs and bear were in their chiefest battle, lo the mighty hand of God upon them. The gallery that was double, and compassed the yard round about, was so shaken at the foundation, that it fell (as it were in a moment) flat to the ground, without post or pier, that was left standing, so high as the stake whereunto the bear was tied.'

Paris Garden, being both public and wooded, had some of the characteristics of one of the seedy corners of our modern parks. It was, according to William Fleetwood, the recorder for London, a 'bower of conspiracies', whose thick-growing willows offered a 'notable covert for confederates to shroud in'. In 1578 Fleetwood, who seemed to spend much of his time spying and eavesdropping in Polonius fashion, rowed to Paris Garden in the wake of the French ambassador, whom he suspected of intrigue. But the place was too dark for him to discern anything incriminating.

The Swan

Just east of here stood the Swan Playhouse. The Swan was built by the moneylender Francis Langley in 1595 as competition to the Rose, and was, in its day, the largest theatre in London and one of the most splendid, its pillars cleverly painted in marble 'to deceive the most cunning' eye. Dutch scholar, Johannes de Witt, made a drawing of the Swan's stage and a part of its auditorium that was later copied by a fellow scholar and friend giving us the only image we have of an interior of an Elizabethan playhouse.

The Swan had a chequered history. After only two years it was closed down following a production of *The Isle of Dogs*, a lost play by Thomas Nashe and Ben Jonson that was a bit too critical of Elizabeth's government. In 1602 it was back in business, but not for long. A confidence trickster named Richard Venner collected a house-full of takings for an entertainment called *England's Joy,* and absconded with the money' without offering a show. The enraged audience revenged itself by destroying the 'hangings, curtains, chairs, stools, walls' of the playhouse. The only surviving play known to have been performed at the Swan was Thomas Middleton's great comedy of 1613, *A Chaste Maid in Cheapside.*

St George's Circus

Turn right on Meymott Street and left on Hatfields; at the end turn left on The Cut and right on Blackfriars Road. The road extends to St George's Circus, which now covers St George's Fields, a large patch of open ground where John Gerard once picked water violets. The fields were also a mustering and training ground for militias. In *Henry VI*, the Duke of York's Irish army is dispersed and ordered to regroup the next day at St George's Fields where they 'shall have pay and everything you wish'. If Shakespeare is to be believed, a windmill stood on the fields, a place which Shallow, newly reacquainted with Falstaff, suddenly recollects:

SHALLOW: O, Sir John, do you remember since we lay all night in Windmill in Saint George's Field?

FALSTAFF: No more of that good master Shallow, no more of that.

Cross St George's Circus, bearing left, and turn down London Road. Turn right on Garden Row; over George's Road; through West Square and down Austral Street; turn left on Brook Drive, right on Dante Road and left at the end on grim Newington Butts, the site of archery targets and what was probably the first playhouse built south of the river, a dim forerunner of the Rose and the Globe, about which we know next to nothing.

It may have been a proper amphitheatre like the Globe or it may have been a converted inn. It was probably in business from 1575. Strange's Men, one of the early theatre companies for which Shakespeare worked, were ordered to stop playing at the Rose Theatre in 1592 and to transfer for three days a week to Newington Butts. This was a bad idea and the order was rescinded 'by reason of the tediousness of the way', something you'll probably appreciate. Indeed, although in 1594 the theatre was used by a combined troupe of the Admiral's Men (the main company at the Rose) and Shakespeare's own Lord Chamberlain's Men, the Newington Butts playhouse never really caught on. The company's daily takings for some early Shakespearean fare such as *The Taming of the Shrew* and *Titus Andronicus* were a miserable 9 shillings. It was too far out of the way.

The Elephant & Castle

Keep going in the same direction towards Elephant & Castle. The Elephant & Castle was a smithy, later a pub, whose sign bore the crest of the Cutlers' Company, dealers in ivory. Anyone who uses the bus or tube will know that this vast traffic island is usually referred to as 'Elephant', and there's an exchange between Sebastian and Antonio in *Twelfth Night* that often raises a knowing laugh with those who live south of the river:

> Hold sir, here's my purse.
> In the south suburbs at the Elephant
> Is best to lodge.

Shakespeare's Illyrian pub, though, was in fact on Bankside, near the Globe and, appropriately, doubled as a brothel. Keep walking on this side of the traffic islands until you will reach one of the entrances to the underpass. Follow the signs to Elephant & Castle Underground Station.

FURTHER INFORMATION

AROUND ST PAUL'S
St Paul's. Open daily; entry to services is free, of course, and on week-days these are at: 7.30am (8.30am Saturday), 8am, 12.30pm, 5pm (Choral Evensong); on Sundays at 8am, 10.15am, 11.30am (Choral Eucharist), 3.15pm (Choral Evensong), 6pm.

BARBICAN AND CHEAPSIDE
St Giles without Cripplegate. Open from 9.30am–5.15pm, Monday to Friday; 9am–12 noon Saturday.
The Guildhall. Usually open when not in use. Telephone 020 7606 3030.
The Museum of London. Open 10am–5pm, Monday to Saturday; 12 noon–5.50pm Sunday. Admission free.

CLERKENWELL AND SMITHFIELD
St Etheldreda's. Open occasionally.
St John's Gate and Museum. Open daily. Admission free.
The Charterhouse. Tours on Wednesdays from April–August by arrangement. Tel: 020 7251 5002 (the Clerk to the Brothers).
St Bartholomew the Great. Open Monday to Friday, 8.30am–5pm; Saturday and Sunday, 10.30am–1.30pm.
St Bartholomew the Less. Open weekdays 7–8pm, with services midday–1pm; Sunday services 11am.

BLACKFRIARS TO MONUMENT
The Monument. Open daily, 9.30am–5pm. Admission charged.

BISHOPSGATE TO LONDON BRIDGE
St Botolph without Bishopsgate. Open 8am–5.30pm Monday to Friday.
St Andrew Undershaft. Usually open 9am–5pm Monday to Friday.
St Helen's Bishopsgate. Usually open 9am–5pm Monday to Friday.

THE TOWER AND THE WHARVES
The Tower of London: Open March to October, Monday to Saturday, 9am–5pm; Sunday 10am–5pm; and November to February, Tuesday to

Saturday, 9am–4pm; Sunday and Monday 10am–4pm. Admission charged, concessions; children under 5 free.

BANKSIDE
Southwark Cathedral. Open daily. The Southwark Cathedral visitor centre and exhibition is also open daily 10am–6pm.
The Golden Hind. Open daily, but hours are variable.
Shakespeare's Globe Exhibition. Open daily, 10am–5pm. Joint tickets for the Rose Theatre Exhibition are available.

ALONG THE STRAND
National Portrait Gallery. Open weekdays 10am–6pm; Sunday 12 noon–6pm. Closed public holidays. Admission free.
Prince Henry's Room. Open Monday to Saturday 11am–2pm. Admission free.

WESTMINSTER TO LAMBETH
Jewel Tower. Open 10am–6pm, last admission 5.30pm.
St Margaret's, Westminster. Open Friday 9.30am–3.45pm, Saturday 9.30am–1.45pm, Sunday, 2pm–5pm.
Westminster Abbey. Open Monday 9.45am–3.45pm, Tuesday 9.30am–3.45pm, Wednesday 9.30am–7pm, Thursday 9.30am–3.45pm, Friday 9.30am–3.45pm, Saturday 9.30am–1.45pm. No tourist visits on Sunday. Admission to the nave and cloisters is free. There is an admission charge to Poets' Corner and other areas.

THE INNS OF COURT
Temple Gardens. Open 12 noon–3pm May, June, July and September.
Middle Temple Hall. Occasionally open by appointment; telephone the Treasury Office, 020 7427 4800.
Gray's Inn Hall. Occasionally open by appointment; write to the Treasury, South Square, Gray's Inn, London WC1.
Temple Church. Open Monday to Saturday, 10am–4pm.

ST JAMES'S AND WHITEHALL
The Queen's Chapel and the Chapel Royal. Open for services on Sundays at 8.30am and 11.15am and on weekdays at 12.30pm on Holy Days (as advertised). The Queen's Chapel is open from Easter Day to the end of July, the Chapel Royal from October to Good Friday.
The Banqueting House. Open Monday to Saturday, 10am–5pm.

HAMPTON AND HAMPTON COURT
Garrick's Lawn. Open daily from 7.30am to dusk; the temple itself is open on Sundays only, April to September, 2–5pm.
Bushy Park. Open on Sundays throughout the year; it is also open on weekdays, but there is sometimes limited access from September to November when the deer are culled.
Hampton Court. Gardens open from 7.30am to dusk. The palace is open 27 October to 29 March, Monday 10.15am–4.30pm, Tuesday to Sunday 9.30am–4.30pm; 30 March to 26 October, Monday 10.15am–6pm, Tuesday to Sunday 9.30am–6pm.

DEPTFORD AND GREENWICH
St Nicholas' Church. Open 10am–2pm, Monday to Friday.
Greenwich Park. Open from 7.30am to dusk.

ST PANCRAS TO MARYLEBONE
British Library. Open Monday, Wednesday, Thursday and Friday 9.30am–6pm; Tuesday 9.30am–8pm; Saturday 9.30am–5pm; Sundays and Bank Holidays 11am–5pm. Admission free.

SHAKESPEARE IN THE RESTORATION
St Giles in the Fields. Open Monday to Friday, 9am–4pm.
The Banqueting House. Open Monday to Saturday, 10am–5pm.

THE AGE OF GARRICK
Theatre Museum. Open 10am–6pm daily. Admission free.
St Paul's, Covent Garden. Open 8.30am–4.30pm daily.

ROMANTIC SHAKESPEARE
Theatre Museum. Open 10am–6pm daily. Admission free.

VICTORIAN SHAKESPEARE
Theatre Museum. Open 10am–6pm daily. Admission free.
National Portrait Gallery. Open Monday to Wednesday, Saturday and Sunday 10am–6pm; Thursday and Friday 10am–9pm.
St Paul's Church. Open daily 8.30am–4.30pm.

LAMBETH AND SOUTHWARK
The foyers of the Old Vic, Young Vic and National Theatres are usually open daily.

BIBLIOGRAPHY

A book – even so unscholarly a book – which is entirely dependent upon the achievements of others should own its debt to a few of the many secondary sources read, paraphrased and, no doubt, abused.

Biography
I have relied chiefly upon Samuel Schoenbaum's *William Shakespeare: A Documentary Life* and to a lesser extent on *Shakespeare, A Life* by Park Honan. I have also used J. E. Neale's great *Queen Elizabeth I* and Charles Nicholl's enthralling reconstruction of Marlowe's death in *The Reckoning*.

16th- and 17th-century theatre history
I have drawn upon the monumental multi-volume achievements of E. K. Chambers in *The Elizabethan Stage* and Glynne Wickham in *Early English Stages,* and upon Andrew Gurr's *Playgoing in Shakespeare's London* and *The Shakespearean Stage 1576–1642*, Jean Wilson's *The Archaeology of Shakespeare*, Bernard Beckerman's *Shakespeare at the Globe* and Lukas Erne's *Shakespeare as Literary Dramatist*.

Later periods
I found useful *The Cambridge Companion to Shakespeare on the Stage* edited by Stanley Wells and Sarah Stanton, Michael Dobson's *The Making of the National Poet: Shakespeare Adaptation, and Authorship, 1660–1769, Shakespeare in the Theatre: 1701–1800* by Charles Beecher Hogan, Ian McIntyre's *Garrick*, A. C. Sprague's *Shakespeare and the Actors: The Stage Business in his Plays, 1660–1905, Shakespeare on the Stage* and *William Poel and the Elizabethan Revival* both by Robert Spaight, *Shakespeare and the Victorian Stage* edited by Richard Foulkes,*Shakespearean Constitutions: Politics, Theatre, Criticism 1730–1830* by Jonathan Bate, *Victorian Spectacular Theatre, 1850–1910* by Michael M.Booth, and *The Shakespeare Revolution: Criticism and Performance in the Twentieth Century* by J. L. Styan. The exemplary *Oxford Companion to Shakespeare*, edited by Stanley Wells and Michael Dobson, was invaluable for many periods and subjects.

London
I have profited from a collection of excellent recent histories of London, in particular those by Francis Sheppard, Stephen Inwood and Roy Porter. I must also acknowledge T. F. Ordish, who in his *Shakespeare's London*

crossed some familiar territory in 1904, V.S.Pritchett whose *London Perceived* has helped to sustain my affection for the city, the infallible Ben Weinreb and Christopher Hibbert, authors of *The London Encyclopedia,* and the topographical labours of Adrian Proctor and Robert Taylor, creators of *The A–Z of Elizabethan London.* Peter Blayney's *The Bookshops in Paul's Cross Churchyard* must take the credit for any accuracy which may be contained in my attempt to evoke a long-vanished trade in the precincts of St Paul's.

Anthologies and collected editions

I have cited quite a few authors other than Shakespeare in the text, usually from collected editions, but a number of anthologies were helpful. *The Romantics on Shakespeare*, edited by Jonathan Bate, *Johnson on Shakespeare* edited by, *Shakespeare Criticism 1623–1840* edited by D. Nichol Smith, *On Shakespeare* by George Bernard Shaw, edited by Edwin Wilson. Stanley Wells's *Shakespeare in the Theatre: An Anthology of Criticism* was invaluable, as was *Eyewitnesses to Shakespeare: First Hand Accounts of Performances, 1590-1890,* edited by Gamini Salgado. John Gross's entertaining *After Shakespeare* drew my attention to some recondite areas of Shakespeare's literary legacy. I also enjoyed reacquainting myself with ideas found in Jonathan Bate's *The Genius of Shakespeare* and Gary Taylor's *Reinventing Shakespeare.*

Quotations

Gary Taylor and his co-editor Stanley Wells also prepared the edition from which quotations are taken: *The Complete Oxford Shakespeare.*

A BRIEF LIFE OF SHAKESPEARE

WILLIAM SHAKESPEARE (1564–1616)

1564 Born to John and Mary Shakespeare probably at Henley Street, Stratford-upon-Avon

1571-72 Probably starts at the Grammar School in Stratford

1579 Probably leaves the Grammar School

1582 Married Anne Hathaway in or near Stratford

1583 Susanna born

1585 Twins Hamnet and Judith born

1585-92 The 'lost years', sometimes believed to have been spent 'school-mastering in the country'. Probably spent in part as a hireling player in London.

1590-94 Working in London as freelance or with the Earl of Pembroke's Men; early performances probably include *1, 2 & 3 Henry VI*, *The Taming of the Shrew*, *Titus Andronicus* and *Richard III* at the Theatre, Curtain and Rose playhouses as well as on tour and at Court

1592 Robert Greene attacks Shakespeare in his *Groatsworth of Wit*, the earliest indisputable allusion to Shakespeare in London

1593 Publication of *Venus & Adonis*

1593 Probably joins Lord Chamberlain's Men, becoming shareholder, actor and company playwright at the Theatre in Shoreditch as well as on tour and at Court

1596	Living near St Helen's Bishopsgate
1595-98	Early performances include *Romeo and Juliet*, *A Midsummer Night's Dream*, *Richard II* and *1 & 2 Henry IV*
1596	Hamnet dies
1597	Buys New Place, Stratford
1598-99	Theatre in Shoreditch dismantled; the Globe built on Bankside
1599-1601	Living in Southwark. Early performances of *Julius Caesar*, *As You Like It*, *Twelfth Night* and *Hamlet*
1601	John Shakespeare dies
1602-04	Living with Mountjoy family in Silver Street, Cripplegate Ward
1603	Death of Elizabeth I and accession of James I; Chamberlain's Men become King's Men
1603-06	Early performances include *Othello*, *King Lear*, *Macbeth* and *Antony and Cleopatra*
1607	Susanna Shakespeare married John Hall in Stratford
1608	King's Men acquire a large chamber in the old Blackfriars Priory and use it as an outdoor playhouse
1608	Mary Shakespeare dies
1608-11	Early performances include *Coriolanus*, *The Winter's Tale*, *Cymbeline* and *The Tempest*
1609	Publication of *The Sonnets* (probably written 1592–8)
1612	Living in Stratford
1613	Globe is burned down during performance of *Henry VIII* and rebuilt the following year
1614	Shakespeare dies in Stratford
1623	Anne Shakespeare dies. Publication of the First Folio of Shakespeare's plays

INDEX